STUDYING PLAYS

STUDYING PLAYS

MICK WALLIS

Lecturer in Drama, Loughborough University

and

SIMON SHEPHERD

Professor of Drama, Goldsmiths College, University of London

A member of the Hodder Headline Group
LONDON • NEW YORK • SYDNEY • AUCKLAND

First published in Great Britain in 1998 by
Arnold, a member of the Hodder Headline Group,
338 Euston Road, London NW1 3BH

http://www.arnoldpublishers.com

Co-published in the United States of America by
Oxford University Press Inc.,
198 Madison Avenue, New York, NY 10016

British Library Cataloguing in Publication Data
A catalogue entry for this book is available from the British Library

Library of Congress Cataloging-in-Publication Data
Wallis, Mick.
Studying plays / Mick Wallis and Simon Shepherd.
p.   cm.
Includes bibliographical references and index.
ISBN 0 340 73156 7. – ISBN 0 340 70571 X (pbk.)
1. Drama–Explication.   I. Shepherd, Simon.   II. Title.
PN1707.W32   1998
808.2–dc21   98–19097
CIP

ISBN 0 340 70571 X (pb)
ISBN 0 340 731567 (hb)

2 3 4 5 6 7 8 9 10

Production Editor: Rada Radojicic
Production Controller: Priya Gohil
Cover Design: Andy McColm

Typeset in 10/12pt Sabon by J&L Composition Ltd, Filey, North Yorkshire
Printed and bound in Great Britain by MPG Books, Bodmin, Cornwall

Contents

Words in **bold** are in the Glossary, together with other useful words.

For Connie, Graham, and Reg, with love

Acknowledgements

Thanks are due to Mick Mangan, Terry Stevenson and Christine White for their expert advice; to Drama Section students at Loughborough University for helping develop these materials in class; and to Christopher Wheeler of Arnold for his patience, good humour and constructive criticism.

We owe a debt, too, to Manfred Pfister. We have acknowledged his direct influence several times in this book. But, in addition, his example of systematic analysis, so assiduously conducted in *The Theory and Analysis of Drama*, has guided our own independent enterprise as a whole.

|1|

Getting started

In Shakespeare's *A Midsummer Night's Dream* (1594) there is quite a funny scene which shows a group of workmen rehearsing a play. They are getting in a mess about the proper way to stage their script.

Their problem is one which a lot of people share. How does the play which we read as a script relate to the play which we see as a performance? For many of us the business of reading a play is rather unsatisfactory because we continually have the sense that what we are looking at is only words on a page and that those words have yet to come alive in the mouths of real human beings standing on a stage. It is much more pleasant and satisfying to read a good novel, because the novel is designed to be words on a page. Open a novel and you've got everything you need in front of you; open a playtext and you have to start imagining the things that aren't there – how it might look and sound, how an audience might react.

1.1 Reading the play

It is because the playtext is such a strange – incomplete – object that it seems useful to have a guide as to how someone might get the most out of dealing with this object. Our overall aim is to enrich people's reading of plays so that the activity is not only thoroughly satisfying but also exciting. In doing so we hope to discover a lot more about the relationship between the two sorts of 'play' – the script and the performance. So we should end up being able to avoid the comical bewilderment of Shakespeare's 'mechanicals'.

1.1.1 Play as book

The first thing to realise when we open a playtext is that the words in front of us are not designed to function in the same way as the words in a novel or poem. These words are designed to become a performance – or, to put it more strongly, they are designed to *produce* that performance. How do they produce a performance? At a basic level they do so by instructing not only what is to be said but how it is to be said, and to whom, and in what context, and with what actions, and in what space. So the words of the playtext in front of us contain a great deal of different sorts of information; they are issuing a lot of instructions for making the performance. We shall be showing soon how these instructions operate.

For now, however, let's continue thinking in general terms about how we approach this strange object, the playtext. Many people begin reading a play in the same way as they begin reading a novel or a magazine. They are curious to know what the story is, they want to follow it through as it unfolds. Without an author, a narrating voice, to guide us, as there is in a novel, we tend to set about extracting the main outline of the story for ourselves. And the places where that seems stated most clearly tend to be chunks of dialogue which are usually spoken by the important characters. So our eyes skate over the other bits, which seem less relevant. And in particular we often leap completely over the bits in italics, which seem to be instructions only of relevance to actors and designers. So a reader will attend to us when we say: 'This book will show you how the playtext produces the performed play' but ignore the direction *(they say this in a helpful manner)*.

The bits in italics are described, and usually dismissed, as stage directions. But, as we hope to show you, much of the dialogue also contains directions. Indeed, it is very rare that you read what someone is saying without at the same time also being given the information about how it is to be said. It is the second part of that reading process (learning about the 'how') which has to be learnt as part of the discipline of studying plays. This is the point at which we face the fact that because the words of a playtext are designed differently and function differently from the words of a novel, so they need to be read differently.

The dialogue in front of us is busy doing a lot more than telling a story. It is, as we have said, creating images, movement, a stage world; and at the same time it is addressing itself to the audience, telling them how to watch, alerting them to significances, making them feel comfortable or making them feel worried that nothing is quite what it seems. You may feel that all this stuff about images and attitude to audiences is cooked up by the director, designer and actors once they have read the play. Our suggestion to you, in this book, is that you can find it all in the playtext for yourself. And indeed, it is designed to be found in the playtext – as we said above, the written form of the play has a job of work to do. That job is nothing short of shaping what we call the 'production' of the play. For whoever has written those words has imagined them as a performed event. They have not been written to exist on the page; they have been written to shape or *produce* the performance, the production. That doesn't mean to say that there is only one correct production of each play. All sorts of different interpretations in different societies can happen. But it is still nevertheless true to say that each written text contains an *implied production*. The chapters that follow will reveal some of these implied productions to you.

Before we move on, however, let's summarise the relationship between the written thing, that strange incomplete object, the playtext and the performed thing, the show with real people and spaces, the production. Our summary, shown in Fig. 1.1, is in the form of a diagram.

PLAYTEXT

dialogue   stage directions

PERFORMED TEXT

character   dialogue   space   action

Fig. 1.1

Chapters 2 to 5 in *Studying Plays* are organised around these four basic elements of the performed text as it is shaped, scripted, 'produced' by the dramatic text. In those chapters we shall set out methods and terminology for analysing the playtext in relation to these elements. Before you get on to those chapters, however, we want to push a bit further with our exploration of the relationship between playtext and performed text. In order to do that, we'll look at a couple of examples.

1.1.2 The playtext into performance

Imagine a stained-glass window in a Christian church, in which a chaste young woman, the type of woman who is a virgin until marriage and faithful to her husband thereafter, kneels and prays to God. The stained-glass window shows us the image. We are interested in her as a picture which signifies innocence, rather than in the details of her life.

And now imagine the same image made by a performer on a stage. As she kneels, she speaks:

> Here I kneel.
> If e'er my will did trespass 'gainst his love,
> Either in discourse of thought or actual deed,

. . .

I cannot say 'whore';
It does abhor me now I speak the word;
To do the act that might the addition earn,
Not the world's mass of vanity could make me.

These are lines spoken by Desdemona in Shakespeare's *Othello* (1602–4, 4.2.152–65). The young bride has been accused by her husband Othello of being unfaithful. We can take the lines as evidence of her guiltlessness and purity, and of her pain at being wrongly suspected. But if we also note that she is kneeling, we start to see that Shakespeare is here constructing a formal picture, an emblem, rather like that in a stained-glass window. As we get better at this, we might also see – and find ways to describe (as we show later) – how the very rhythm of the lines which open and close the speech produces a stillness on the stage.

But let us look a little more widely. Also on stage are Desdemona's servant Emilia, and her husband Iago, Othello's right-hand man, who has deceived his master into suspecting Desdemona. While Emilia is agitated and suspects foul play – 'I will be hang'd if some eternal villain . . . Have not devis'd this slander' (ll. 131–4) – the villainous Iago feigns innocence and tells Desdemona, 'I pray you be content' (l. 166). Indeed, Desdemona's lines just quoted are made in the same speech which she begins, 'O God! Iago, / What shall I do to win my lord again?' (ll. 149–50).

What we have, then, are two pictures, one inside the other. Inside is the emblematic Desdemona, pure and innocent. But the total stage picture is of Iago manipulating Desdemona into her posture of defeat, and revelling in it. Surrounding the emblem of innocence is the emblem of villainy and deception. This double emblem is part of the way in which this scene produces meaning for an audience.

Here, then, is clear evidence of the importance of remembering always that the dramatic text is a script for activity on a stage.

As an exercise: Refer to the scene in *Othello* just discussed and sketch out a short account of it of your own, attending to stage emblem as much as to other matters such as psychology and language. Look again at any Renaissance play you are studying or have read and see if you can find other emblematic moments, other stage pictures.

Let us now turn our attention to another woman with a dodgy husband, Nora in Ibsen's *A Doll's House* (1879), the play which we shall be coming back to throughout this book. We are well into the third and final act. Nora has a secret – that she forged her dying father's signature in order to secure a loan, which she then used to take her seriously sick husband away on convalescence. He has been ignorant of this fact and Nora knows that knowledge of it would anger and disgust him, probably destroying their marriage. But a man called Krogstad knows the truth and has written a letter to Nora's husband, Torvald Helmer, spilling the beans. Nora knows this. Helmer has just carried his mail into his study:

> NORA: (*wild-eyed, fumbles around, seizes* HELMER's *cloak, throws it around herself and whispers quickly, hoarsely*). Never see him again. Never. Never. Never. (*Throws the shawl over her head.*) Never see the children again. Them, too. Never. Never. Oh – the icy black water! Oh – that bottomless – that – ! Oh, if only it were all over! Now he's got it – he's reading it. Oh no, no! Not yet! Goodbye Torvald! Goodbye my darlings!
>
> *She turns to run into the hall. As she does so,* HELMER *throws open his door and stands there with an open letter in his hand.*
>
> (p. 92)

Helmer is indeed furiously angry. When Nora tries to explain herself, that she acted out of love, Helmer tells her, 'Oh, don't try to make silly excuses.' And when she becomes still more agitated and says, 'You're not going to suffer for my sake. I won't let you' – sharing with him her suicidal thoughts – he snaps back, 'Stop being theatrical' (p. 93).

We might be inclined to look at Nora's speech and think that this is just a bit of old-fashioned, melodramatic, over-the-top writing. But if we note how it stands out from the rest of the play; if we note Helmer's own comment about theatricality (other translators have him say, 'Stop being melodramatic'); and if we look at the stage directions concerning the cloak and shawl, we start to see something much more interesting going on.

As will emerge later in our account of the play – and, we hope, in your reading of it – Nora is indeed being 'theatrical'. She is living her life just now *as if* it were a melodrama, or a play with a melodramatic drive to it: a happy and just conclusion will, she imagines, suddenly emerge by some miracle out of desperation. Nora wants both to kill herself – to make a huge sacrifice – *and* to have Helmer stop her from doing so because he loves and values her. But life is not like that.

There is more than this. Ibsen lets the audience also imagine it is watching a play that works like a melodrama. Nora's speech and actions will at first have been taken at face value (even if they might have sounded a little old-fashioned) as the depiction of a desperate woman. Helmer's riposte to her breaks into this sympathetic response from the audience, and 'frames' the moment as melodrama.

And then a little later on, Krogstad relents and returns the only evidence of Nora's guilt – an IOU – to the couple, torn to shreds. Helmer is beside himself with joy: 'Nora! No – I must read it once more. Yes, yes, it's true! I'm saved! Nora, I am saved!' (p. 95). Indeed, the play could quickly end hereafter. The crisis has passed. But Nora has learned her lesson. Her husband cannot hear her love. What they must do is sit down and talk. And eventually she leaves, famously slamming the offstage street door.

What Ibsen does, then, is not only show that Nora has been locked into a 'theatrical' frame of mind. He also shows that Helmer *and the audience* have been locked there as well. What have they been doing sitting there in the auditorium anyway? Waiting for a happy end? Life is not like that. As readers of the play we would miss all of this startling challenge if we were merely concentrating on the story of Nora's development.

1.1.3 Reading the performance

Our two examples have taken us into quite complicated territory. They do not simply show how the written playtext instructs a performer to move or to deliver lines, or how a stage picture is created as a context for those lines. They also show how the attitude of the audience is shaped. In the case of Desdemona the audience is encouraged to regard her in two ways – as the emblem of a virgin and as a real woman falsely accused. In the case of Nora the audience is encouraged to adopt a somewhat sentimental attitude to her, and then, rather challengingly, Ibsen shows them how false this attitude is.

The task of controlling the audience's attitude to the stage is one of the key considerations of the playtext. This is what caused most grief to the mechanicals in *A Midsummer Night's Dream* (3.1) – they did not know how to present the lion in the story without frightening the ladies in the audience (and to frighten their audience may have cost them their lives). They had to find a means of showing a lion which would be taken seriously as a lion without being taken so seriously that people were frightened. The playtext's requirement of a lion led directly into consideration of how an audience watches. Where has this taken our argument about the playtext?

We have suggested so far that the playtext *produces* the performance, in the sense that it carries information which can be used by the acting company in constructing a performance (how people move, what pictures are made, etc.). Now we are suggesting – in addition – that the playtext seeks to *produce an attitude to* the performance: its pictures are designed to lead the audience towards particular sorts of interpretation. By manipulating the audience's recognition of melodrama, and by subverting expectations derived from different sorts of drama, Ibsen was challenging the fantasy solutions offered by other sorts of drama in favour of a drama which shows life as it 'really' is.

When we start using words such as 'subvert' and 'challenge' we make the business of watching a play seem very far from being passive and relaxed. That is not to say that it need not be passive, if a person so wants, but for someone picking up on the signals, recognising the language, the business of watching becomes very much more active – the performance is, in a sense, being 'read'. And it is usually offered as something to be read. In order that we acknowledge this fact, and remember it, let's now alter a couple of terms we have been using until now. Instead of merely talking of the performance as an end point, a 'production', let's now refer to it as the *theatrical text* – a text because it is something to be read, but read in the theatre. And to remove that slippery word 'play', let's change 'playtext' to *dramatic text*. The implication is now that two sets of reading go on: the dramatic text is read on the page, the theatrical text is read by an audience from the stage. So the production is not a stopping-point, it is pushing the audience somewhere new: to new thoughts about 'emblem' or 'melodrama', for instance.

1.1.4 How does reading performance happen?

If an audience responds to something as realistic, and then discovers it's melodrama, this implies that audience members bring a certain amount of knowledge about drama with them into the theatre. More than that, it implies that they agree to respond to the play according to how they think the play wants them to respond. If it looks like pantomime, you start to respond to it as pantomime (and you don't shout 'Look out behind you!' when you're watching *Hamlet*).

This readiness of an audience to respond appropriately is called convention. The root of the word 'convention' is to do with agreement (see R.Williams 1976: 70). When we watch Renaissance dramas we acknowledge the convention that asides cannot be overheard by others on stage; or, at grand opera, we agree to the logic that a heroine dying of tuberculosis can still sing hideously high notes. Shakespeare's mechanicals got themselves in a pickle because they were in a muddle about conventions: they could have assumed their audience would agree to accept the stage lion as a real lion. Conventions are in fact very handy, and no performance is ever without them (for, at the minimum, we agree to let the performance happen on the stage without walking onto that stage uninvited ourselves). We respect the convention in order for the thing to happen in the first place.

But it also has to be said that conventions change. We no longer use the aside, or look for emblems. What past audiences accepted, present audiences may find unacceptable. We often use the word 'conventional' to mean something which is old-fashioned, where the conventions have gone past their use-by date. But, as we have said, all performances work with conventions – it is just that some conventions feel old and hence noticeable, while others that are contemporary don't seem to be conventions, but just natural. And when new conventions are coming into being they might feel strange, difficult, unintelligible. Ibsen's audience may well have found melodrama old-fashioned, a residue from the past; but they may also have felt that his new conventions, the conventions of Naturalism, were presenting them with shocking or inexplicable material: the doorslam became notorious. To us, by contrast, the conventions of Naturalism feel like a residue of the past as we head towards other sorts of theatre. But, as you'll note from television dramas, Naturalism is still being used. We can make sense of this situation, first, by adopting the terms given by Raymond Williams (1977) – residual, dominant, emergent (where 'dominant' is the convention most preferred at the present); and then we can acknowledge Williams' point that all three sorts of convention can be seen in use at any one moment. Thus in the Desdemona extract we saw how the creation of an emblem (a medieval practice) coexisted with the new Renaissance writing of psychologically complex characters. You could try observing similar coexisting conventions on a night's television.

So the way that the dramatic text establishes and manipulates the conventions of the theatrical text can in turn question or challenge an audience, or indeed give them pleasure. When we watch those mechanicals rehearsing we find them funny not only because of their mistakes about how to do a play, but because the play they are rehearsing is itself old-fashioned. Now if a reader or an audience had no knowledge of conventions, they would be ignorant of this whole context to the lines spoken by the mechanicals. And the experience of reading the play, in whatever respect, would be not just thinner but rather wrong-headed. We shall try to ensure that by the end of this book you are a more subtle reader of dramatic and theatrical text, able to enjoy the mechanicals without sharing their mistakes.

1.2 Stage directions

These are the bits on the page which are not spoken by characters. We know they're not for speaking because they're in *italics*. Readers often skip over them rather fast. But they work with the dialogue to script what characters do, to produce the production. So, before we move on to the chapter on Characters, let's pause to have a closer look at these bits in italics.

1.2.1 *What do stage directions do?*

Stage directions script a variety of things. In the short extract from *A Doll's House*, for instance, there are instructions regarding facial expression, vocal delivery, gesture and basic actions, costume, 'kinesics' (moving about the stage), 'proxemics' (blocking), space and props.

Fig. 1.2 sets out the various functions of stage directions. You may want to adjust or add to it.

As an exercise: Take a passage from the play you are studying which includes stage directions: explore the range of things scripted by those directions.

STAGE DIRECTIONS

scenic arrangements	actor(s)/characters
lay-out of stage	delivery of dialogue
furnishings	bodily state
props	emotion
	proxemics (blocking)
	kinesics (movement)

Fig. 1.2

1.2.2 *What is the relationship between the stage directions and the dialogue?*

Since dialogue not only contains a story but also makes directions for action, character and space, it is often assumed to be the most important of the two elements which comprise the dramatic text – it seems to have more bearing on the production. The preferential treatment of dialogue over stage directions is institutionalised in the practice which refers to *Haupttext* (German for 'high text') and *Nebentext* ('ancillary text') in place of dialogue and stage directions respectively (these are the terms of Roman Ingarden, which are explored in Aston and Savona 1991). But this is actually a partial, and thus misleading, version of the relationship between stage directions and dialogue.

In many cases stage directions work in conjunction with dialogue, explaining it: such stage directions may be called *conjunctive*. But there are some plays, such as Beckett's *Acts Without Words 1* and 2 (1958, 1960), where stage directions have completely replaced dialogue. In other plays dialogue is suspended for long passages: thus, in all of Act 3 scene 3 of Galsworthy's *Justice* (1910), the unjustly imprisoned Falder roams distractedly about his prison cell, the box-like **proscenium stage** transformed from familiar living space to a place of mute entrapment.

Stage directions can, then, take precedence over dialogue. But they can also act in tension with or against dialogue. These sorts of directions may be called *disjunctive*. Manfred Pfister (1988: 48) provides a good example, again from Beckett. *Waiting for Godot* (1955) ends with the following exchange:

VLADIMIR: Well? Shall we go?
ESTRAGON: Yes, let's go.
(*They do not move.*)

The same contradiction between their intended actions and what they actually do is scripted to happen at each act end. Its repetition drives the point home: we assume in life that intention leads to action, and we expect to see this affirmed on stage, but Beckett refuses.

1.2.3 Implicit stage directions

We have already suggested that dialogue contains 'implicit' stage directions, and we have seen an example: when Shakespeare gives the actress Desdemona the line, 'Here I kneel', he indicates quite directly that the speech is to be played kneeling.

It was common practice in Renaissance plays to embed the stage directions in the speeches, to have people say how they were moving and where. With this in mind if you look at the opening of *Hamlet* (1601), you will observe that the characters tell us what the image is: ''Tis now struck twelve', ''Tis bitter cold', 'Have you had quiet guard', 'good night' (1.1.7–11).

Once you get used to looking for the implicit directions in Renaissance plays, you will find them in many later sorts of drama. The custom of writing fairly full stage directions only began in the nineteenth century. And even since then, many directions are still embedded: in *Double Vision* by the Women's Theatre Group (1982) this exchange takes place: 'Shh, I'm watching. It's educational. Leeds United.' 'Oh God, he's so patronising.' (p. 37). The dialogue tells us not only that they are watching television, but also that, as it goes on, it is a quiz programme. There is no other stage direction.

As an exercise: Take a scene from the play you are studying and identify all the different implicit stage directions in the speeches.

1.2.4 The changing importance of stage directions

If you look at the opening of *Hamlet* in the edition by Hibbard (1987), you will find this at the top of the scene: '*Enter Francisco, a sentinel, who stands on guard. Enter Barnardo, to relieve him.*' This direction has been invented by the editor. He has done it to make the play easier to read. Even at the cost of interfering with Shakespeare's text, he wants the play to look like a proper playtext would look in 1987.

What has happened between Shakespeare's time and the editor's is that plays have turned into books. Shakespeare could count on the fact that his actors would be used to picking up the implicit stage directions. Many plays until well into the nineteenth century were written on the basis that actors would automatically note not only these directions but also the conventions within which acting and speaking were to be done (someone who specialised as a melodrama villain would know the sort of walk and gestures that were to be supplied, much as a session musician knows the harmonic arrangements that are required). When, however, dramatists wanted their play to be done differently, when they wanted to resist the regular treatment that the actors would have given it, they needed to supply stage directions to insist on precise detail: '*This speech is not to be spoken in a tone implying hardship*' (Robertson, *Caste* 1867: 144). In stage directions of this sort, you can see a tension between the dominant and the emergent conventions (as we described them earlier), between what the actor would normally do and the new thing the dramatist wanted.

This tension between actors and dramatists became very apparent in the late nineteenth century, when a group of writers who were trying to 'reform' the drama found that commercial managements were not interested in their serious and political plays. Lacking much prospect of frequent commercial production, they published their plays to be read as books. This meant supplying sufficient information to make them easily readable by people who were novel readers rather than actors. Thus if you look at a play by one of these new political dramatists, George Bernard Shaw, you will find not only detailed descriptions of the action but expressions of opinion that seem much more than a direction to actors: thus, '*Externally he is pretentious, booming, noisy, important. Really he is that obsolescent social phenomenon the fool of the family dumped on the Church by his father the patron*' (*Mrs Warren's Profession* 1902: 227). The same sort of thing appeared years later: a character note describes '*that middle-class womanhood, which is so eminently secure in its divine rights, that it can afford to tolerate the parliament, and reasonably free assembly of its menfolk*'. This is John Osborne, *Look Back in Anger* (1956) (p. 39). The stage direction has turned into a supplementary and mostly unperformable part of the text. Shaw's prefaces to his plays became as famous as the plays themselves (and *Mrs Warren* was published as a book about four years before it was performed). This tradition continues in the work of Edward Bond, whose plays are accompanied by poems which are published in the programmes for the performance.

Thus from the sort of stage directions, their presence or absence, their quantity and content, you can deduce something of the conditions prevailing when the play was written, and the play's relationship to dominant conventions.

> As an exercise: Look at a number of plays pulled randomly from the shelf or found in an anthology of plays of various date. Comment on the different ways in which stage directions figure in them. Try to map out for yourself what this implies in terms of their different moments of creation.

2

Characters and persons

2.1 Expectations about character

Many of us who are interested in drama would say that this is part of our more general interest in people. It is in plays that we can extend our reflection on human action in a variety of circumstances. There is indeed a rich variety of characters to admire, pity, blame, suspect or be curious about. For some of us, especially setting out on a study of drama at school or college, this 'interest in people' is quite securely grounded in a forceful notion of what a proper stage person should be. It seems to be common sense that an adequately scripted character is a 'fully rounded' one, that our encountering the character on stage should be just like our encounter with real people in daily life.

We expect, for instance, to be able to place them as a recognisable social type; but also that they have hidden depths to their personality that will only gradually become apparent to us. Similarly, we expect that their motives will only gradually become discernible, as we match their actions to their words and learn to hear the implications of what they say as much as the surface content. We expect that the story of their past has some bearing on their behaviour in the present. And we expect them to adapt to changing circumstances, to develop.

As in life, our response to a dramatic character may be to judge them. We might scan the playtext (or review the performance of the play) for evidence of the character's motivations, to solve the riddle of their behaviour, to find the fatal flaw of character or crucial choice of action that brings about their fate, if unhappy.

But this set of expectations clustered around the idea of the 'rounded character' is in fact only a fairly recent one. It only became fully established in the early years of the twentieth century. It is quite specific to Western culture.

One of the things we shall do in this chapter is to unpick what we mean by a dramatic 'character'. What do stage persons do, and how? What might 'roundedness' consist of? What other conventions of character are there?

In other words, we shall be suggesting what questions – for all of us as *analysts and performers* of the drama – are most pertinent to ask about dramatic character. The sorts of question we suggest will not be ones about blameworthiness or virtue, or whether the characters are rounded or not. This need not deny that many plays do indeed invite the judgement of the *audience*: our question will be how, and on what terms? And neither need this shift of emphasis deny our own interest in people. That interest will not only be justified, but also enriched by the questions we all come to ask. To start, it will be useful to continue our account of the Ibsen play.

2.2 Three aspects of dramatic character

Recall from Chapter 1 that Krogstad knows Nora's guilty secret and so holds power over her. One of the critics who saw the first production in Copenhagen complained: 'That his makeup bore evidence of the mark of Cain did not surprise me; it is of course traditional at the Royal Theatre to reveal to the audience at once who you are.' (For initial press reactions, see Marker and Marker 1989.) He complains, then, that this is an old-fashioned sort of stage person: one who is obvious from the start. The character is too simply drawn for him. Moreover, it is based on a racial stereotype, and one that has become a regular feature of too many plays – the stage Jew as villain.

The basic complaint, then, is about the character's *conception*. Krogstad had been conceived too simply, and conceived on an unacceptable basis. *Character conception* is our first aspect of character.

If Krogstad was conceived too simply for the critic, the implication is that, for him, a complex characterisation is the best standard. But some characters are simpler than others. We can think of 'simple' and 'complex' as two ends of a sliding scale.

To establish our other two aspects of dramatic character, let us consider what many had come to feel was 'old-fashioned' by 1879. The 'well-made play' is a formula commended by Eugène Scribe to fellow writers and audiences alike in Paris in 1836. Scribe's maxim was that people went to the theatre to be entertained rather than to be improved, and that by picking out elements from past models of dramatic writing – from ancient Athens through the Renaissance to melodrama – it is possible to arrive at a formula for the delivery of such entertainment: simple action, easily recognisable characters, intrigue and secrets, points of crisis and entanglement, a just conclusion. (For a consideration of the well-made play in England, see Taylor 1967.)

The well-made play is driven by the plot. At its most basic, the characters are mere devices – like the characters in a video-game now – placed there to make the plot work. These 'stock' characters – ones easily taken down from the shelf, held in stock for repeated use – merely serve the plot. The

monological characters of melodrama had easily found their way into Scribe's formula. Yet of course one aspect of even complex characters is their function in the plot. Nearly all characters move the action on in some way or another.

An important aspect of the vast majority of stage persons is their *plot function*. This is our second aspect of dramatic character.

Now, in Ibsen's play, it turns out that Krogstad has himself committed a misdemeanour in the past, one not dissimilar from Nora's forgery. Since then he has been treated as a social outcast. It has been very difficult for him to find work. His plight contrasts with Nora's outwardly comfortable position. In the play's design, he is a *foil* to Nora – a point of comparison. And there is a second foil in the play. Nora's old friend Mrs Linde returns to town after a long absence in the first act. Because of circumstances beyond her control she has had to become a very independent person. Her life has not been easy. As Nora in the course of the play comes to strive for her own independence, our knowledge of Mrs Linde acts as a point of reference for what that might imply.

If a character is being used as a foil, this is purely for the audience's benefit. We do not have foils in real life, because there is no audience. A character's function as foil is specific to the fiction. It is part of its formal design. Our third aspect of dramatic character is *formal function*.

We can find more formal functions in *A Doll's House* – aspects of character which are specific to the 'rhetorical' dimension of the play, the way it 'speaks to' its audience. Take Mrs Linde. In her first long conversation with Nora, we learn about Mrs Linde herself, but Ibsen uses the scene to develop and reveal to us Nora's own attitudes and give us hints about her past. We learn about Nora through her dialogue with her friend. The character Mrs Linde is, then, being used here as a *confidante* – the person to whom the protagonist speaks privately and in earnest, thus revealing their inner thoughts to the audience. And Dr Rank is in the position of the *raisonneur* – the regular character of the nineteenth-century Parisian stage, often a doctor, who explains things, makes sense of the situation, reasons things out for the sake of characters and audience alike.

Apart from the brief period of stage Naturalism – and leaving aside conventions dominant in TV and film drama – theatre has always had recourse to characters serving a directly formal function. To foils, confidantes and *raisonneurs*, we can add choruses and narrators. These sorts of character remain important in theatre today – because there is always a live audience to be explained to.

From our discussion of the Ibsen play, we have drawn out three aspects of dramatic characters in general:

- *Character conception* – from stereotype to psychological complexity;
- *Plot function* – how the characters serve the plot;
- *Formal function* – characters or aspects of them specific to theatrical communication: narrators, confidantes, foils, etc.

Note that these are *aspects* of character and not separable types. Any one stage person will combine at least the first two. We shall explore these three aspects further below. But doing the following exercise will be of use now.

> As an exercise: Sketch down the names of characters from two or three plays you are studying or know, and consider each in terms of the three aspects we have listed: (1) Are the various characters simple or complex? Do you discover a sliding scale of complexity? Do they seem to be based on what they are to represent – like their class, age or typical behaviour, like villainy – or are they based on the idea of the complexity of human psychology? Or maybe both? (2) What is their plot function, if any? That is, how do they make the plot work? (3) Are there any formal functions you can spot? That is, do some characters directly serve the 'rhetorical' functioning of the play, the way it argues things with the audience?

2.3 Mapping characters

A useful way to begin the analysis of a play is to draw up a 'family tree' of the main characters. What relationships do they bear to one another? Fig. 2.1 makes a start on *King Lear*.

While it may begin with actual family ties, our diagram goes on to map out the characters in terms of their given 'value' in the drama. Very roughly, then, we have separated out forces for good from forces for ill. Note, too, that our map shows the groups of characters involved in the plot strands centred on Lear and Gloucester respectively.

Fig. 2.1

At a more detailed level, we can map out significant similarities and differences between characters. We might, for instance, consider that each of these characters makes some sacrifice which contributes to Lear's eventual coming to rest. So each makes a sacrifice and each has some sort of quality that helps redeem Lear, as Fig. 2.2 illustrates.

	Cordelia	Kent	Edgar	Fool
sacrifice	fatherly love/power	king's love/power	embraces absolute poverty/feigned 'madness'	stays with Lear/risks unwelcome honesty
redeeming qualities	loyalty/Romance figure/'Christ' at end	loyalty/yeoman values	basic humanity/ Romance chivalry at end	popular wisdom/ truthful/sense out of nonsense

Fig. 2.2

We have placed them in rank according to social order and have started to sketch out the sort of sacrifice and redemptive quality associated with each. This is just a beginning. When we look a little more closely at our map and the play, other shapes will emerge. Our simple table above might for instance prompt us to think more about 'value'. So Kent reduces himself, but comes to represent traditional yeoman values, the very stuff of Renaissance 'Englishness'; Edgar as Poor Tom is basic humanity without social organisation; Cordelia both quickly becomes a figure from Romance (see the way France speaks of her in the first scene, 1.1.250 ff.) and at the end speaks like Christ (4.5.15–17; 23–4). The characters set these values to work within the play.

Similarly, we might choose to map single characters or character groups. We might come to think it too simple merely to categorise Regan and Goneril as 'forces for ill'. It is clear that their father has been belligerent and headstrong. We might start with something like Fig. 2.3.

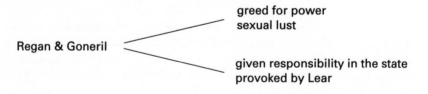

Fig. 2.3

If we read more about Renaissance culture, we find that women in all sorts of art and reference, including plays, sermons, tapestries, paintings, fables and other stories, were often stereotyped into one of two positions, very crudely that of the 'virgin' and the 'whore', so we might want to make a map like that in Fig. 2.4.

Lear's vision (and who else in the play?)	Cordelia, Regan, Goneril	Shakespeare's vision (what the playtext 'says')
	virgin–whore	

Fig. 2.4

One task of commentary on the play is to see to what extent Shakespeare uses this virgin/whore **binary** in the actual design of his woman characters, as opposed to what other characters say about them.

None of what we have sketched out here provides the 'answer' to what the play means or to what any one character fully means. But it begins the work of modelling how the play, through its characters, *produces* meaning for its audience. It looks at what the play *sets in play*, how it sets up the theatrical text to be read by the audience.

2.4 Developing the aspects of dramatic character

2.4.1 *Character conception*

In this subsection we develop further our notion of character conception.

2.4.1.1 MODE AND BASIS

The critic who complained about Krogstad thought that the character had been conceived too crudely, that it was a theatrical stereotype (the villain), and that it was based on a racial stereotype (the wicked Jew) as well. He wanted something more complex.

In fact, Ibsen progressively reveals Krogstad to be a complex personality: not only does he feel terribly wronged, and is able to speak about this persuasively; he also resumes a tender relationship with Mrs Linde. Both what that critic felt was missing, and in fact what Ibsen seems later in the play to supply, is Krogstad as a complex character based in some psychological truths.

So, taking the cue from our example, we can usefully make two distinctions. The first is between simple and complex characters – let us call this the *mode* of character conception. The second is between the mode and what it is based on, what underlies it. So let us call this the *basis* of the character conception (see Fig. 2.5).

2.4.1.2 VARIETY AND COMBINATION OF BASIS

The question of the basis of character conception was raised in the exercise at the end of section 2.2. As the mapping exercises following it suggested, characters almost always 'stand for' or act as representatives of something in a play.

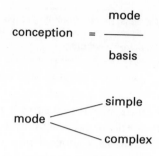

Fig. 2.5

They may typify a *social class* (Willy Loman in Miller's *Death of a Salesman*) or a *moral position* (Bonario in Jonson's *Volpone*), for instance. They may represent a *fundamental drive*, like greed (Volpone in *Volpone*). In other plays by Jonson, such basic drives are conceived of in terms of the scheme of **humours** developed earlier by medieval physicians. Furthermore, 'Volpone' derives from the Italian word for 'fox'; other predatory characters in the play have their names derived from words for vulture and raven; Mosca, from the Italian for fly, is very quick and feeds off decay and waste. The characters are based in animal *fable*. Or the most important thing about a character in the play might be their behaviour, the choices they make in life – that is, they may stand for a particular sort of *ethic* (Antigone, who insists on a proper funeral for her brother who has died in a fight; and her royal father Creon, who resists this because it will displease the gods and bring the city into disrepute, in Sophocles' *Antigone*). The character Amalia in Cherríe Moraga's *Giving Up the Ghost* is an 'earth-mother' figure. Representing both Chicano (Mexican) culture and nurturing, she is conceived in *mythic* terms – she brings into the play what are felt to be eternal qualities especially associated by some feminists with women, and felt by them to be suppressed in dominant Western cultures.

Recognisable values and opinions, human qualities and situations, are set to work in these plays through the bases of their character conceptions. The character 'mobilises' these qualities, sets them to work in the play.

Character basis cuts across distinctions between different modes. We tend to distinguish characters in complex mode from simple ones on the evidence of their *psychology*: we witness the workings of their thoughts and emotions as they unfold in the changing circumstances of the action. But it is perfectly possible to have a psychological basis for a *simple* character – someone who clearly typifies a certain sort of 'mind-set' – especially in comedy. Alan Ayckbourn's comedies are full of such creatures.

Psychology is not only, or even necessarily, the basis for complexity. Characters may, for instance, be *ethically* complex – consisting of conflicting behaviours and their justifications for that behaviour. Antony and Cleopatra in Shakespeare's play are both good examples of ethical complexity.

Equally, we may be able to see a number of different bases all strongly at work in a character. Volpone is a good example – he is a *moral* type, conceived of in terms of both *humour* and animal *fable*.

Let us review what we have established in this subsection so far. We have identified, in alphabetical order, the following bases of character conception: *fundamental drive; ethical; humoural; fabular; moral position; mythic; psychological; social class*. This list is not, of course, exhaustive. It is what our examples threw up for us. When reading or rehearsing a play, a first question needs to be, what are the bases of conception of the various character conceptions? You will find your own words and phrases. We have listed more terms of our own, in our own language, in Fig. 2.6.

Let us make a couple of clarifications. By 'historical' basis for a character, we do not simply mean that the character is drawn from history as a source. You could make all number of stage characters out of the records of

cultural	Sam and Willie *vs.* Hally in Fugard's *'Master Harold'* . . . *and the boys*;
discursive	speaking from a particular sort of position, e.g. a pessimist, Marxist, royalist (see below, section 2.6);
emotional	Katherina in Shakespeare's *The Taming of the Shrew*;
epochal	from a distinct 'time' in relation to other characters, e.g. Kent and Cordelia in Shakespeare's *King Lear*;
formal	basis confined to the play's rhetorical aspect, e.g. narrators, chorus;
generic	stock types, e.g. the wicked squire in melodrama; or typical of another genre than the main one of the play (e.g. Cordelia);
historical	e.g. Oppenheimer in Kipphardt's *In the Matter of Robert J. Oppenheimer*;
pastiche	quoted from a different genre, e.g. the Gods in Brecht's *Good Person of Setzuan*;
pathetic	designed to move the audience, e.g. Laura in Williams' *The Glass Menagerie*;
poetic	i.e. representing a poetic force, like Nemesis, e.g. Death in *Everyman*;
psychological	late Naturalism, but also e.g. Mathias in Lewis' *The Bells*;
social prejudice	race, class, gender stereotypes;
'universal'	archetypes, e.g. Man and Woman in Toller's *Masses and Man*.

Fig. 2.6 More descriptions of character bases

Robert J. Oppenheimer's life, for instance – a tragic hero, a sad clown. But in Kipphardt's documentary play, the character appears *as* historical record. If we note that the play also invests the character with an ethical basis, we can start to unpick how it works. Similarly, some modern plays use ancient myth as the source of their characters, but do not use them mythically. Sartre's play *The Flies* (1942) uses the Greek myth of Orestes to make an image of Nazi occupation of France.

What we have called 'universal' and 'mythic' bases above are quite similar. Maybe they are the same thing? If we were writing an essay about both Toller's play and Moraga's, we would need to spend some time thinking about what we meant by each. Identifying the bases makes us clarify our commentary and analysis.

Note also that some bases are interdependent with the other two aspects of character besides conception that we noted in section 2.2 above. What we call a 'formal' basis here corresponds to a character's 'formal function'. A character with a 'generic' basis – the stock type – is likely to be there to serve the plot.

Lastly, let us note that there need not be a single basis for any one character conception. This will usually only be the case for very simple characters. We can expect to find a variety of bases – though one of these might, in our understanding of the play, appear to be the *dominant basis*.

2.4.1.3 VARIETY AND COMBINATION OF MODE

We began by distinguishing between just two modes of character conception – simple and complex – and by then suggesting that we can see these as two poles of a *continuum*. Some characters are simpler than others. Meanwhile, out of our table of bases there have emerged some *specific sorts* of simpler character: archetype, stereotype, type. We shall meet another specific mode – the 'personified abstraction' – in section 2.7.

An *archetype* is a character standing for something held to be universal. So, Woman is a character supposedly representing the essence of womanhood. Even though archetypes are always open to challenge, we usually think of them as being conceived of without malice or deliberate prejudice. Dealing in *stereotypes* is usually felt to be a much more blameworthy activity: if characters are consciously conceived as stereotypes, this must involve some degree of aggression. Yet sometimes theatre allows such aggression in the name of health – as in moral and political satire.

We might talk of social *types* and moral types. When we do, we implicitly point to the wider world beyond the theatre. The theatre is one place among many – including, for instance, journalism, TV news, gossip, sociology, religious parables – where we cluster different people together into convenient groups in order to think about the world and our culture. A type – which can surely be a good thing or a bad thing, depending on how it is used – is simply a representative of one such perceived cluster.

Brecht tends to deal in types (e.g. Pelagea Vlassova in *The Mother*), though he insists that his theatre is there to demonstrate that people can *change*. 'Type' rather suggests fixity. So the mode of the relatively simple characters in Brecht's plays might better be described as *model*. Brecht is not alone in creating characters which are there to be considered, pondered over from a critical, curious distance. A model is both a replica of something and something that we can 'model', meaning 'reshape'. In Brecht's theatre, actor and audience imaginatively reshape the character – they see how adaptable it is to different circumstances, how it might have taken different decisions. This is meant to replicate our own choices in life.

So we have now generated, as well as our sliding scale from simple to complex, a list of specific modes: *archetype, model, stereotype* and *type*. You may find that you want to add more.

Given that any character might have a number of bases, it may well be that the mode of the character is simple in some respects and complex in others. While Pelagea Vlassova, Brecht's *Mother*, is ethically complex, many find the character to be based on a very simple gender stereotype – albeit probably unconsciously on Brecht's part. Shakespeare's characters Othello and Cleopatra are both quite complex in psychological terms. But there is plenty of evidence in *Othello* and *Antony and Cleopatra* that Shakespeare sets up scenes to play off stereotypes (which he may or may not have agreed with) of women and black people against one another (see e.g. Wallis 1995).

As an exercise: Look at the characters from a few plays you know and decide on both mode and basis for the conception of each. Remember that there can always be more modes than one. And maybe a character is psychologically complex, yet still a racial stereotype.

2.4.2 *Plot function – actantial analysis*

In some instances (much farce, for instance), it is clear that the main function of the stage persons is to serve the plot. Even when this is not the case, the functioning of the plot can be seen as 'calling up' the need for characters – even very rounded ones. Thus Rosencrantz and Guildenstern need to be invented to get Hamlet to England.

A useful conception here is that of *actantial analysis*. Deriving from a study of Russian folk tales, this model is especially relevant to *quest narratives*. A useful and brief account can be found in Aston and Savona (1991: 36–42). Basically, the idea is that there are various functions to be fulfilled by the characters in order for the narrative to operate. For instance, there needs to be a hero (called the 'subject of the quest'), an object of the quest (what is being sought by the hero – maybe a lost sister, or the answer to a question), a helper and an antagonist. Characters in a quest narrative can be seen as different sorts of 'actant', that is, as fulfilling these various basic roles.

Many dramatic texts are themselves quest narratives. (Think of a number of Hollywood action adventures, for instance.) An 'actantial analysis' of a dramatic script regards characters purely in their mutual relation to the quest – though this and the object of the quest may change.

So, for instance, an actantial analysis of *A Doll's House* might begin by noticing the following. First, we can regard Nora as the subject of the quest, a miraculous change in her husband's attitude as its object, and Krogstad as an antagonist. But as the play develops, Krogstad not only suffers a change of heart and destroys the evidence of Nora's guilt, but his antagonism itself can be read as a force helping Nora along on her newly-to-be-discovered quest – that of self-determination.

The play can be analysed in terms both of psychological motivation and of quest narrative. And it is best understood in both these ways, in relation to one another. To *reduce* the play to psychology misses its rhetorical effect – the way in which it works persuasively on its audience. Either the audience experiences the change of quest along with Nora – or it watches her realising that a new quest awaits her. We are all subjects of one quest or another.

There are, of course, other narratives than quest narratives, in which characters are closely tied to the plot: Aristotelian tragedy, for instance, which we discuss elsewhere.

2.4.3 Formal function

This can be crucial not only to particular plays but to whole systems of theatre. The most celebrated is that of classical Athens, where the Chorus **mediates** between the main actors and the audience. They watch as if on behalf of the audience and comment between the episodes on the action, evaluating what has happened, predicting what might happen next. Often they are divided into two semi-choruses who debate with one another. The Greek chorus often has a group identity, such as old men. It speaks from a recognisable position.

The Greek chorus is thought to derive from religious practice. The tragedies were written for an annual event which was part religious festival, part civic competition. But the festivals and the tragedies written for them were most significantly occasions of communal reflection, when both valued myths and ideas about the new city state were publicly thought through. The chorus is a fundamental part of this public dialogue.

In *The Fireraisers* (1961), Max Frisch makes fun of the way modern **bourgeois** people think about their society and their place in it. Between the scenes, a chorus of Firemen come on stage and enact what is a pastiche (see above, Fig. 2.6) of the Greek chorus.

2.5 Character articulation

In this section we look at the *articulation* of dramatic characters. When we articulate an idea, we give it a particular shape in order to put it across to our hearers. Similarly we are concerned here with particular shapes to do with characters, and what these shapes do in relation to the audience. We shall be looking at three sorts of character articulation: *external* (how characters as whole things are articulated before an audience); *internal* (what shapes, or internal articulations, there may be in any given character); and *logical* (the shape of the *selection* of characters put before an audience, the *dramatis personae*).

Let us start with an external articulation.

2.5.1 *Positioning*

You will probably be familiar with the regular and useful distinction between *sympathy*, 'feeling for' a character, and *empathy*, 'feeling with'. The latter is often held to be the best form of relationship to be had with a character. But such a claim ignores the vast variety of ways in which plays can work quite genuinely – and as great pieces of art, entertainment or politics – without an ounce of it. Famously, Brecht wanted his audiences to keep a *critical distance* from his characters. Similarly, most comedy relies on – invites – the audience to maintain an *objective* rather than subjective relationship with the persons.

'Subjective' and 'objective' may need some explanation. Put simply, subject means 'self'. Object means 'other'. If I take a subjective view, it is my own: maybe I think only of my own interests, or rely only on my own knowledge. If I have a subjective relationship with a fictional character, I imagine myself in their situation. But if I take an objective view, I try to treat my own immediate perceptions as being of no more value than those of others, and gather in evidence and try to come to a conclusion that all other reasonable people would agree with. If I have an objective relationship with a fictional character, I look at them from the outside, look at them in their own situation.

So 'subjective' and 'objective' are each used in two interconnected ways. They refer both to the *attitude of* the viewer and to the *attitude to* the thing viewed.

If I make a subjective response to a real person, I am being very closely engaged with them. But: I may mistake them for myself, or only think of them in terms of my own interests, or fail to see their own choices given their situation. If I make an objective response to a real person, I am watching them very closely, understanding what they are and where they are. But: I may then 'objectify' them, treat them merely as an object. Theatre makes play with subjective and objective responses to characters – to *fictional* persons. And theatre makers in modern times have argued much about which is the best attitude for theatre to invite from the audience.

Clearly, stereotypes are objectified characters; types are characters to be viewed objectively; sympathy is more objective than empathy. Our job must now be to describe *how* empathy, sympathy or objectivity is scripted to happen, how the dramatic text positions the various characters before the audience.

Let us not forget that in the midst of this is a very basic sort of positioning – the sheer fact that we are looking at a figure on the stage who by convention sees and knows less than we do. This is the situation of *dramatic irony*. Usually a matter of dialogue and plot – words said to one character and not another, something that happens without a character's knowledge – we can also usefully think of a very physical example: 'Look out behind you!'

2.5.2 Registers of performance

George Taylor of Manchester University does a very useful exercise with students which we can link with our last subsection. The difference is that we are here concerned first with the actor, not the audience. Using practical examples, he asks how we can describe the various relationships between an actor and the role they play. Clearly, the way the actor acts significantly affects the way the character is positioned before the audience. Our own term for this set of relationships – between actor and role, and between stage and auditorium – is *register of performance*.

Different sorts of dramatic script invite or assume different registers of performance. And what is invited or assumed is a matter not only of the type of play (say, farce or tragedy), but also the prevailing theatrical conventions (see 1.1.4). Doing George Taylor's exercise might generate the following series:

> Presentation
> Narration
> Demonstration
> Representation
> Imitation
> Impersonation
> Identification
> Realisation
> Possession

If I *impersonate* a police officer, I fool you into believing that I am one. I can *present* Boadicea if I dress up in robes, helmet and shield and stand in a tableau. Maybe as performer I also tell her story, *narrate* her from the tableau. You see the picture and hear the words.

Nowadays, the *identification* of performer with role is perhaps dominant.

It is commonly supposed to constitute 'proper' acting. But as we said at the start of this chapter, this assumption is very local to our time and culture. It emerges most strongly at the moment of Naturalism, becomes encoded in the Stanislavskian system, and via the 'Method', as developed by Lee Strasberg and others in New York, feeds into cinema and then television (see Shepherd and Womack 1996). We might consider that television, in presenting and framing actual slices of life alongside fictional texts, has been a key factor in promoting this sense of what is 'good' or 'proper' acting.

If the rule of identification emerges strongly in the late nineteenth century within Naturalism, then this can be related to the fact that Naturalism as a *movement* – it had declared aims – insisted that art should *accurately reflect* life. This insistence on an objectivity that was 'scientific' can itself be related to a project of laying bare the brute facts of modern life under capitalism – in particular, the double standards pertaining to women, the facts of poverty and the hypocrisies of organised religion. It was this emerging movement which Ibsen was reaching towards in *A Doll's House*.

Yet cultural workers like Brecht in Germany from the 1930s insisted that Naturalism could only show *surface appearances*. What mattered for Brecht were the larger structures of society and history in which individuals and collectives choose between one action and another. The audience should be encouraged to concentrate on these structures and their own relationship to them, rather than becoming bound up with the fate of one individual. They should become more objective. To become embroiled in the minute details of a personality is like not seeing the wood for the trees. And it invites a fatalistic attitude, the sense that things cannot change, that environment entirely shapes and limits ('determines') the individual. According to his analysis, the best way of gaining a clear understanding of social life and individual behaviours and responsibilities – which must include our ability to *change* things – is to *typify* situations and persons, to show them in their general aspect, and for performers and audience alike to stand 'outside' the staged situation. The actor *demonstrates* the character. This, said Brecht, was now a more *realistic* form of theatre.

Theatre makers like Grotowski and Artaud in the first half of the twentieth century invited performers to be totally *possessed* by their role. The performer became something like a religious celebrant, sacrificing themselves to the act of acting. Often the confessional or self-sacrificial activity of the performer was much more important than any detail of the fictional person as such.

One of the most immediate and powerful ways of being possessed by a role is to act in mask. And this of course includes the comic mask. The performers of the Italian *commedia dell'arte* (see Rudlin 1994) played characters based on fundamental drives; the mask helped them enter fully into those drives.

It might be difficult for many Western spectators to feel empathy with Grotowski's tortured religious celebrant. But do we not also expect of

Hollywood stars like Robert de Niro that they also sacrifice themselves to their role, become obsessed by the part? We probably do. So does Hollywood's ultimate embodiment of Stanislavskian 'method' offer empathy? Or an awesome spectacle?

Very commonly, now, we hear five notions put in combination as the recipe for good acting: *'rounded character'* – taken to mean both *plausibility* and *psychological complexity* – *identification*, and *empathy*. Probably the most respected commendation of empathy comes from Aristotle, who described how Greek tragedy worked (see also 2.5.3, below). The audience must empathise with Sophocles' Oedipus, for instance, in order for them to feel and then purge the emotions of pity and fear at the end. But what register of performance do we imagine held sway in Athens in the 5th century BCE? How like today's dominant recipe was it? Imagine Robert de Niro in platform boots, masked, declaiming verse to an audience of thousands in the outdoors. Imagine a chorus, singing and dancing in highly rhythmic fashion, **mediating** the character and the plot to the audience between each short episode. Accidentally killing your father and then marrying and having sex with your mother is a terrible ethical bind, but Sophocles does not write this situation with much psychological complexity. The proposition is terrible enough to draw us in – and Oedipus is a figure deserving of our respect. This, and the drive of the plot, are what construct empathy. And what can 'roundedness' mean in these circumstances? That we know what sort of child Oedipus was?

As we write, a theatre critic is complaining on radio that in his most recent movie, a famous film actor loses himself so much in the role, that he disappears. So identification clearly has its problems if the actor forgets to *project* something to the audience. For this critic, *realisation* (see the list above, p. 24) fails to communicate.

'Character' only exists in the context of the variable and specifiable relationship that we have called register of performance. Dramatic texts are written in the expectation of performance, and performance modes differ from culture to culture, time to time. And recall that while each of these various registers may turn up in a variety of historical or cultural contexts, we shall want to begin to understand how they operate – and what significance they have – in each of those *particular* contexts. Brecht learned some tricks from the Early Modern stage: but emblematic, demonstrative playing means something different in a Marxist context from a Renaissance **humanist** one.

As an exercise: (1) What is the register of performance assumed by the dramatic text you are currently reading? What sort of relationship between performer and role does it support? How subjective or objective is the audience invited to be? How? (2) Play with the table of registers of performance on p. 24 – what might each of the words listed describe? Are there words you would add or substitute?

Let us now move to more 'internal' questions of character articulation.

2.5.3 Dynamics

It is common to speak of 'character development', though rather ambiguously. Some people mean that the character changes (matures or learns), others that character detail becomes progressively apparent to us – rather like the way a photographic print develops. We prefer to discuss this second sense under the heading of 'delivery': see below, 2.5.6.

Character dynamics are clearly very much tied up with the plot. Characters change because of what happens in the action. And character dynamics work differently on the audience according to what sort of positioning the character has in relation to the audience. The most familiar case is surely that of the protagonist in Aristotle's description of Greek tragedy just raised in 2.5.2. Here, plot and character are strongly interdependent, and the audience tracks each closely through the contract of empathy. The character rises, suffers a change of fortune, falls and finally meets a catastrophe. Drawn into this dynamic, the audience are positioned to share in the *anagnorisis* – the character's recognition of their fault, or *hamartia*. Augusto Boal (1979: 25–47) gives a very concise summary of Aristotle's tragic scheme – though it's important to be aware that he is criticising it at the same time (4.1.9).

An unpublished play done by the Communist Unity Theatre in London in 1937 plays with the conventional relationship between plot and character dynamic. Towards the end of Herbert Hodge's *Cannibal Carnival*, Joe the Policeman suddenly – and for no reason set up by the plot – 'comes over all class conscious' and joins the oppressed against the oppressors. A question is being asked about just what sort of narrative in the real world – what sort of politics – would make real policemen and others like them change sides.

There are two sorts of change a character might undergo. They might change *in themselves* – become more humble, wise or generous. Or they might change *their situation* – become married, dead or prosperous.

In *A Doll's House*, Nora develops from being naïve and childish into a mature woman who can clearly see that she has been living a lie. She becomes committed to her own self-discovery. Her situation changes from a security which was also, however, a trap, to a liberty which is also, however, a step into the dangerous unknown. She has lost her children.

2.5.4 Continuity and discontinuity

People develop in life – they learn as they get older, for instance – but they remain the same person. The majority of stage persons are similarly *continuous* characters. But others are *discontinuous*.

As models of human potential for adaptability, Brecht's characters are intended to be taken by the audience a scene at a time. We should not look for a character 'through-line' of the sort Stanislavski recommended to his actors, but look at the character afresh in each scene. Indeed, Brecht is suggesting that we ourselves are discontinuous, that we can reinvent ourselves if we want to. He makes a somewhat crazy parable out of this idea in *Man Equals Man* (1926).

Some characters are split on stage between two actors. Noël Greig has Sam in *Poppies* (1983) witness himself as a much younger man. And in *The Good Person of Setzuan* Brecht famously has one actress play two roles, the generous prostitute Shen Te and her hard-nosed male cousin Shui Ta – whom she has invented. While Shen Te invents her cousin within the fiction, we are invited to watch as if they were two people. In this 'split character' Brecht examines the rigid gender system he sees in cahoots with the capitalism he criticises. To survive as 'feminine', Shen Te needs the 'masculine' aggression of Shui Ta.

Some critics complained that Nora's psychological development in *A Doll's House* was implausible. The development we noted in 2.5.3 was too sharp for them. But just as we have seen that Ibsen sets up Krogstad as a stage villain only then to reveal complexity, so Nora at the start seems to have been set up deliberately as a false signal. As Marker and Marker (1989) show, Nora in the opening moments is drawn as a stage type very popular in 1879 – the delightfully innocent, young, happy, carefree yet devoted housewife. She is an ideal type from the romantic drama that many in Ibsen's first audience would have admired – and they would have expected her to end the play yet more happily married. The actress who played her, Betty Hennings, was famous for playing such parts.

Naturalism – the movement which Ibsen was finding his way towards, helping to establish, in this play – began primarily as a movement concerned with the relationship between individuals and their environment: the social, historical and biological constraints put upon their self-realisation as fully human individuals. It was concerned with the contemporary, with the here and now. Often it was pessimistic, suggesting that we are all somehow trapped (see 5.1.3). But it was primarily a *critical* movement. It challenged **bourgeois** convention. It suggested that it was time to learn new roles in life, to stop living according to old rules and assumptions – because these were damaging to us.

We saw in the last subsection that Naturalism aimed to lay bare the true facts of contemporary life. It wanted to unmask hypocrisy. It took an *ironic* attitude – it assumed that there is a truth to be found behind appearances.

Ibsen's play has a deeply ironic structure. Not only does Nora discover that she herself has been playing a role which stifles the 'true' one she might find in life: the audience also discover that the pleasant fictions on their stage mask the reality surrounding them – and that the theatre is a place where they have tried to sustain such fictions about their own lives. Just as the play suddenly splits from being an apparently well-made play into something much less comfortable, so Nora *as a presentation to the audience* splits from stage type to ethical and psychological complexity.

Of course, Nora's naïveté at the start is part of this psychological complexity. But for the play to work as we suggest it was intended to, the audience must only realise this *after* they have at first taken Nora in as a simple character. Ibsen gives the actress a hugely challenging yet very exciting task – to play Nora *both* as continuous character *and* as discontinuous character. She is being invited to juggle two registers of performance with great skill (see Cima 1993).

> As an exercise: Look at one play you are studying and sketch out the various character dynamics. Which characters change, and how? How does this relate to audience response through positioning? Are all the characters continuous? Do you know of any plays in which there are discontinuous characters?

2.5.5 *Character conception as authentication or point of interest*

The critic who complained that Nora's development was implausible may himself have been in tune with the emerging conventions of Naturalism. But, even while the conventions of close psychological identification between actress and role were not yet established, the majority in that first audience could have accepted what we might now find artificial or stagey acting as a vehicle for communicating the truth of a psychology. *All theatrical watching is conventional*: we accept the signs made by the theatre as referring to something in real life, or to something in a fiction which we can somehow relate to real life. Through the lens of late-Romantic acting styles, then, that audience will have expected to see 'truths' about their lives, or life in general.

The actor's words and gestures do not need to be indistinguishable from those of real life in order for an audience to take and accept them as signs which are 'true' – which gesture persuasively towards real life. In other words, any number of acting styles, or registers of performance, can *authenticate* the performance, act as a guarantee that the stage is worth watching, that something meaningful is going on.

In the German city of Weimar in 1800, at the theatre of Goethe and Schiller, what helped authenticate the performance, to make it 'real' in relation to life and human value, was a *gracefulness* of bearing, the use of only the right hand for gestures, and the use of only particular gestures with definite meanings (4.2.3.2).

Brecht insisted that a truly realistic drama must delve beneath and beyond the obvious 'given' of a particular situation, or the details of a particular life. Thus it is the *distance* between performer and role which helps authenticate the Brechtian stage.

The notion of *'character effect'* might help us here. It simply refers to the constructed *illusion* of a whole personality – complete with inner consciousness, past history, spleen, kidneys and grandmother – which certain dramatic texts strive for, and perhaps most do effect to some degree. We can usefully ask the question, what actually produces this illusion, how is it achieved? Alan Sinfield (1992) has suggested, for instance, that the character Hamlet appears 'rounded' because there is an *excess of meaning* related to him. It is not so much either that we know everything about him, or that we know little and so become curious about him as if he were real. Rather, Sinfield suggests, it is because we know more than we need to – as we do about people close to us in real life.

We have established that Naturalism, the movement Ibsen helped install in the theatre, was typically concerned with the split between life as it appears and how it actually is. At the level of character there is the split between the role the character plays in their life, and the underlying reasons – what it is that motivates the playing of that particular life-role. The audience are not invited to relish the task of finding out the complex truth of the character, of filling or rounding out psychological being, of solving the 'riddle' of character. It is the struggle to find a meaningful role to play in life which is the actively interesting part. The *crisis* of role, not its 'roundedness', is the fundamental *point of interest*.

So, at the beginning, the complex characters of Naturalism were to some extent split or discontinuous characters. The complexity of characterisation was at one and the same time a point of interest (because of the crisis of life-role) and an emerging means of authenticating the theatrical event.

What has happened since is that the point of interest has subsided, while psychological complexity as character effect has become the dominant mode of authentication.

'Serious' dramatic texts thereafter have increasingly come to offer the players clues about character which they must interpret and, increasingly, come to their *own* sense of. Naturalism as it developed became a drama about very particular individuals: the actor's interpretation of the role became a key factor in the meanings playtexts made for an audience. It is this work that was addressed by Stanislavski's 'system', the set of exercises he developed for actors at the Moscow Arts Theatre early in the twentieth century.

So we are now in a position to see that the 'obvious' recipe of rounded character, psychological complexity, identification and empathy is only quite local to our own circumstances, and developed in circumstances that have now passed us by. And, as some still newer, some rediscovered and always various ways of playing are developed with theatre audiences of today, we see that recipe gradually falling into residue.

2.5.6 *Delivery*

Recall from 2.5.3 that by *character delivery* we mean the way that a character is progressively revealed to us. We shall look at two things – how the character is revealed to the audience in performance; and how they are delivered on the page in the playscript. Let us start with the first, delivery in the performance text.

In some plays the audience gets to know the character straight away. In others the character unfolds to them as the play progresses. This is what we mean by *character delivery*.

Let us use the example of the British TV detective series *Inspector Morse*. Character here is conceived psychologically. Fairly complex portraits are made of people we might recognise, and they typically doubt themselves, tell themselves or others half-truths or half-lies, and seem to be disturbed by a shadowy personal history. As an audience we can be interested in them 'as people', as well-drawn and detailed portraits of folk just like us. But is this really what is offered as our main point of interest?

In terms of *plot* what holds and indeed drives our interest along is the puzzle of evidence about the crime, and its gradual unravelling for us and for the detectives. Included in this is the ironic distance between our own knowledge or guesses and those of Morse. And it is here in particular that the *delivery* of character becomes important. What this series did so well, and what is a staple of its genre, is its *enigmatic* delivery of character. We see a character make a statement on screen. She is perhaps the lover of the murdered man. As she speaks, we not only listen to her words, but we also watch her eyes mist over, hear the catch in her voice. We are aware that we are in the presence of 'subtext' – that we glimpse the real role beneath the publicly lived one – yet we cannot just now ascertain what the reality is. There is a secret to be discovered. And we are to encounter several such characters, several potential suspects, in the course of the programme.

A psychological 'conception' of character helps authenticate this detective fiction for its medium, for television – which, as we suggested above, mostly cannot tolerate 'implausibility' of personation except in comedy. What is principally delivered is a deliciously complex web of clues, and much of our enjoyment is gained from tracking those clues to some sort of conclusion. But part of our enjoyment, too, is precisely the game of 'fathoming out' those who are suspects or whom we have come to suspect are later going to be revealed as suspects. The split between reality and lived role becomes in this case part of the apparatus of intrigue and irony in the drama. We are not principally interested in the relationship between people and their environment, or indeed in the complex working of a particular psychology, but in the repeated thrill of suspicion and discovery. Irony is not confined to the plot. Suspense operates both at the level of the plot *and* at the level of character delivery.

Let us now turn to the way in which the dramatic text delivers character to the actor.

Of course, any actress worth her salt will enter fully into the life of the character she plays, will make it fully 'rounded', will work hard to understand her motivation at various points in the play, particularly in relation to her more general motivations, her conscious and unconscious life-aims. And, of course, what can be gleaned or imagined about her life offstage – including before the start of the action – is important grist to this mill. She will bring all of this information to bear on every moment in the play's action.

But everything that is 'obvious' in the last paragraph we now know to be obvious only for the plays of later Naturalism and its residue. The actress playing Nora will miss half her part if she reads the play through that set of spectacles.

Shakespeare and other actors of his day – around 1600 – got their parts all right. They received the role they were to play. But a 'part' was precisely that – a roll of paper (a 'role') – on which just the lines they were to speak and their cues (the line immediately preceding theirs) were written. There was no such thing as the book of the play to refer to – and nobody was going to copy out the whole play a dozen times, just for the sake of a production. Why? The reason is because both character types and certain sorts of speeches followed fairly predictable patterns – and because actors specialised in particular sorts of role. Parts might well be written for them. In addition, consider that verse writing very efficiently scripts breath, body and emotion (3.4.2). As we established in Chapter 1, the Renaissance stage worked emblematically as much as it did psychologically. A piece of verse might suggest an emotional state, establish the character's expressivity; but the situation in which the speech was to be delivered was always very clearly drawn. Indeed, the verse itself often helps make the emblem (3.4.2). It is speech and emblem together which make the clearest sense, deliver the most potent 'truth' – not the character's 'through-line'. We pointed to an obvious Renaissance stage emblem – Desdemona kneeling – in Chapter 1. But we should be ready to see every scene, and every part of a scene (4.1.19), in a Renaissance play as a fresh emblem, a fresh stage picture.

Our final thoughts on character articulation now turn to the selection of characters.

2.5.7 *The* dramatis personae

The persons in a Classical Athenian tragedy – apart from the odd messenger who brings bad news – are grand people: princes, queens, military heroes. Aristotle later assumed that only people of rank would attract empathy – while superheroes and gods would not, because they are too unlike us.

Shakespeare's stage, what used to be called the 'Golden Age' of English drama, has characters of a much wider social range; though those of lower class tend to be the comic characters. It is often suggested that Renaissance dramatists were thinking, consciously or not, about the whole social fabric because society was changing so rapidly. It is also sometimes suggested that this was a time of increased democratic feeling.

In the prologue of Nicholas Rowe's *The Fair Penitent* (1703), the actress speaking the prologue declares that this is no tragedy of princes, but of ordinary middling sort of folk. Middling folk now wanted to see themselves on stage in serious situations.

Miller's *Death of a Salesman* (1949) has as its protagonist a lower-middle-class shoe salesman.

What classes of people are represented in the drama, and what sort of roles they play, tell us much about the culture in which a theatre operates, and the role it plays within it. That it was an *actress* delivering Rowe's prologue is, of course, significant in itself. Women were not allowed on the professional stage in England until the Restoration in 1660. Most of the major characters in plays written today are probably still male.

As an exercise: (1) To what extent does character conception authenticate the play you are now studying? How? What else do you need to know to decide? Is character conception itself a point of interest in the play? Are there, for instance, crises of life-role, or various sorts of character conception at work in the play? (2) Look at character delivery in the dramatic text. Does the author make clear signals to the player, for instance in an opening stage direction? On what must the player base their performance? (3) Look at character delivery in the theatrical text. How is the audience scripted to experience the character? Is all revealed at once? Only gradually? How, and why? (4) Look at the *dramatis personae* from a number of plays. What conclusions do you draw?

2.6 Further aspects of dramatic character

There are three further aspects of dramatic character for us to consider, following on section 2.2.

2.6.1 *Discursive function*

One possible basis of character conception we suggested in 2.4.1.2 was 'discursive'. The character speaks a particular discourse, a way of talking about the world which is structured in a particular way (3.1.5.4). Thus, for instance, Dr Rank in *A Doll's House* turns out not to be the *raisonneur* we expected.

He is rather a resigned sort of chap – ready to die, a bit sad with life, and believing that his illness is the result of his father's dissolute life.

Now, this discourse of being resigned to the fact that your life is shaped/determined from the outset is not just important to Dr Rank personally. It is a proposition that Ibsen clearly wants us to think about and consider. So while Rank does not state this as a world-view as a *raisonneur* might, his character nevertheless contributes to what the play itself seems to be 'saying to' or 'discussing with' us. In the same play, Helmer suggests to Nora that a criminal parent will corrupt their children just by being with them. Nora believes him and abandons her children. This sort of question was on many lips in 1879. So the discourses of characters can contribute to the discourse of the play as a whole.

But this sort of contribution is made by more than what the characters say and do. Their character dynamic will be significant – what happens to particular sorts of person, and why. And by 'particular sort' we need not mean 'sort' in real life. Our mapping exercise in section 2.3 helped us organise the *dramatis personae* according to their *value* in the play's scheme. Part of the play's discourse – its structured way of speaking about the world – is what it shows happening to particular sorts of value.

As an exercise: Inspect character discourse, and the dynamics of characters who seem to bear particular sorts of value, in any play you are studying. Sketch out an account of the discourses the play seems to be dealing in.

2.6.2 Aesthetic function

Characters can deliver sheer pleasure – because of the way they speak or the way they behave; because they are such outlandish, or typical, characters; or because they are so wonderfully subtly or deliciously crudely drawn. Alongside all the other five functions we consider, and connecting with them in ways we can play with in our commentaries, is this question of the direct pleasure witnessing a stage character brings: what we shall call the *aesthetic aspect* of character.

2.6.3 Vehicle

In some sorts of theatre, the character is principally there as a vehicle for the performer's special skills. This is the case with various sorts of clown, like *Arlecchino* (Harlequin) in the many scenarios of the *commedia dell'arte* (Rudlin 1994). We might say that, among other things, the character here is a *vehicle* for the performer. Some of the Italian Dario Fo's characters written for his own brand of political clowning were derived from the *commedia*. The part is a vehicle for the display of his own comic skills, though Fo regards those skills as a vehicle in turn for progressive political satire.

2.7 Character at work

We have come a long way since the opening of this chapter. Let us end it by looking at a few examples of character at work, to review what we have learned.

Let us return once more to Krogstad as a stage villain who turns out not to be one. We have said that he feels wronged by society. But Nora herself wrongs him. In the first act, she is very pompous about her husband's new job as bank manager. She promises Mrs Linde that she will get her a job there. She crows about this to Krogstad, whom she treats with absolute disdain. When she learns that Krogstad has been a clerk at the bank and was recently fired by Helmer she has to back-track and insist that she meant him no harm. Ibsen here ties a nice knot for Nora and audience alike. For Krogstad is indeed a threat to Nora, because he alone knows her secret. He is, for the time being, the villain of the piece. But part and parcel of his 'villainy' is his class status. Nora is a snob, and the audience are thrown into this collision of the stage type they can comfortably hate and Nora's embarrassing echo of their own habitual class prejudice. People are not what they at first appear.

The medieval '**morality**' play *Everyman* (*c.*1498) concerns the fate of a character called Everyman. He stands for all people – all men. God sends Death to stop him on his complacent way and to prepare for the end of his life, for the judgement to come. He resists, and tries to find a way of delaying. He asks various characters – like Friendship, Kindred and Goods – to help. But eventually, finding his quest for delay an impossibility, he sets out on a new quest to make atonement for his sins in life. His helpers now are such as Knowledge, Confession and Good Deeds; so, in the end, he dies well. Morality-play characters like Greed, Sloth, Patience and Confession have since been called 'personified abstractions' – ideas and values important to us are made into whole characters on the medieval morality stage.

The dramatic writing that was powerfully emergent in the Renaissance period in England gave the effect of an inner personality. It portrayed an individuality which is at least as important as, and comes before, one's social position; and it portrayed individual *expressivity*. The emergence of this sort of writing is one important element of a cultural practice which is itself part of a massive transformation of social and economic conditions. While there are arguments as to the relationships between them, these changes can be specified as the emergence of capitalism within and against feudalism; the rise of Protestantism; **humanism**; and sceptical reasoning.

Yet alongside this emergent 'psychological' writing in Renaissance plays is the sort of 'emblematic' writing we have identified. The logic of the 'personified abstraction' – a clear and definite basis to the conception of the character – remains as an active residue from the past. So, in Renaissance plays, two different ways of writing character occur side by side, and we appear to be invited to 'add them together' to get the complete picture. The same character is frequently composed of both psychological and emblematic aspects. To read a Renaissance play as if it were Naturalism or a TV soap is, quite clearly, to misread it, to miss its own rhetorical procedures, the way it works persuasively on us.

But personified abstractions are there on the TV screen, too. In a much less declared way, contemporary **dramaturgy** almost always uses particular characters, if not to stand for, then at least to *conduct* particular qualities – to enact them in particular situations ('Men Behaving Badly'). The 'type' is more than a sort of clearly outlined, cartooned representative of a recognisable social group. It is not simply a case of making the picture of the individual character clearer or easier to handle. The abstraction, the deliberate bracketing off or downplaying of psychological complexity or personal history, allows questions to be asked about typical *beliefs and actions*. Soaps and detective dramas are good cases in point. This does not, we would contend, make them 'bad' dramas. If it did, it would make much of Aeschylus, Sophocles and Euripides bad, too.

All characters are in some way or another 'models' of human behaviour. This chapter has set out a number of ways in which we can think and write about what sort of models there are, and how that modelling works.

|3|

Dialogue

3.1 The workings of dialogue

3.1.1 *Theatrical communication*

Let us start by stating the obvious: what is said on stage is designed to be heard by the audience. When one character speaks to another, he or she sends a message – about themselves or their desires or what happened last week – to the other character, who receives this message. But this onstage communication itself, involving both sender and receiver, can be thought of as another message, one being sent from the stage to the audience – again about character, action and circumstance, but always a slightly different message from that between character and character.

In theatre, then, there are always two lines of communication. First there is communication between characters. Second, there is communication between the stage and the audience. Our own preference is to speak of this second message being sent from the *stage*; others, like Mick Short (1989), speak of it being sent by the *author*. Both are reasonable ways of putting it.

Stating the obvious can help us think about varieties of theatre and varieties of character. In stage Naturalism and almost all TV and films, the audience 'overhear' what passes between characters. But in medieval drama and still in the Renaissance, in Brecht's theatre and much TV situation comedy, the fact that a message is being sent to the audience is not hidden but rather declared, either implicitly (in the attitude of the performer: see 2.5.2) or explicitly, by a character speaking directly to the audience or camera.

Let us think briefly about the character who stands and speaks alone (*solus*) on stage. In a soliloquy such as Hamlet's famous 'To be, or not to be' (3.1.55 ff.), we can imagine that we are overhearing. Maybe he is talking to himself – or maybe the convention is being assumed that we are hearing his thoughts. But our best bet is to assume that, in Shakespeare's time, speaking *solus* always includes the convention that the character is speaking directly to the audience. Hamlet – and the stage he is on – is discussing the purpose of existence directly with us, as well as with himself.

In the famous opening speech of Shakespeare's *Richard 3* (1592/3), Richard stands alone and tells the audience directly about three things. First, he sets up the situation, that of peace after war. Then he describes himself, as being unfit for such tranquil times. Thirdly, he tells us what he is going to do, which is trick his way to power. Richard here acts as Narrator (or Presenter, Chorus) to his own play. Many plays have such special characters dedicated to announcing the theatrical presentation. But this speech – especially its middle section, which is based on the self-presentations of the medieval **Vice** – is fun because it tells us more about Richard than he plans to tell us himself. Here, after all, is a man who *revels* in his wickedness (see Clemen 1986).

Narrators, asides (when a character turns away from a conversation to comment on it or their real purpose in it), self-presentations, soliloquies and choric songs remain an important part of the dramatic repertoire today. And always implicit, though often explicit, in *all* dialogue, is that second line of communication we have noted between stage and auditorium.

As an exercise: Look at a chunk of stage dialogue and distinguish between onstage communication and communication between stage and auditorium. What makes the difference? Seek out various examples of *solus* speaking or choric song and describe them as pieces of communication.

3.1.2 Functions of dialogue

We are concerned in this chapter with dialogue as something spoken on the stage. What does it deliver to the audience? Looking back now to Chapter 1, Fig. 1.1, we can start with the following:

- *conversational exchange between characters* (see section 3.2, below);
- *information as to time and place*;
- *information about action* (what has happened elsewhere: see 4.1.16);
- *actual enactments* (like accusations, confessions: see section 3.3);
- *information about characters* (how they speak and what about; what is said of others).

This makes a useful checklist when reading stage dialogue. We can now stand back a little and see just what it is designed to deliver to the audience at any one time.

The weighting of these various functions will differ throughout the play. Most begin with some sort of *exposition*. While information about time and place will be scattered throughout, an audience is typically told about the here and now at the beginning. Exposition may be declared – say, a Narrator gives it – or 'woven in' to the dialogue. If the play begins when the action it is concerned with has already begun (say, the murder has already been committed, or the feud between the families has lasted three generations already), the exposition may refer in detail to past events. Plays such as this are said to begin *in medias res* (Latin: 'in the middle of things'). When delivered by a character, exposition is both information about the situation and previous action, and implicit information about the character. Most exposition, then, also delivers the character's 'perspective' (4.1.16.3). Consider, for instance, Nora's conversation with Mrs Linde in Act 1 of *A Doll's House*.

Information about characters is embedded in dialogue in a number of ways. As well as what others say of them, we have each character's own *expressivity* – the sort of tactics they use in conversational exchanges (3.2, below); what they say about themselves (though we need to distinguish between what *they* say they are and what *we* make of this given the circumstance of its saying); their typical mode of expression, throughout or in various circumstances (are they rational, passionate, devious, tender . . . ?); their declared or implied beliefs.

3.1.3 Ideolect and sociolect

All of us speak in a particular way. We have a recognisable style of speech. Perhaps we use irony a lot. Do we tend to insinuate things? Are we crisp and to the point, or loquacious? Do we use simple words and sentences, or obscure words and tangled syntax? A person's particular way of speaking is called their *ideolect*. Dialogue often establishes stage character through ideolect. Think of Wilde's Lady Bracknell in *The Importance of Being Earnest* (1895).

Yet social groups also share a common way of speaking. This goes beyond accent. In Britain, the way in which people from Liverpool present themselves and interact with others, the way they put things, is recognisably different from the way people from Tunbridge Wells do these same things. The same goes for agricultural workers versus City of London office workers. A shared style of speech is called a *sociolect*. In plays, sociolect quickly establishes the character's social origin or status.

Clearly, ideolect is often at work in comic characterisation, and sociolect in making stereotypes. But these are not the only possibilities.

As an exercise: Look at one scene from a play and sketch out the various ways in which stage dialogue is designed to work on the audience.

3.1.4 Dynamics

In this subsection we are concerned with the push-and-pull of dialogue – both between characters and between the stage and the auditorium.

3.1.4.1 THE DYNAMICS OF EXCHANGE

Even with simple characters we are drawn into the cut and thrust of an argument, or the verbal embraces of young love, or the stunned response to bad news. Regardless of characters or the details of the fiction, let us say that *dialogue demands its own empathy* – we easily imagine ourselves in such a situation; these exchanges are ones that could be ours; it might be our own story. Such exchanges most certainly will have happened in our own *real* story.

Drama plugs into our most basic desires, fears and wants. Just as the clown slipping on the banana skin makes our stomach turn, so the threat from the outsider makes us look over our own shoulder. All of us feel threatened in some way, and theatre stimulates that fear and many other basic feelings. We easily – automatically – imagine ourselves as part of the situation shaped by the dialogue. As we wrote in 2.5.1, 'Look out behind you!'

So while dialogue constructs character and action, and we can become good at describing this, we also need to show how local bits of dialogue involve the audience in the cut and thrust of position-taking, challenge, triumph, defeat; the securities of meeting and embrace; the joys of recovering lost ones; the thrill of verbal abuse and profanity; the feelings of isolation but also relief when confessing guilt. Then we are going much further in describing how the play as a whole works on the audience.

This aspect of the dialogue can best be shown in a diagram (see Fig. 3.1). Is it a stand-off between two forces of equal strength? A meeting of minds? Or maybe it is an **apostrophe**, in which the speaker reaches beyond the immediate situation, to address someone or something not present – like a god, nature or a dead hero?

It may be that a particular sort of exchange occurs several times throughout a play or scene. If so, then perhaps an opposition between specific characters, or some other sort of relatedness like trust, love or suspicion, is being gone over again and again. Or perhaps the dynamic between them changes over time. Either will be significant. And some plays are *full* of, say, questionings, or clashes, or people talking past one another. If so, we need to spot this and comment. Section 3.2 below on conversational exchange will help in this work.

The dynamics of exchange can sometimes be formalised. An example is *stichomythia* (Greek, 'stitch rhyme'), in which two opposing interlocutors repeatedly turn what their opponent has said around to make it the pretext for a fresh attack. The argument feels as if it will be never-ending. They are implacably – and creatively – opposed. A famous example is the argument between Antigone and Creon in Sophocles' *Antigone*:

meeting of minds　　　　　*stand-off*　　　　　*apostrophe*

A　　　　　　B　　　A⟶　←B　　　A　　　　　　B

X

complex exchange

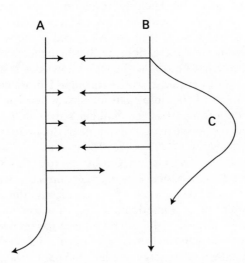

Fig. 3.1 Sketching the dynamics of exchange – some examples
In the complex exchange, B dominates the conversation by drawing C into agreement, and by
questioning, commanding or insisting on things to A. Eventually, A fires off a parting sally and
quits.

ANTIGONE: Ah the good fortune of kings.
           Licensed to say and do whatever they please!
CREON: You are alone here in that opinion.
ANTIGONE: No, they are with me. But they keep their tongues in
           leash.
CREON: Maybe. But you are guilty and they are not.
ANTIGONE: There is no guilt in reverence for the dead.
           [etc. etc.]

(scene II, p. 270)

Stichomythia quickly develops the opposing sides of the argument. It concentrates the argument. And, especially when done in emulation of Greek examples such as this, it is a point where the dramatic text declares its own artifice, the fact that it is composed.

3.1.4.2 STRUCTURAL DYNAMICS

In Section 3.1.2 above we noted that dialogue delivers *exposition* – it provides information to the audience. A great deal of drama uses suspense to move an audience and to maintain its attention. In the TV courtroom drama, we know that the truth is there to be found. If the world is just, then the characters we like *must* end up innocent. If dramatic irony works on us by giving us more information than any one person in the fictional world, then suspense works in the opposite direction. *Someone* knows the truth, but that is not us just now. Then the revelation comes and we feel release. Both withheld exposition and anticipated action (she says she will be revenged on him: we wait to see how, when and if she will succeed) create suspense, and both are the creations of the dialogue. This management of the dialogue with regard to the audience's knowledge is an important part of the play's overall design. It works through a movement between non-delivery and delivery of plot information. This activity of holding back and releasing information is part of the dialogue's *structural dynamic*.

Another aspect of the structural dynamic of dialogue is the way it scripts the sheer *verbal energy* of the stage. We can let a word drift from our mouths or force it out. The 'Get' in 'Get off my foot' has a different 'attack' if I say the sentence with patience or in anger. Similarly, we can inspect how the energy of dialogue at the start of a scene affects the scene's 'attack'. Is the dialogue urgent or composed? How does this scene hit us, or invite us in? And what is its 'cadence'? Just as a sentence has its rise-and-fall pattern or even tone, so a scene has its own cadence too. The cadence comes from the shape of the dialogue's energy as much as that of the action. And then, is this scene which is full of violent language followed by one of whispers or gentle laughter?

In scene 13 of Brecht's *The Life of Galileo* (1943), Galileo's friends wait in suspense to learn whether the Inquisition will get him to recant his heterodox views on the motion of the earth. While their talk is urgent and excited, Brecht makes this a scene which *shows* suspense rather than making us feel it, by the technique used throughout this play, and regularly by him elsewhere, of using scene-titles. A placard on stage has already told us that the scene will show that Galileo recants. Brecht deliberately removes the suspense. His scene-title blunts the 'attack' of the scene. He wants us to concentrate on some other things instead. Here are people making a drama out of Galileo, treating him as a hero and the object of suspense. And downstage is the figure of Galileo's daughter, praying. Yes, indeed, we see that Galileo has driven Virginia into religious superstition. But she is also part of the general *gestus* of the scene (see 4.2.3.2): that's to say, Virginia is not the only person in the scene who believes in miracles.

As an exercise: Inspect the dynamics of exchange and structural dynamics of dialogue in any play you are reading. How do particular exchanges work to draw in the audience? Is audience knowledge manipulated? How? How does dialogue structure the 'feel' or 'energy' of scenes and the succession of scenes? Use sketch diagrams to help your analysis.

3.1.5 More functions of dialogue

3.1.5.1. TEXTUAL REGISTER AND EXPRESSIVITY

In 3.1.2 above we identified the expressivity of characters as one aspect of dramatic dialogue: characters speak about themselves, express emotion, and reveal aspects of their character through the ways they relate to people. *Textual expressivity* is another aspect. We can think of this in terms of the play's *register* from time to time or throughout. Consider part of the closing moments of *King Lear*:

KENT:	Is this the promis'd end?
EDGAR: Or image of that horror?	
ALBANY:	Fall and cease!

(5.3.263–4)

While not a declared chorus, the characters are speaking *as if* a chorus. The three half-lines melt into one another across the different speakers; all speak of the same thing. The three men are here an onstage audience to the terrible events that we, at our safer distance, have also witnessed. As people within the fiction they are responding to events that have 'really' happened. But the lines are also a piece of self-presentation by the play. In the playhouse we respond to the composed, formal nature of this dialogue.

Consider that verse in itself puts a play into a different register of expression. While all dialogue is composed, much prose dialogue is designed to hide this fact. It is *pseudo-colloquial*, pretend everyday speech. But verse is language which draws attention to itself *as* a composition. It frequently confers a sense of dignity and seriousness on the play. Hence the regular distinction made between *verse for tragedy* and *prose for comedy* in Renaissance playtexts.

All the same, verse can be used for comic effect – like the 'old-fashioned' verse Shakespeare has the mechanicals and the players use in *A Midsummer Night's Dream* (1594) and *Hamlet* (1601) respectively, or the tightly rhyming, sparky verse which gives Bartlett's translation of Molière's *The Misanthrope* (1666) such a comic lift. In his play *Job Rocking* (1987), the different sorts of verse create what Benjamin Zephaniah calls a 'theatre of rhythm' (p. 144). We look a little more closely at how stage poetry works below (3.4).

3.1.5.2 FORMAL FRAMINGS: PROLOGUE AND EPILOGUE

Plays of the Restoration in particular are marked by speeches to be made outside of the play's action, but most certainly as an important part of the stage presentation. Spoken by a performer out of role, yet inevitably also associated with the role they do have, these prologues and epilogues might well refer to the content of the play. But their main functions are to speak on behalf of or in celebration of the author; defend stage practice against its detractors; seriously or impishly criticise other playwrights; establish an often witty relationship with the audience; and add to the speaker's charm and authority as a professional. We are mistaken if we ignore these as part of the play.

3.1.5.3 THEME

Read an introduction to any Shakespeare play and you will find that there are themes of nature, or kingship, or Christian redemption, or some such else. A common exercise to be given in class or examination is to set off in search of theme and imagery, to see how one supports the other (for example, animal imagery may contribute to a theme of human nature.) While all plays have their themes, it is verse which tends to support imagery (metaphors and similes) and allusions (to fable or Classical learning); these in turn set up one or several *frames of reference* for understanding the action and characters. They declare what the play is about.

It can be the case, of course, that a playwright is showing off a bit, or attempting to heighten the tone of the play by introducing such explicit thematic material. But in the best plays, imagery and allusion are not bolted on as if to illustrate the theme. Rather, for the playwright they have become the terms in which the subject matter, the story, *needs* to be handled and imagined.

And neither is theme confined to dialogue. It is also constructed by the characters and their action. 'Spotting' a theme by spotting imagery and allusion is only the beginning of really getting down to thematics. A list of quotations is not enough. With which character is the image connected? In what way? In what circumstances is it uttered? What relationships can we map between such characters, and what does this do to **articulate** theme? What do the plot and its resolution – if any – do to the shape of the theme? How do the various themes in the play relate to one another? Diagrams will help.

3.1.5.4 IDEOLOGY AND DISCOURSE

In the table of modes of character conception in Chapter 2, we used the terms 'ideology' and 'discourse'. They are related, but subtly and usefully different. For our purposes here, let us take 'ideology' to mean a fixed belief. Perhaps I believe in the Christian god, or capitalism, or hanging for murderers. It can then be said, with no offence to believers, that I have a distinctive religious, political, economic or judicial *ideology*.

But in a more diffuse way, I may habitually talk in terms of things these days having gone downhill; or as if I truly expected that the goodness of heart of special people would always magically save the day. In these cases I would be speaking either pessimistic or romantic *discourse*. A discourse is a structured way of speaking about the world. Ideology and discourse interlink, of course. A feminist believes in the rights and value of women, and that men have frustrated these – this is her ideology. But she also uses feminist discourse – a structure of arguments, assumptions and analysis – to think about and argue for that cause. Characters may speak from an ideological position; they may also set up a particular discourse for the audience to interact with.

When Edmund in *King Lear* (1605/6) says, 'Now, gods, stand up for bastards' (1.2.22) he is speaking a discourse of self-determination. He introduces into the play – and acts upon – the spoken assumption that people can make themselves into what they want to be. Power and wealth come from what you do in your life, not from your status at birth. When he speaks this line, he has just performed a nasty yet *amusing* trick on his superstitious father. Opposing Edmund's discourse, Shakespeare sets the discourse of loyalty spoken and performed by Kent and Cordelia. Both of them speak and act from the assumption that there is a bond of mutual respect between ruler and ruled, father and daughter. But all this does is to provoke Lear into sending them into exile. Meanwhile, Edmund quickly turns out to be very cruelly selfish. Both discourses, then, have their downside. Many commentaries on the play note that it is written at a time of great and rapid change in the basic social and economic fabric of England. The feudal system, with its discourse of mutual bondedness, was being displaced by capitalism, with its discourse of self-determination. The play seems to show the old system in hopeless decay, and the one supplanting it as potentially very dangerous. This clash of discourses happens within a framework of more general discourses scattered throughout the play about human needs and desires, power and government, the nature of humanity, popular knowledge, and redemption through faith.

So 'discourse' might prove to be a better word for us to use than 'theme'. All of us speak our own set of discourses. Each character will speak theirs. In many plays, character discourse is being offered to the audience to interact with – one of the key functions of such a character in the play is to carry and perform this discourse. Imagery and allusion intensify discourse, make it more recognisable as the thing we call 'theme'.

A play like *Lear* (there are many) sets up a system of discourses that interact with one another. The action sets them in play with one another.

We have said that discourses, sometimes clearly foregrounded as 'theme', often set up *frames of reference* for understanding the play. Some plays contain any competing discourses within them in a single discourse which acts as a sort of 'outer frame' – the audience is invited to regard it as superior to the others. We could call this the play's *discursive frame*. The discursive frame of all Brecht's plays after around 1930 is Marxism. Within it, he sets up discourses of ethical behaviour, imperialism, gender relations, human nature, and so on.

3.1.5.5 SENTENTIAE

Often we may feel that a character is the author's mouthpiece, that by this means the author is 'laying down the law'. A more polite way of saying this is that the author is being *sententious*. Many Renaissance plays have characters deliver lines like Delio's '*Integrity of life is fame's best friend, / Which nobly, beyond death, shall crown the end*' (5.5.120–1), which conclude Webster's *The Duchess of Malfi* (1614). Since it comes at the end, is spoken by a morally worthy character, and is set out as a unit of verse, we can take it as a message coming (somewhat) directly from author to audience. Proverbial statements such as this are called *sententiae* (sing. -*tia*). When, in the same play, the tyrannical Ferdinand thanks Bosola for his plain speaking with the *sententia*, '*That friend a great man's ruin strongly checks, / Who rails into his belief all his defects*' (3.1.92–3), he is speaking good sense but with utter insincerity. The lines thus come to have an ironic relationship to Ferdinand himself.

We can think of *sententiae* as bits of discourse specially foregrounded by a play.

In some plays we may find characters delivering *sententiae* that establish their discursive position rather than that of the author; or sententious characters (this is their ideolect) who do not speak so formally.

3.1.5.6 SIGNATURE

Many playwrights have their distinctive style. Not only the language which their characters speak, but also such features as the patterning of speeches, the pace of action, the relationship between action and event (see 4.1.1) are recognisably theirs. Wilde's epigrammatic and ironic style, and Orton's later emulation of it, declare the presence of the author behind the text. It is as if the play were being 'signed' by the author. When we sign a letter we are saying, 'This is my message to you.' A distinctive style which declares authorship is called *signature*.

Caryl Churchill's skip-connecting (where one character picks up on the middle of the previous speaker's speech and responds to that, often before they have finished) in *Top Girls* (1982) instantly became her 'signature' – even though it has not been her regular style. Pinter's pauses have been part of his.

3.1.5.7 PLEASURE

Let us not forget that composed language not only persuades, it also gives pleasure. We go to the theatre to witness art as much as fiction. Our commentaries need to attend to the direct pleasures written into stage speech as much as to its dramatic content.

Pleasure is not confined to effects of beauty. Language can be surprising, acrobatic, wonderfully various as well as magnificently measured.

Of course, the relative beauty of speaking will be part of the system of ideolects at work within a play. Maybe the 'good' or 'high' characters speak well and the 'bad' or 'low' badly – though villains often get the best lines!

As an exercise: Review this section, with plays you know in mind. How would its various suggestions help you to comment on them?

3.2 The workings of conversation

What goes on in a conversation? Linguists have for some time studied the ways in which people interact through talk in everyday life. The insights and methods of analysis developed in this branch of study, Sociolinguistics, can help us in ours. So we are here concerned with the *interpersonal* functions of stage dialogue – what passes between character and character. If, later on, you want to pursue these ideas in more detail, a good place to start is with Short (1989), from whom a number of topics have been borrowed here. Herman (1995) provides a book-length study.

Let us imagine a conversation between two people. They take turns. A says something, B responds:

(1) A: Lovely weather we're having.
(2) B: It's gorgeous. Have you come far?
(3) A: Took about twenty minutes walking. The bus takes longer. It goes all round the houses. Imagine trudging all round the estates in a bus in this heat, full of screaming kids with their

buckets and spades. No, I'd rather walk, me. I've always been
a walker, really.

(4) B: The sea's so calm, isn't it?

(5) A: You a walker?

(6) B: If I want exercise, I prefer to swim.

(7) A: Get yourself some stout boots, old girl. Otherwise you'll get
blisters.

(8) B: I'm going for an ice-cream.

What comments can we make?

3.2.1 *Turn-taking*

Participants in a conversation take turns. What they say invites a response.
In the first exchange (1, 2) A's opening gambit is to make a statement. B
affirms by making a similar one, and then invites A to respond to a question.
If the conversation continued like this, we would have a succession of cues
and responses:

A: cue
B: response – cue
A: response – cue
B: response – cue
     . . . and so on

Looking at (6), we see that response and cue need not be separated out for
the conversation still to run smoothly. B has responded to A's question by
inviting comment on another form of exercise: the cue for a further response
has been made.

The conversation ends when the chain of cue and response is broken.
Here, at (8), B breaks off the conversation by declaring her departure.

3.2.2 *Types of turn*

There are three obvious types of conversational cue: statements, questions
and commands. Each can be responded to differently. Here are some suggestions:

statement affirm
                deny

question answer
              refuse to answer
              ask for qualification

```
command    obey
           question
           refuse
```

Remember that a response can itself constitute the next cue. You ask how big I am and I ask for qualification of your question: 'Do you mean how heavy or how tall?' Or you tell me to pick up your bag and I say, 'I daren't, because of my back.'

Clearly, the preponderance of a particular type of cue in a conversation from one party or another can be significant, especially if it changes over time. I begin my job interview answering the questions fired at me, each answer merely cueing my interviewer's next question; then I negotiate room to make some statements of my own; having gained confidence, I ask a few questions myself. If I am not terribly impressed by what I am hearing, perhaps I demand to know what their policy is with regard to equal opportunities (and see Pfister 1988: 148–54).

We shall return to questions, commands and statements below, in section 3.3.

> As a short exercise: (1) Inspect the types of turn at work in the conversation above; (2) play with making different responses to the cues.

In passing, let us note that drama improvisation games depend very much on the easy flow of cues and responses back and forth between the participants. Failing to provide cues to your partner 'blocks' the game.

3.2.3 Topic control, initiation of exchanges, and lexical control

All the same, one of the factors that makes improvised, real-life or scripted dialogue interesting is its departure from regularity. Unexpected or unwarranted responses are made to cues, and those responses become the cue for the conversation to take a different direction.

B's casual question at (2), which merely contributes to an exchange of pleasantries, is met at (3) with what threatens to be a life-history from A. B tries to divert from this by talking about the sea and swimming at (4) and (6). But A persists with talk about walking, to the extent that (7) is no response at all to (6), but rather a continuation of A's own (5).

A has tried to hog the conversation, to lead it in a particular direction. B responds by trying to return the conversation to an exchange of pleasantries – or, perhaps, to take control of it herself , 'digging in' around the topic of swimming. A major feature of this short conversation is a struggle over *topic control*.

Note also that B attempts to begin the conversation afresh at (4) with the switch from walking and the estate to the sea. She does this in some desperation. But other speakers may habitually initiate exchanges because they are, for instance, in positions of authority (the interviewer) or are very sociable or supportive people. B takes A's (1) for just such an opening. Both the character habits and the local details of *initiation of exchange* are useful things to spot.

Suppose that A had been bossy in a different way, not by insisting on the topic of conversation, but rather by doing this:

    (4) B: The sea's so calm, isn't it?
    (5') A: Placid.
    (6') B: I think I may take a swim.
    (7') A: Go for a swim.
    (8) B: I'm going for an ice-cream.

A's (5') is not so much an affirmation of (4) as a correction to it – confirmed by the further 'correction' of 'take' to 'go for' at (7'). A is trying to insist on how things should be expressed, what the proper words and phrases are. A is attempting to take *lexical control* (see Short 1989: 156–67).

> As a short exercise: Improvise a conversation between a hospital patient in a cancer ward and their visitor. Play with topic control, lexical control and the initiation of exchanges.

3.2.4 *Length of turn*

A takes control first by talking at length at (3). Even if there were no struggle over topic control, the long turn might well signal a desire to dominate the conversation. Imbalance of *length of turn* is one indication of power difference in a conversation.

But we cannot make it a rule that long turns mean domination. Consider, for instance, a confession to a priest. Have you sinned? A long answer signals the worthiest surrender to mercy or justice. Here, speaking at length is a way of surrendering.

Similarly, while it has been suggested that short turns of equal length – like (1) and (2) above – signal an easy familiarity between the speakers, we might also imagine such a rhythm at work in a fierce argument or, say, the questioning of a truculent offender by a police officer. *Stichomythia* (3.1.4.1, above) is a battle of wits conducted through short exchanges.

So, too, long and equal turns might signal deep intimacy, but they might also result from two people trying to speak their own monologue.

Length of turn, then, is a significant factor in the dynamics of conversation, but there are no absolute rules for its interpretation. We can make useful observations about length of turn in conversations we meet in dramatic dialogue if we attend to

- *relational factors*: Has the length of turn changed in the course of this conversation? Is this bit of dialogue different from the last or next? Why?
- *combinatory factors*: What other markers are there for intimacy, power-difference, etc.? (examples might be tone of address, topic control)

Length of turn, if we attend to relational and combinatory factors, is one piece of data we can use in our commentary on dramatic dialogue. It is one important characteristic of the conversation being staged. But note that it also contributes to the feel of the stage, its 'temperature' or energy, the rhythm of a scene. This is as much a proper part of our commentary as is attention to what is going on between the characters. Consider how length of turn gives a different feel to a Pinter play as compared to one by Ayckbourn.

3.2.5 *Terms of address*

Our two conversationalists do not refer to one another by name. Perhaps they are a little familiar with one another, perhaps they have only just met. We cannot tell from the conversation itself. But there is one act of naming, and that does tell us something. At (7) A calls B 'old girl'. This is a very familiar and potentially deprecatory term of address. We can tell that A and B do not know one another well, from A's question (5), 'You a walker?' Clearly, then, A is being presumptuous or insensitive or both. Perhaps this, as much as the one-sidedness of the conversation, makes her break it off.

The adult in the Catholic confessional is addressed as 'My child' and responds with 'Father'. Butler and aristocrat refer to one another as 'Your Lordship', or 'Lady Margaret', and 'Jeeves' respectively. The policewoman who has stopped me for speeding calls me by my first name, and I call her 'Officer'. The male interviewee for the job is addressed as 'Mister O'Toole' but addresses none of the interviewers by name, out of deference. One of the panel calls the female interviewee '*Ms* O'Toole' with such a deliberate emphasis that it signals hostility.

So an important marker for the type of relationship between characters – and for the breaking of the rules of decorum such relationships entail – is the system of terms of address the speakers employ (Short 1989: 154–6). Are surnames or forenames used, and who by? Are there terms of endearment or of insult? Do such usages change in the course of the scene or play? Are the usages scripted so as to appear appropriate to the circumstances, or not?

An obvious point of reference for us are the names Torvald and Nora use in *A Doll's House*. In Act 1 they call one another by these forenames, but

Torvald also calls her 'squirrel' and 'songbird'. She uses no such diminutive in return, though she refers to herself in the same terms. In Act 3, Torvald still refers to her as his 'songbird' but without her compliance: she has 'changed' (p. 96), and no longer surrenders to Helmer's attempts to dominate and contain her.

So we have in this play a pattern, an '**economy**', of naming: there are significant differences between characters and from one time to the next. A good account of this economy of naming would tackle the irony Nora is scripted to employ in Act 1 when she refers to 'we larks and squirrels'(p. 26). She is proud of her secret, and her use of the plural challenges Helmer's power to condescend. A good account would also note Helmer's extension of this patronising familiarity into criticism and correction of Nora's behaviour: he calls her (in translation) 'squanderbird'.

We have just used the phrase 'patronising familiarity'. But not everyone would agree with us. While we would rather not chat with them ourselves, there are no doubt still some folk around who would find Helmer's naming of his wife sweet, loving and perfectly normal. Certainly there were such people at the play's first performances, as contemporary reviews attest (see Marker and Marker 1989: 46 ff.). Ibsen seems to offer his first audiences a conventional picture of domestic bliss, which they come to find sickening as the play progresses and as they look back at its beginning. They seem to be prompted to change in tandem with Nora.

The prevailing social conventions, both those in the theatre and those supposed in the fiction, are important factors in our interpretation of these patterns of naming. When in 1956 John Osborne has Jimmy in *Look Back in Anger* say to Alison, 'Bears and squirrels *are* marvellous' (p. 34), he seems certain to be prompting us to squirm. And any *aficionados* of the theatre in his audience would surely instantly think of doll's houses.

In modern English we refer to the second person as 'you', whether one or many, familiar or stranger. In French, the once singular and plural forms *tu* and *vous* respectively have fallen into a usage which signifies familiarity. In the singular, *tu* is used with lovers, friends, family and pets, while *vous* is used with strangers and others deserving respect in both singular and plural. It is usually insulting, then, to address your teacher as *tu* or your husband as *vous*. Several languages have a similar 't/v' rule. Consider the German *du* and *Sie*. English *used* to, in the distinction between 'thee/thou' and 'you' – and this is significant for Renaissance and earlier texts. In fact, English *still does* have such a distinction in its 'non-standard' regional dialects.

In reviewing *terms of address*, we have looked at *naming systems* (forename, surname, title); *pronoun systems* ('you'/'thou', but consider also 'Come here, you' instead of 'Come here, Miss Persaud', and the patronising 'does she want a choccie, then?' spoken directly *to* her); and *given names* (pet names, familiars like 'old girl', insults like 'fat bastard').

As a short exercise: (1) List out the names you are called by various people and in what circumstances; (2) skim through a scene or scenes of a play, list out the terms of address deployed by whom to whom and when; and comment.

3.2.6 Conversational maxims

We noted above that an easy flow of conversation depends upon the orderly alternation of cue and response. We also noted that some responses are less appropriate than others, as when, for example, B goes off at a long tangent at (3) and fails to respond pertinently to A's 'swimming' gambit with his advice on boots at (7).

The philosopher H. P. Grice has suggested that conversation is a co-operative activity which assumes certain rules or maxims (see Short 1989: 150–4). The co-operative principle is maintained so long as our utterances obey the maxims of

- *quantity*   give the right amount of information (neither too much nor too little)
- *quality*   try to be truthful
- *relation*   say something pertinent (don't go off at a tangent)
- *manner*   don't be long-winded and be clear (avoid prolixity, ambiguity and obscurity)

Some suggest additions to this list. One we might find useful is

- *respect*   give your interlocutor their due (give them the respect they deserve)

Dialogue is often interesting, informative and key to the action when one or more of these maxims is *broken*. There are four ways this can happen:

- *quietly violate* a maxim   e.g. deceive
- *opt out* of the co-operative principle   e.g. claim a right to silence
- *avoid a clash* by breaking one maxim   e.g. tell a lie to be kind
- *brazenly flout* a maxim   e.g. when the customs officer asks if you have anything to declare, reply 'Nothing but my genius'

At (3) A breaks the maxims of quantity and relation, quite possibly through quiet (unintentional?) violation. Perhaps at (7) the maxim of relation is brazenly flouted. That would depend on how the line was played. Our maxim of respect is also broken at (7).

While A hogs the conversation at (3), the maxim of manner is not broken in a strict sense, since the expressions used are not long-winded in themselves. (A does not say 'their gleaming buckets of red and blue, spades of vomit yellow'.) But perhaps the *curtness* of 'Placid' at (5') ought to count as breaking that maxim? And it maybe also breaks the maxim of respect?

Once again, we should avoid thinking that there are hard and fast rules. Grice has provided us with a very useful – and *flexible* – framework which can help us spot, analyse and comment on significant exchanges in a scripted conversation.

As an exercise: (1) Taking any of lines 1 to 8, or a line a partner feeds you, compose responses that break maxims of the co-operative principle in conversation. Try to break them in different ways. (You might even try setting up a stack of cards with 'quantity', 'relation' etc. written on them. At each go, turn over a new card.) Discuss the results. (2) Scan a scene or scenes of a play you know and pick out any broken maxims. Comment on their role in the action, character drawing, construction of irony, comedy, etc.

3.2.7 *Conversational and conventional implicature*

The idea of 'subtext' is a familiar one to most students of drama. A character says one thing but we know they mean or are thinking another. Perhaps a stage direction has told us this directly; perhaps they are contradicting something said before or after; perhaps they are contradicting or simply not saying what we have come to understand of their true motives from a whole assembly of such information. The idea is most familiar in the context of Stanislavski's prescription that the actor find the character's 'through line' and a psychological 'inner truth'.

The notion of *implicature* in linguistics takes us into similar, but slightly wider, territory. 'Implicature' is a bit like 'implication', and, to be frank, for our own immediate purposes we can treat the words as meaning the same thing.

When B above at (8) says she is going for an ice-cream, she is perhaps quietly violating the maxim of quality in order not to break that of respect. Or maybe she breaks it simply to make an easy exit. What seems to lie behind her words is something like the *conversational implicature* that A is a jerk and that she has had enough of the running monologue. She does not say it directly, but makes the clear implication. Remember that audiences often know more than the characters. A conversational implicature may sometimes be scripted to be clear to the audience, but not to the character being addressed. If this were a sketch for performance, fun could be had just as well by having A remain oblivious to the implicature, or by spotting it and . . . well, responding or not?

When A at (3) above paints the picture of the bus and the estate, the conversational implicature is that s/he is above the ordinary. The character does not directly make this claim, but it is made all the same. But the speech also comes near to the *conventional implicature* that *all* housing estates and *all* public transport facilities are unpleasant. A implies that everyone in their right mind despises such places. Conventional implicatures are often marked by the use of connectors like 'indeed' or 'so' or 'in truth'. A might say something like, 'Indeed, it is a very shabby route through the estate.' Conventional implicatures mark out the speaker as part of or an aspirant to a particular social group; they declare that they share the appropriate standards.

Short (1989: 150) shows how Wilde scripts conventional implicatures for Lady Bracknell. He also shows how, in *A Man for All Seasons* (1960), Bolt scripts the character Rich's discomfort when under interrogation. For instance, when Norfolk asks, 'When did Thomas give you this thing?', Rich replies, 'I don't exactly remember.' The 'exactly' breaks the maxim of manner, but quite unintentionally on the part of the speaker (p. 154). Bolt won't have looked up *unintentional implicature* in a text book in order to script this discomfort. But the notion of it helps us understand how his scripted language is *working* – both in the conversation and between the stage and the auditorium.

3.2.8 Scripted conversations

Through the ruse of a short scripted conversation, we have here explored some of the interpersonal aspects of social (real-life) conversation identified by social linguists. Now, clearly it would be a dull playwright – and a confused one – who sat down to script dialogue according to these 'rules'. However the playwright comes at the act of scripting dialogue, though, that dialogue will to a greater or lesser degree share the basic aspects of social language. The rules social linguists have identified come automatically to us in conversation, and just as automatically to the playwright.

None the less, all dramatic dialogue is a *representation* of social conversation. The unwritten rules operate in a more condensed, more efficient way. And sometimes we can spot the playwright exploiting the rules, pushing the dialogue into bigger, clearer shapes to the point that the artifice becomes delightfully clear. Pinter, Wilde and Orton come to mind.

So are we to make tables, use our calculators on the text? Do we need to scan every speech for conversational implicatures, weigh the speeches of every character? Not at all. But a sound working knowledge of the basic principles set out in this section will

1 give us the tools to write more precisely and subtly about bits or aspects of dialogue we might anyway have recognised as significant;
2 keep us attuned so that we can spot more examples still.

And let us remember what dialogue is for. A knowledge of the interpersonal functions of conversation can

3 inform our choices on the rehearsal floor.

3.3 Speech acts

3.3.1 *Speech as action*

Let us now pick up on statements, questions and commands which we identified as sorts of conversational cue in the last section (3.2.2). The philosopher J. L. Austin was interested in what utterances *do* in the world. In his book *How to Do Things with Words* (1962), he developed his idea of *speech acts*. Speech can have a direct effect, in the same way that a punch in the face or a tender kiss can. This idea of 'doing things with words' has proven to be a useful tool for analysing what dialogue does on the stage, too. An extended account of speech acts can be found in Elam (1980: 156–70); our account here is based on this.

Austin starts by distinguishing between two sorts of utterance:

- *constative* utterances   stating facts
- *performative* utterances   doing something with words e.g. commands, requests, vows, namings

For the time being we can use 'speech act' and 'performative utterance' to mean the same thing.

The first line of *A Doll's House* is a command. Nora tells her maid, 'Hide that Christmas tree away, Helen.' Our first impression of Nora made by this 'performative' is of someone who is in control of her situation: she is exercising power.

The last line in the first brief appearance on stage of an earlier heroine, the Duchess in Webster's *The Duchess of Malfi* (1614), has a similar effect. After some short exchanges with her brother, she gathers up the courtier Silvio:

> DUCHESS: You are for Milan?
> SILVIO: I am.
> DUCHESS: Bring the caroches [coaches]: we'll bring you down to the haven.
>
> (1.2.146–7)

Her first entrance establishes the Duchess as a confident and powerful woman who instructs servants and organises men.

Surely neither of these performatives is there by pure chance. Each of these playwrights is scripting words for a female protagonist who, in the course of either play, is to conduct a struggle of self-determination in the face of male prejudice and control. Note that as well as the performatives, we have in each example a hint of what is to come. Nora commands the tree to be *hidden* – she fears something. The Duchess gives the courtier a lift – she is easy and familiar. Not everyone in the play – least of all her brothers – will like this.

While both of these speeches are performative – they get the servants to do things – neither is of great direct significance to the action of the play. But elsewhere, performative utterances are the very stuff of stage action: they change the situation (see 4.1.1). Consider the first scene of *King Lear*.

As soon as Lear enters, he makes commands: 'Attend the lords of France and Burgundy' . . . 'Give me the map there' . . . 'Know that we have divided / In three our kingdom' (1.1.33; 36–7). Note especially that Shakespeare scripts a command ('Know that') where he might have got the same information across with a constative ('we have divided'). The line thus has similar force to what might have been scripted as an action in the present: 'I hereby divide'. (Note that we can now add 'proclamations' to our list of performative utterances. Add others that occur to you as you get used to this work.)

Lear does not ask his daughters which of them loves him most, but commands them: 'Tell me, my daughters' (1.1.47). When he does use a question, it is followed by a command: 'What says our second daughter? . . . Speak' (1.1.66–7). What kings do is command; their function is to rule. But this flood of commands helps establish Lear as headstrong. It leads up to the disastrous proclamation: 'Here I disclaim all paternal care' as he banishes Cordelia from his heart and home (1.1.112). This speech act performs a key action of the play, as do his 'I do invest you jointly with my power' to Cornwall and Albany and his 'take thy reward' which banishes Kent (1.1.129; 172). There is something wrong in this play with the commanding function of kings. If we recall the idea of the formal stage 'emblem' from Chapter 1, we can now spot one in this scene quite easily. Lear says to the dukes: 'This coronet part between you' (1.1.138). We do not do Shakespeare justice if we say that Lear is using a metaphor and means 'divide up the kingdom'. He is scripted to refer to '*this* coronet'. There is clearly a solid object in his hand or held on a cushion by a flunkey, a real crown. What are the men to do with it? Lear is commanding what is either impossible or intrinsically and *unnecessarily* destructive. If there is a metaphor here, it is this deeper one about the consequences of Lear's actions. Attention to speech acts has helped us find it.

Note that a speech act or performative utterance may contain a *performative verb* like 'invest' or 'disclaim'. Other examples are 'I pronounce', 'I deny', 'I accuse'. Above, we have made Lear majestically underline one of these performative verbs by saying, 'I *hereby* divide'. But performatives can be delivered without specific performative verbs. Commands or questions, for instance, can be accomplished by simply saying 'Bring me my hat' or 'What is your name?'

Playwright Noël Greig does a nice rehearsal game in which he asks actors to find a performative verb to prefix every line they are to speak: '*I command you*, What is your name?' It is a good way to play with motivation and line delivery. It's fine in such a game to let the performative verbs open out into unexpected territory: 'I suggest'; 'I implore'; 'I insinuate with every bone of my body'.

As an exercise: Find all the performative utterances in Act 1 scene 1 of
King Lear. Tabulate them according to type and identify the speaker of
each. Comment.

3.3.2 *Illocutionary force and perlocutionary effect*

Would it be useful to think of constative utterances (statements) in dramatic
dialogue as having the function of relaying information to the audience
('Lovely weather we're having') and performative utterances ('Die, you
dog!') as having the function of furthering the action? Not quite! First, we
should consider that a statement of fact can change the situation. For example, as the melodrama nears its conclusion, the young woman declares: 'I am
your lost daughter.' Second, a performative utterance might be delivered in
the apparent form of a constative. Lear says: 'Ourself, by monthly course,
. . . shall our abode / Make with you by due turn' (1.1.131–3). Strictly speaking, he is merely stating a fact about the future. But clearly he is insisting
that what he says will be the case. The line is, again, a command.

So it looks as though we have here two 'constative utterances' working
like speech acts. The speakers are doing things with their words.

Having made his distinction between constative and performative utterances, Austin collapsed it. (It seems that he was in fact planning to do this
all along. The title of his book is deceptively simple; it jokingly pretends to
be just like a book on 'How to win friends'. He wanted his own audience to
think speech acts through with him. We are doing that now.) As Elam (1980)
recounts, Austin's work and that of J. R. Searle developed towards the
proposition that we think of *every* utterance – every speech act – as being
composed of three subsidiary kinds of act:

- *locutionary act*   (uttering something meaningful)
- *illocutionary act*   (the act performed *in* saying something)
- *perlocutionary act* (effects produced on the hearer *by* saying it)

So now we can be more precise. When Lear says: 'Here I disclaim all paternal care' (1.1.112), the illocutionary act is one of disclaiming. But its perlocutionary effect is to banish Cordelia. And when he says: 'Ourself, by
monthly course, . . . shall our abode / Make with you by due turn' (1.1.131–
3) he performs the *illocutionary act* of commanding his daughters and sons-
in-law. But Lear ends up being bounced between them with an ever-decreas-
ing retinue. The *perlocutionary force* of the utterance is weak. We might
consider that Shakespeare then scripts for Lear a terrible divide between the
illocutionary force of his vows and his calls upon heaven or nature and the
perlocutionary effect of these utterances.

The idea of 'illocutionary force' is a useful one. If we think across to

Physics, we can note that forces have direction and amplitude (size). Illocutionary acts can have a different force according to the circumstance. If I tell you to 'Go', for instance, I might be dismissing you from the room, encouraging you to go to the rave, or advising you to see a counsellor. When the Duchess of Malfi tells her steward Antonio to 'Raise yourself' (1.2.338), the illocutionary force of those two words is exquisitely ambiguous. They are in the act of gently seducing one another. He has lower-class rank but she, according to convention, has the lower rank in gender. She is both commanding him, and inviting him to stand as her equal. The delicious 'wobble' of that moment does two important things. It expresses a beautiful balance in their relationship; and it suggests that they are performing a dangerous balancing act from which they might fall. In addition, the fact that she has already called him her 'upright treasurer' (1.2.294) makes her command easily taken as a sexual pun. As well as the wobble around status, there is one around chastity and sexual directness. Our attention to illocutionary force has helped us to pinpoint and to describe this small but important moment in the play's design.

> As a short exercise: Look back at the table made in the last exercise. Find examples where the notion of illocutionary and perlocutionary acts or force would be useful in writing about action or character. A hint: we have looked briefly at Lear; why not start with Kent?

3.3.3 The limits of locution

We have given little emphasis so far to the locutionary act, most usually thought of as the successful utterance of a meaningful sentence. At first sight, this would seem to be a 'given' upon which the more interesting areas of illocution and perlocution rest.

But drama is often concerned with extremes, and it is at some extremes that we find locution under pressure. First let us consider an emotional or spiritual extreme. Shakespeare's King Richard has just dreamt of ghosts in *Richard 3*:

RICHARD: What do I fear? Myself? There's none else by.
Richard loves Richard; that is, I am I.
Is there a murderer here? No – yes, I am.
Then fly. What, from myself? Great reason why –
Lest I revenge . . .

(5.3.182–6)

We might say that Richard here has to struggle towards successful composition: he himself is uncomposed ('beside himself'); he struggles to maintain his world-view; and he struggles to compose the sentences with which he makes sense of the world. While Richard just about manages to put sentences together, we shall find other characters in other plays unable to do that. In Winsome Pinnock's *Talking in Tongues* (1991), Leela's *'speech becomes a garble'* (p. 233) as she tries to express her rage about the racism which oppresses her and the feelings of 'pain and absurdity' (p. 226) surrounding her own violent reaction to it. Yet this collapse of standard locution also rhymes with Sugar's story which opens the play, in which 'talking in tongues' figures as a healing process. In the Bible myth, those who talk in tongues speak an ancient universal language, from a time when humanity was united. Pinnock suggests that 'one of our quests is to find our way back to one another' (p. 266).

For our second extreme of three, let us start with a constative utterance which does not change the situation. Such a statement might at least be said to involve the very basic illocutionary act of making sense. But if I say: 'The handle on the banana is Belgian today', I may be grammatically correct but will be making very little sense to you. Is the sentence meaningful or not? There is nothing wrong with it as a sentence.

If a character said that line on a stage, we might be persuaded – though uncomfortably – that bananas in their world did have handles, and that these were apt to change nationality. Short (1989: 147) shows how, in the 'Absurdist' *One Way Pendulum* (1959), N. F. Simpson has the characters set up a bizarre world in just this way. The perlocutionary effect on the audience is to persuade them – for the purposes of watching the play – that such a situation exists (see 5.2.12 on dramatic worlds).

In Act 1 of Beckett's *Waiting for Godot* (1955), Pozzo has the otherwise mute Lucky perform this speech:

> Given the existence as uttered forth in the public words of Puncher
> and Wattman of a personal God quaquaquaqua with a white beard
> quaquaquaqua outside time without extension who from the heights
> of divine apathia divine athambia divine aphasia loves us dearly with
> some expectations for reason unknown but time will tell . . .
>
> (p. 43)

This is just one tenth of it. Though for the most part grammatically correct, it seems that it will go on for ever. While the repeated 'quaquaquaqua' mimics the Latin *qua* one might find in philosophical discourse, it also sounds like a stuttering absent-minded professor, a machine run out of control or a duck. When we get to 'divine', it seems that words are fighting in his mind for the right to substitute one another. Beckett here makes metaphysical discourse (i.e. concerning the nature of existence) sound like nothing more than talking to fill up space.

But as is clear from the above, a disparity between successful locution and making conventional sense can also deliver pure playfulness, a delight in the way that language *constructs* sense. It might also lead us into serious consideration of the power of language to construct our view of the world around us. We shall meet with the persuasive power of what at first seem to be mere locutions later, in 3.3.5.

As a third extreme of locution, let us consider language which is so elegantly composed that it seems to be skating on thin ice. At the opening of *The Duchess of Malfi*, Antonio delivers a speech which describes his idea of the ideal court:

> In seeking to reduce both State and people   5
> To a fix'd order, their judicious King
> Begins at home. Quits first his royal palace
> Of flatt'ring sycophants, of dissolute,
> And infamous persons, which he secretly terms
> His master's master-piece, the work of Heaven,   10
> Consid'ring duly, that a Prince's court
> Is like a common fountain, whence should flow
> Pure silver-drops in general.
>
>   (1.1.5–12)

Consider the **syntax** of the second sentence. To what does the 'which' in line 9 refer? After some work, we shall conclude that it must be 'his royal palace' (l. 7). To deliver this logical connection with clarity the actor has to keep absolute poise, producing and then setting aside the 'dissolute and infamous persons' as if they were a parenthesis. In other words, Webster is scripting for Antonio an extremely poised, elegant and discriminating ideolect (see 3.1.3). The speech as a whole (we show here only an extract) flows gracefully, and divides into two contrasting halves: Antonio deals first with the ideal court and then with its antithesis. The very shape of the speech repeats his fountain image, suggesting not just a natural spring, but a graceful and delicate monument.

3.3.4 Felicity conditions

When Kent challenges the wisdom of Lear's actions, he does a few things that we should by now be able to pick up on and describe with some ease. He uses commands ('See better' 1.1.157). He starts by calling his master 'Royal Lear' but soon descends to the more abrasive 'Lear' and 'King' (ll. 138; 157; 159). He is driven by his need to tell the truth (to observe the maxim of quality); but given the circumstances, his words break the conversational maxim of respect.

But Kent is, of course, doing his proper duty. He assumes that, as part of the aristocracy, he *must* correct the monarch when he is in danger of doing wrong. This is, indeed, part of the contract of mutual respect between them.

Yet Lear has torn up that contract. His wilfulness has changed the conditions in which Kent now speaks. The warning has not been made in the happy – felicitous – circumstances in which it might succeed. And so Kent is driven, or drives himself, to an extreme.

So *felicity conditions* are key in life to making successful conversational gambits. And drama often depends on the mismatch between the illocutionary acts of characters and the conditions in which they make them. Two more examples are close at hand.

First, recall how Nora in *A Doll's House* boasts to Krogstad in Act 1 of her influence over her husband, whom she hopes will employ Mrs Linde. Her bid for superiority misfires because, unknown to her, Helmer has just fired Krogstad, who now believes she has persuaded him to do this as well.

Second, let us return to *The Duchess of Malfi*. In the closing moments of the first act, the Duchess and Antonio perform a marriage ceremony on themselves. This is technically permissible in her society. She celebrates with the words: 'What can the church force more?' (1.2.404). As the play unfolds, we learn how infelicitous the circumstances for those words in fact are. The church – one of her two brothers is the Cardinal – can force her very brutally to submit.

In addition to felicity conditions, linguists refer to sincerity conditions – we are supposed to mean what we say – and preparatory conditions – we have to set the scene for our utterance to be successful (see Elam 1980: 161–3).

3.3.5 Presuppositions

Kent, Nora and the Duchess all presuppose that they are safe to say what they say. It seems practical – pragmatic – at the time. They make the *pragmatic presupposition* that what they say will have the desired effect. So we have found two ways of saying the same thing. Another way of saying that much drama depends on a lack of felicity conditions for what characters say is that they make false pragmatic presuppositions.

Again, without losing ourselves in a forest of tables, lists and diagrams, let us see what other sorts of presupposition have been proposed, and what consequences these have for our analysis of dramatic dialogue.

Short (1989: 145–8) reviews work on *existential* and *linguistic* presuppositions. If we recall the example of *One Way Pendulum* (3.3.3, above), we witness the basic activity of talking about something in a way which takes its existence for granted. So *existential presuppositions* are at the heart of the way in which dialogue sets up the fictional world for us. A character says, 'I'm going to see the fairies', and we take it for granted – we 'suspend our disbelief' – that there are fairies in their world.

It is a fact of life – or at least of the general arrangement of language – that we are more inclined to challenge what a sentence claims than what it takes for granted. So the very structure of sentences provides us with a way of *insinuating* things – literally, to 'curve' (*OED*) something into the conversation, say something indirectly. If I say: 'My brother can beat your brother at football any day', you might think I am exaggerating or lying about his prowess. But you most likely accept that I have a brother in the first place. Disguise and deception are part of the common stuff of drama. *Linguistic presuppositions* play their important part in that game.

3.3.6 *Grice's maxims and the audience*

We saw in 3.2.7 how an implicature passing from author to actor and audience can script, for instance, a character's discomfort. But we can usefully take things further than Short (1989) does.

There are occasions in plays – and sometimes plays as a whole – which we feel are sending a 'nod and a wink' to the audience. We raised this idea when discussing authorial signature (3.1.5.6, above).

At the opening of Joe Orton's *The Ruffian on the Stair* (1966), Mike is shaving at the sink. Joyce comes from the bedroom of the flat with a breakfast tray. The first lines are:

JOYCE: Have you got an appointment?
MIKE: Yes, I'm to be at King's Cross Station at eleven. I'm meeting a
    man in the toilets. (*He puts away his shaving materials.*)
JOYCE: You always go to such interesting places.

Regardless of what implicatures we may later learn are passing between these two characters (and we learn of none), these opening lines set before the audience the proposition that 'meeting men in the station toilets is interesting'. To many in the 1966 audience, that statement would break the maxims of relation and perhaps manner. It seems not to be pertinent to anything, to be an obscure thing to be saying.

But for homosexual men in the audience, and other people who knew about 'cottaging' – meeting up in public toilets to find sexual partners and most likely to have sex there and then – the proposition would be hilariously, embarrassingly and dangerously clear. From their point of view – and, we can guess, Orton's – Orton is deliberately flouting the maxims of quantity and respect. He is insulting his 'straight' audience behind their backs, and saying much more than is 'necessary'.

There isn't really any implicature here in the strict sense. But Grice's maxims, when we apply them to the stage–audience axis, can give us access to the **rhetorical** attitude of a play or playwright.

What makes this example even more fun is that it is very similar in manner to Pinter's *The Birthday Party* (1958). Orton is making a pastiche. Pinter at that time was famous for producing sensations (implicatures) of hidden threat in his plots and situations. The idea of a ruffian on the stair in Pinter suggests a violent young outsider who will disrupt peace and maim individuals. Orton plays with the fact that for some middle-class gay men, a ruffian on the stair suggests the convenient proximity of a 'bit of rough' – the cherished fantasy of a working-class sexual partner (see Shepherd 1989).

Here we see Orton working up a specific bit of irony, a sort of dare from the stage to the audience to see what he is really saying. But we can use Grice's maxims in more general terms, too, to think about the way that a play situates itself before the audience. Does it present itself according to the accepted conventions? Or does it 'go too far' or 'give too little' in some respect or another? Does it offend the sensibilities of the audience? And if so, why? Is it for the sake of it, or so that some other assumed maxim of theatrical communication ('truth-telling', say) can be maintained? Grice's maxims offer us a very useful model for spotting and then describing how some plays break the currently assumed conventions of the dialogue between stage and auditorium. And we might also say that such plays are 'speaking a deviant discourse' (see 3.1.5.4, above).

3.4 The stylistics of theatrical prose and verse

When studying poetry, it is usual to call on *stylistics* – a variety of ways to analyse how the verse works. This analysis then helps develop and structure a commentary on the poem. Thus the commentary might attend to rhythm, alliteration, syntax (the way the grammar works), metaphor, simile, and so on. All these contribute to the 'feel' of the poem as well as what it says.

Clearly such techniques will be of use when making a commentary on a piece of verse drama. What we find will not only tell us how the playwright is writing verse. Much more importantly, it will also tell us in some detail how meanings are being fashioned and how the playwright is making the actor speak. We have in fact already begun this work when we looked at Antonio and Lucky's speeches in 3.3.3.

The job of stylistics when applied to a dramatic speech, then, is to investigate it as a *theatrical* composition.

Stylistics can be brought to bear on any piece of writing, verse or prose. Whether or not we are students of English Language as well as drama, there is much that we can spot without specialist knowledge. The next two subsections demonstrate the sort of work that can be done.

3.4.1 Prose analysis

At the opening of Tennessee Williams' *The Glass Menagerie* (1945), the character Tom Wingfield '*strolls across the front of the stage*' . . . '*stops to light a cigarette*' by a fire-escape. . . and '*addresses the audience*' thus (we have numbered the sentences for later reference):

(1) Yes, I have tricks in my pocket, I have things up my sleeve. (2) But I am the opposite of a stage magician. (3) He gives you illusion that has the appearance of truth. (4) I give you truth in the pleasant disguise of illusion. (5) To begin with, I turn back time. (6) I reverse it to that quaint period, the thirties, when the huge middle class of America was matriculating in a school for the blind. (7) Their eyes had failed them, or they had failed their eyes, and so they were having their fingers pressed forcibly down on the fiery Braille alphabet of a dissolving economy. (8) In Spain there was revolution. Here . . .

and the speech goes on. Let's comment on how it unfolds for an audience:

(1) 'Yes' answers nothing other than an assumed accusation or comment. The speaker is 'one ahead' of us, but at the same time seems defensive. He then says the same thing twice, with identical **syntax**, connected by a comma. Saying something twice can be for emphasis, but may also suggest redundancy, a waste of words. Maybe the comma produces a 'drift' in the sentence?

(2) Clear metatheatrical reference: this is about the show as theatre. So who is speaking? The author? Is this character its 'author'?

(3) and (4). Expands on (2). Again, two syntactically identical statements. This suggests a clear opposition, yet the line is difficult to grasp because the difference is mainly produced by the swapping of 'illusion' and 'truth'. The sentences mean the opposite to one another, but are very similar.

(5) and (6). Repetition again, 'I turn back', . . . 'I reverse'. These redundancies seem scripted to produce a 'poetic' or 'epic' feel to this speech as it goes on.

(6) – But the repetition now supports a *turn* from the 'I' of the presenter – the pronoun is used six times – to what he is presenting. This sentence marks a point of division in the speech. While the sentences have so far been short, and simple in terms of both syntax and vocabulary, this one is long, a little more complicated, introduces adjectives ('quaint', 'huge') and a major metaphor. This metaphor is ironic – the positive idea of matriculation clashes with the conventional idea of blindness as a misfortune.

(7) Opens with another repetition / opposition structure ('them' – 'eyes') and then *flows on* through the comma, into an extension of the 'blindness' figure. Violence is connoted – 'forcibly' and 'fiery'. There are two disjunctions here. First, 'fiery' is unconventionally paired with 'Braille'. Second, the clear signal that both 'alphabet' and indeed 'fiery' suggest is paired with 'dissolving'. Both the long stretch of the metaphor across two sentences and these disjunctions may script two feelings: first, an ironic attitude on the

part of the speaker; second, the bewilderment of those people from the 1930s (as opposed to the clarities of Spain).

Making sketch notes in this sort of detail helps us get close to the way in which the dramatic text is working on its audience. The next step will be to write an account of the speech using what we have identified. Clearly we cannot do this for the whole play. But when commenting on a speech, we should always be ready to go into such detail rather than just repeating the surface meaning.

3.4.2 *Verse analysis*

Let us return to Desdemona's speech that we first met in Chapter 1. Here it is in full:

O God! Iago,	149
What shall I do to win my lord again?	150
Good friend, go to him; for, by this light of heaven,	151
I know not how I lost him. Here I kneel.	152
If e'er my will did trespass 'gainst his love,	153
Either in discourse of thought or actual deed,	154
Or that mine eyes, mine ears, or any sense,	155
Delighted them in any other form,	156
Or that I do not yet, and ever did,	157
And ever will – though he do shake me off	158
To beggarly divorcement – love him dearly,	159
Comfort forswear me! Unkindness may do much;	160
And his unkindness may defeat my life,	161
And never taint my love. I cannot say 'whore';	162
It does abhor me now I speak the word;	163
To do the act that might the addition earn,	164
Not the world's mass of vanity could make me.	165

The speech divides into four sections: 149–152 (urgency); 152–157 (composure – the start of the formal stage figure); 157–160 (eruption of urgency from within the composure); 160–165 (recomposure). The speech stages a struggle between urgency and an attempt to remain composed.

- Line 149 is shared with Iago, who has been winding Emilia up. Desdemona *interrupts* him, first with a cry of desperation and then with a direct address to him. The words go in different directions.
- 150 is end-stopped: this question could be a heading for the speech (for character and audience).
- Then 151 flows quickly into 152 through enjambment combined with simple words and regular iambic measure. The passage is marked by physical movement – gestures to Iago and to heaven, leading to the mid-

line syntactical break at 'Here I kneel' (152). The new sentence forces a pause in the still-regular iambic measure. If the performer delivers the line at an even pace, the kneeling is a sudden drop to the floor; if she kneels as she speaks the first half of the line, the even measure times a slow sink down. Movement and short simple phrases are to be replaced with verbal elaboration.

- 152–7 are made formal, statuesque, by using pairs of lines similarly headed: 'If e'er' / 'Or' / 'Or' in an argument structure which holds back the main verb ('forswear'), which finally arrives, climactically, in a line starting with a reversed stress and with an internal rhyme (dearly/forswear me). We *hear* the ornate syntax: the speaker has an articulate intelligence. Within the sequence its general shape of repetition and coupling is echoed in miniature: 155 'mine' . . . 'mine' with another 'or'; 157–8 repeats the shape, now speeding up through the enjambment made swifter by the 'And'. This formal arrangement makes the temporary rupture more violent, with the parenthesis 'though he . . . divorcement' at 158–9; it is as if the increasing pace of the overall rhetoric is fighting a battle to contain the emotion that motivates it. It briefly shows itself before the argument continues.

- After the climax of 'forswear me' there is a new stillness produced by the simplicity, the repetition of 'unkindness may', and the fluid link between 'my life' and 'my love'. Within that stillness is all the force of resolution – the change from 'defeat' to 'never taint', but seemingly understated (the 'And' of 162 has the force of 'But' or 'Yet').

- The crucial *forced* internal rhyme of 'whore' and 'abhor' across 162–3 is, cruelly, almost a pun: the word men use of women falls apart in her mouth. She is *wresting* composure out of the situation, speaking the dreaded word with fragile poise.

- 164–5 end the speech with sounds that make the words *solidify*, through two sequences of euphony: 'a*ct* / th*at* / m*ight* / addition' . . . 'm*a*ss / m*ake* / *me*' and through the huge syntactical inversion (in the shape of chiasmus: one word order mirror-images the other); which is also coupled with the weird metre – the chaos of the opening of the final line, and its 'feminine' ending. This is formal public composure with a suggested mass of feeling, the chaos of stress, beneath it.

3.4.4 Architectonics

Opening a copy of Schiller's *Mary Stuart* (1800), one is struck by the physical shape of the print on the page. There are great slabs of speech. Characters typically speak several verse lines at a time. This grandeur and weightiness translate onto the stage. The play in performance often feels solid yet also graceful, like a huge bridge or building might, defying gravity by being massive yet also beautifully balanced.

Schiller's play and others of its type make obvious the physical feel of the dialogue's outward shape, which in other cases might be, say, slabby, spiky, or sparse. An important part of the design of such plays is the *architectonics* of the dialogue.

|4|

Plot, action and the actor's body

This chapter has two sections. In the longer first one we encounter ways of thinking about plot and action. The shorter second section looks at ways in which dramatic texts either script or assume things about the actual bodies on stage.

4.1 Plot and action

4.1.1 Action and events

What is action? Pfister (1988) suggests a simple and powerful definition: an action is something which changes the situation. Hamlet stabs Polonius through the arras and so has to go on the run. Lear divides kingly power and so the kingdom falls into disarray and he falls prey to his children. Pfister diagrams:

$$\text{action}$$
$$\text{S1} \quad \rightarrow \quad \text{S2}$$

Hamlet's action above is purely physical. Lear's action is accomplished through words. And recall our discussion of speech acts in general: even a seemingly bald statement can change the situation. Cordelia's simple statement 'I love your Majesty / According to my bond' (1.1.91–2) has a devastating effect at the start of *King Lear* – because Lear takes the statement as an act of refusal. High dramatic consequences flow from revelatory statements in many melodramas. In Palmer's *East Lynne* (1874), Lady Isabel has left her husband and is assumed dead. But she returns disguised as a governess, Madame Vine, to nurse her dying child. Her cry 'My child is dead!' (p. 336) reveals that the mother herself is living. It begins the process of her discovery to her husband and their reconciliation before she herself dies.

Is, then, everything that is said and happens on stage 'action' in Pfister's terms? Usefully again, he says not. Consider a play like Beckett's *Waiting for Godot* (1955). The two characters say and do many things, but their situation remains the same at the end of the play as it was at the beginning. They are still waiting for Godot – waiting for something significant to happen.

But the audience do witness many events, from the trying on of boots to Estragon's attempt to hang himself. Similarly, while our day may have been full of events, we might still feel at its end that nothing has really happened: our situation has not changed, we have not changed the situation of others. Pfister uses 'event' to describe things said and done in a play which do not change the situation. His diagram is:

$$\text{event}$$
$$\text{S1} \qquad \rightarrow \qquad \text{S1}$$

In *Waiting for Godot*, the fact that nothing significant happens is central to what the play is about. To some it suggests that there is no ultimate meaning or purpose to life, that in the real world as much as on the stage, we while away the time thinking, arguing, struggling and looking for a truth which will never arrive. Meanwhile, Beckett refused to admit that his play was about anything at all. And so, to some, *Godot* also suggests that plays may appear to be significant acts of communication, but are themselves in fact just events. Taken together, of course, these two interpretations keep chasing one another round in a circle. If we believe life has a point and Beckett's play, by being devoid of meaning, successfully argues that life is pointless, it has challenged our belief. But how can a meaningless play argue anything successfully? This paradox probably contributes to the play's continuing fascination.

Mid-twentieth-century plays such as *Waiting for Godot*, which engage with the idea that life has no ultimate meaning and express this through the construction of paradoxical worlds (see 5.2.12) and dialogue (see 3.2), are part of what Martin Esslin (1968) dubbed 'Absurdism'. Absurdist plays question the value of human existence after 'the death of God' and the purposes of theatre itself.

The point of *Godot* is precisely that it consists *only* of events, and we expect plays (and life) to contain action. We can expect most plays, indeed, to be a mixture of events and actions. But what *is* a change in a situation? Does it include a nuanced change in the relationship between two characters? Must it contribute towards the outcome of the play, its dramatic resolution after the crisis? Suppose there is no crisis?

We need, then, to think of our event–action **binary** as a dynamic one. Most things that happen on stage in most plays can be thought of as having degrees of either event or action. We might even want to think of an 'action' as a special sort of 'event'. An event is anything that happens; actions are events which change the situation. This does not mean that Pfister's distinction is too simple or that it has collapsed. Rather, it can become a subtle tool for use in commentary and analysis.

4.1.2 *Situations and their elaboration*

As we have already discussed, an obvious function of much dialogue is to elaborate character. Another function is exposition, establishing the situation from which the action of the play proceeds. But the changing situations throughout the action themselves are, in most plays, also elaborated. Whole scenes may be given over to this sort of function.

Nora's dance of the tarantella can be seen as a point of crisis. It perhaps moves the action on in the sense that the state of mind it expresses is one which cannot rest in its given situation. Readings of the play which concentrate on 'psychological development' will want to place this scene into a plausible scheme of the changes in her state of mind. Several critics at the time found Nora's psychological development implausible, mainly because they could not believe anyone could really come to leave home and children so precipitately. We could argue with them perhaps.

More recently, it has been argued that the tarantella scene is just one instance in many from the late nineteenth century in which women are represented as fundamentally 'hysterical'. It is a moment in the play when Nora is reduced to a gender stereotype. There is doubtless some truth in this.

But, especially if we think in terms of *gestus* (see below, 4.2.3.2), of something being shown to us with some deliberation, we can also see this scene as an *elaboration of the situation*. The scene explores not only Nora's mental state but also the interpersonal dynamics of power into which she has now fallen. At the most basic level, note how the two men conduct her movements. We may say that she 'expresses' something they cannot themselves see in front of their eyes. But we can also see – are made to see – that they are themselves part-authors of what she has to express. The scene in this sort of reading might be thought of as asking, 'Where are we now?'

Again, to claim that the tarantella scene is an elaboration of the situation does not say everything about it. It does not exhaust all other 'takes' on it. But it is an important take, and one we can keep in our repertoire of approaches to *any* scene. One possible way of looking at the tarantella scene is as a *tension* between Nora as biological stereotype and Nora as victim of the gender system. Perhaps it asks, 'Which is she? Can we decide?' If so, then we are starting to ask questions about the world view, the ideology, of the play as a whole. (As your studies progress, you might come to note that if that question *is* implied, it is one asked by men as subjects [as 'I'] about women as 'others', as objects of enquiry or pity.)

The *degree* of elaboration, through plot, event and scenography, may also give us an indication of the basic concerns of a play and the way in which the play persuades us to accept it as a way of looking at the world (its 'strategies of authentication'). Naturalism, for instance, elaborates scenes and situations both because it is interested in precisely *how* an environment affects 'agency' (that is, it is concerned with actual and possible behaviours, our ability to act in the world) and because the audience are required to believe in the stage as a direct replication of life. Not all plays have these interests.

4.1.3 The theatre of situations

In *Huis clos* (1944), Sartre places his three characters in hell. At the end of the play they are still there. Their situation has not changed. But the play works on its audience with much more urgency than *Godot* does. The hell they are in looks like a middle-class drawing-room, itself also the typical setting of the well-made plays still then dominating Parisian theatres (see 2.2). Each character spends their time justifying their past actions, or rather excusing them as being forced upon them by circumstances. They dramatise their lives. Sartre also engineers a fierce triangular battle for affections between the three. Each needs the approving gaze of another in order to feel fully themselves, yet also feels threatened by being looked upon critically, from 'outside'. This, implies Sartre, is the situation you are in, you people watching this play. Why not recognise the shape of your situation – which is as I have shown you here, you too are in a sort of hell – and change it? Some things, like our need for the approving gaze of others, are unchangeable. But we can be free if we just stop excusing ourselves and act honestly in the present. The door is open (the door to the room is open by the end of the play, but they dare not leave). Walk through it. The point to existence is what we make of it.

These **existential** arguments developed out of Sartre's experiences during the Nazi occupation of France in the 1940s. Paradoxically, he felt, the occupation freed him because he had to think about his situation in the immediate present, and act upon it. Several other of his plays work out the logic of a given situation. *Huis clos* is the most **parabolic** of his 'theatre of situations'. He is not interested in dramatic solutions or in a tidy conclusion to the plot, but in mapping out what a particular situation offers to or demands of human agency.

This emphasis at the level of a whole play is not unique to Sartre. Many of Brecht's plays can be seen as the elaboration of our situation within late capitalism, often through **parabolic** means, as in *The Good Person of Setzuan* (1943). In this play, an important part of the situation is the binary gender system, the rigid ideological separation of 'male' and 'female'. The play concludes with a spoof happy ending which patently leaves the main character in the lurch. In similar territory, Caryl Churchill's *Top Girls* (1982) explores the situation of women faced with the opportunity to become powerful in a male-defined economic system. It opens in a mythic dimension, gathering together powerful women from history for a bizarre dinner party – and ends in realist mode in 1980s Britain. Again, there is no neat ending. Howard Barker's experiments in a 'theatre of catastrophe' deny the audience not only clear plot lines but also clear characters. In order for theatre to take its audience seriously, he argues, 'it must stop telling them stories they can understand' (Barker 1989: 13). A theatre of 'political reconstruction' (p. 17) must 'return the individual to himself' and ask: 'Are we thus?'(p. 20). Barker goes so far as to avoid a clarity of fictional situation in order to shock his audience into considering their own.

4.1.4 Scales of action

We have moved from what constitutes an action within a scene of a play to considerations of whole plays. Can we then usefully think about scales of action? Pfister (1988) proposes we think in terms of *actions*, *action phases* and *action sequences*. Lear banishing Cordelia or Kent is an action. The division of the kingdom of which both of these are parts is an action phase. Lear's journey from belligerent father and king to his death as pitiful seer is an action sequence.

It will often be a matter of our own judgement what we call an 'action' and what an 'action phase' – just like the distinction between action and event. Any reading or account of an artwork emphasises particular aspects of it, gives it a particular shape. We all have different pictures of the same play (e.g. Wertenbaker's *Our Country's Good*: see 6.2.2.3). Our interpretations give, as well as discover, shape; and Pfister's scales of action can help us be sensitive to this.

4.1.5 From Aristotle to the well-made play

Most of us use the word 'action' in more ways than we have so far described. Sometimes we use it to contain both action and event as defined above. Sometimes we mean just physical activity, either the actions a character is performing or the dynamics between bodies on the stage – the 'blocking'. These uses are fine, but we need to get used to being precise about how we are using the word at any one time.

A significant modern usage of the word 'action' we have not raised so far echoes its use in translations of Aristotle's *Poetics* (*c.*350 BCE), part of which discusses the forms of tragedy and comedy in the Athens of the 5th century BCE. Aristotle writes that a proper tragedy has a beginning, a middle and an end. That sounds rather obvious, but let us pursue it.

First of all, Aristotle distinguishes between *drama* (such as Sophocles' *Oedipus Rex*) and the written or spoken story form, *epic* (such as Homer's *Odyssey*). An epic is inclusive and complex: it contains many stories, goes off at descriptive or philosophical tangents, has no single point of departure and no single point of arrival. The drama, by comparison, is concentrated and focused. It has a clear start and end, and concentrates on a single story. Remember that this is what *Aristotle* is saying about Greek tragedy. It is not a universal truth.

Second, Aristotle has a general philosophical position of the natural growth of things. If you take this seed, that sort of plant will grow. Plant it in clay and expect this sort of result. So situations, people and decisions taken in life have their natural development and conclusion. He is not talking either about plausibility or about fate, though many since have cited him as if he were.

For Aristotle, the drama is a place in which this natural growth of things can be re-experienced. This following-through of consequences constitutes the action of the play. By contrast, Brecht deliberately called his dramaturgy 'epic' to challenge what the Aristotelian formula had become by the twentieth century. He argued that it had become a formula for plausibility and for subjection to a supposed inevitability of things. Against an action of seemingly natural unfolding, Brecht developed his own formula of *montage* in which disparate and seemingly disconnected events contribute to the whole argument. Nevertheless, the argument remains *focused*.

While many treat Aristotle as if he were stating what a proper drama should be, the *Poetics* is much more descriptive than it is prescriptive. This, he claims, is what a tragedy is like if it is true to type. He might be describing a leopard. It seems unlikely, for instance, that he would think the emotional release he calls *catharsis* (see below, 4.1.9) very becoming for someone as civilised as himself. As Andrew Ford (1995) argues, Aristotle implies that this untidy affair is much more the thing for women and the lower classes.

Recall Scribe's insistence in 1836 that people go to the theatre to be entertained, not improved, and his formula for the 'well-made play' that included a simple action, intrigue and secrets, points of crisis and entanglement, and a just conclusion. The Scribean formula has helped set a particular shape of action in stone. We can find it at work in many of the most commercially successful plays of the Western theatre from the last hundred or so years. But let us be clear that it is (a) not true of all plays; (b) not necessary for a 'good' play; (c) a particular prescription that comes from particular cultural circumstances. But we can, indeed, find at work in *A Doll's House* five phases of action to fit the formula *exposition – development and complication – crisis – **dénouement** – resolution*.

The play opens by letting us in on Nora's situation, which develops with the arrivals of Mrs Linde and especially Krogstad, and then winds up in intensity to a breaking-point. Nora's departure gives the play a definite ending, at least in terms of pure action.

We might argue that this sort of shape works for many audiences because it gives them the experience of going on a journey. It can be a journey full of risks and incidents, but all is safely distanced from them, not only because they know it is really a fiction, but also because it is rounded off, satisfactorily done with by the time the lights go up at the end. But other shapes can offer similar pleasurable rewards. In 2.5.6 we saw how, in detective fiction, full exposition is delayed to the end. The process of tension and release gives pleasure.

Implicit in the model for the well-made play is a variation in the *pace* of action. Matters speed up in the third and fourth phases. Again, while not accepting the model itself as some sort of rule, it brings to our attention the *effect* of pace of action both throughout and at various moments in a play's duration.

4.1.6 Shape of the action

Our discussion of Aristotle and Scribe raises the question of the whole shape of the action of a play. It is a shape which an audience carries away with them; which informs the way in which they relate to the characters; which affects their pleasure or displeasure. It is also intrinsic, as we saw with Brecht, to the way in which a play argues its point, if it has one – or to the way in which it positions its audience in relation to the events portrayed.

What, then, is the shape of the play you are reading now? Is it 'linear', following events one after another, or does it use montage (see above)? Is there a rise-and-fall pattern? Or is it like the medieval morality play *Everyman* (c.1498), which has a fall-and-rise pattern, even though it ends with a death? Is there a sense of strands being tied together? Does it feel satisfyingly closed off at the end, or is there a feeling of incompletion? Do we feel as if we are on a journey? If so, is it one of discovery or of inevitability? Are we mostly following the journey of one character? Does it mainly explore a situation? If so, do we get the sense of a satisfactory or niggling elaboration? Is it 'objective', or does it take a 'subjective' viewpoint, as in Tennessee Williams' *The Glass Menagerie* (1945)?

We shall develop some of these questions in the next few subsections. But the best beginning *always* is to take a blank piece of paper and *draw* the shape of the action as it strikes you.

Aristotle uses 'action' in the sense of the thing that has been done. For him, the action of the play is our experience of its unfolding to completion. We can retain this sense of the action as an impression of something done that we carry away from the theatre, but our feelings will not always be of completeness.

> As an exercise: Make exploratory sketches of the shapes of action of a number of plays you know – or of films and TV dramas.

4.1.7 *Schechner's open and closed structures*

In his book *Performance Theory* (1988), the North American academic and radical theatre-maker of the 1970s, Richard Schechner, proposes we test two simple models on any play we encounter. Which does it fit? His model for the well-made play, which he describes as a *closed* structure, is roughly as shown in Fig. 4.1.

A and B stand for two people, two forces or two ideas that are in conflict at the start. R stands for their resolution. This might be a happy outcome, but just as easily tragic. Resolution can include tragic recognition and death (see below, 4.1.10). In *A Doll's House* Ibsen teases his audience with happy resolutions, in which Helmer and Nora are reconciled, but also indicates a 'satisfactorily' unhappy one in which Nora drowns herself and Helmer recognises his loss. Nora herself wants an impossible combination of the two.

His second model is for an open structure, shown in Fig. 4.2.

Nothing has happened fundamentally to change the opening contradiction. There have been what he calls 'explosions' (E), but they have not changed the situation. We might therefore as well call Schechner's 'explosions' events. So this second model fits *Waiting for Godot*.

A significant feeling that we may carry away from many plays – especially from the turn of the nineteenth into the twentieth century – is a contra-

Fig. 4.1

Fig. 4.2

Fig. 4.3

dictory one that the thing is finished, but also unfinished. The opening contradiction is resolved, but not satisfactorily. At the end of Chekhov's *The
Cherry Orchard* (1903), the aristocratic Ranevskayas have finally accepted
that history has moved on and begun to abandon their pretence to power,
privilege and wealth. The ex-serf Lopakhin moves into his historic inheritance by buying their cherry orchard for enterprising development. But
Lopakhin is boorish and unfeeling. The orchard will be chopped down to
make way for holiday homes. If the Ranevskayas' way was selfish, patronising and ignorant, petty-bourgeois capitalist enterprise does not seem to
promise humaneness much of a future either. The model, then, becomes a
combination of the closed and open structures, where A might stand for
stability and B for humane values, as shown in Fig. 4.3.

The dotted lines show what Schechner calls the 'ghost' action (because
it lies behind and disturbs the other more recognisable action). Which set
of lines gets dotted depends both on the play and on the way we respond
to it.

> As an exercise: (a) Think through whether *A Doll's House* is closed,
> open or both in Schechner's terms. (b) Try out the models on several
> more plays. If there is more than a single plot (see below, 4.1.12), you
> might find you need to use several models for the one play.

4.1.8 Genre and structure

'Genre' roughly means 'kind'. We discuss the idea of theatrical genres in
more detail later (see 6.4.4). Here let us note that many genres are charac-
terised by a particular shape of action. Most obvious, perhaps, is romantic
comedy, which begins in discord and ends in accord, corresponding to
Schechner's closed structure. Especially if we concentrate on the young
Athenians, Shakespeare's *A Midsummer Night's Dream* (1594) is a good
example. The plots of many romantic comedies also briefly contain, and all
suggest, a time of harmony before the disharmony. The feeling is that there
is a natural order of things to be returned to. More factors – such as, in this

case, a concern with sex and love – contribute to the profile of a genre, and genres have internal variations (a genre is, after all, simply a label given to a collection of similar things). But shape of action is often one of the fundamentals.

Spotting these shapes can help us unpick the way in which a complex play is working. Romance – an idealising form, often set in **pastoral** or classical worlds – also works towards a final synthesis, a return to peace, order and union. In Shakespeare's *King Lear* (1605/6), Cordelia seems to enter a different world – that of Romance – after she is banished. France's vows to her (1.1.250–5) could be seen to announce this. While the play works like an Aristotelian tragedy, with Lear coming to recognition of his fault at the point of death, his reconciliation with the world couples with a Romantic reconciliation with his lost daughter. This contributes to the exquisite feelings on offer to the audience at the end of the play.

Plays that work towards a happy final synthesis are said to have a comic structure. This does not mean that they are all necessarily funny (consider Romance, e.g. *The Tempest* 1610/11), and not all comedies share the structure (consider satirical comedy, e.g. Jonson's *Volpone* 1606).

4.1.9 Boal and coercion

Notwithstanding any details of the fictional world, a play whose structure suggests that 'there is a natural order of things to be returned to' (see above, 4.1.8) will tend to affirm any such feelings an audience has in relation to the real world. In *The Theater of the Oppressed* (1979), Augusto Boal suggests that Aristotle's formula for tragedy is *coercive* – that it forces people to conform to an existing order, by persuasion. He argues that the shape of action and the relationship between spectator and protagonist – that of empathy, where we 'feel with' the character – encourage our desire to conform rather than rebel or resist.

Aristotle suggests that feelings of fear and pity are aroused in the audience, to be purged at the moment when the hero suffers and then comes to recognition (in Greek, *anagnorisis*) of a personal fault or mistaken action (*hamartia*). The Greek word for purging (like lancing a boil or scouring a pot) is *catharsis*. An implication is that tragedy thus helps educate the spectator in the management of their emotion. But Boal asks, in relation to what? If injustice makes us angry, do we need to manage that anger, or exercise it in the real world in order to overcome injustice?

Central to Boal's argument is the notion of *ethos* (see 2.4.1.2 on personal ethical choices). A society's ethos is the way it expects people to act. The ethos of the tragic hero conflicts with the ethos of the society in the fictional world in one single but essential respect, the *hamartia*. According to Boal, Aristotle assumes we will approve of the ethos of the fictional society. The *hamartia*, says Boal, is simply nonconformity. Regardless of the details of the fictional world, Aristotle's 'coercive system of tragedy' encourages us to regard all nonconformity as a fault.

Boal then goes on to look at other dramatic genres, to suggest that a similar coercive structure is at work in them, because they too work through empathy and catharsis and set part or sometimes all of the ethos of a protagonist against the ethos of a society. He asks, what relationship is set up between the ethos of the society, that of the protagonist, and that of the audience?

While Scribe (see above, 4.1.5) suggested that his formula was for the delivery of entertainment, he himself and, later, others used the well-made play to deliver moral messages in the so-called 'thesis play' genre. An example is Dumas *fils' La Dame aux camélias* (1852), also known as *Camille*. Boal (pp. 43–4) discusses this play in his scheme. The action is set in Paris and in the present of 1852. The heroine, Marguerite, is a high-class prostitute. Though she serves 'respectable' society, and it accords her the status of a celebrity, she commits just one 'sin' – of falling in love, and with an upper-class man. From this point her fortunes change: she is hounded, suffers and eventually dies. Boal describes her *hamartia* as 'negative' – it is the opposite, like a photographic negative, of the Aristotelian *hamartia*, because the audience will see love as a virtue and not a vice. But this means that, through empathy with Marguerite and emotional release when she suffers and dies, they will become critical of the social ethos of the fictional world. While they set out in Act 1 finding the stage world a pleasantly romanticised version of their own immediate reality, by the end they are forced to consider the hypocrisy and cruelties of their own social system, their own lives. The play has done *critical* work.

Note that Boal argues that *Camille* is coercive but that it does progressive work. It persuades through stealth, but persuades in the right direction. Questions of form have been central to arguments about politics and theatre since the 1920s at least. One regular topic is the extent to which an audience is 'led by the nose' by the form, or encouraged to think for itself. This debate has also been taken up by film and television studies.

4.1.10 *Tragedy and loss*

Not all tragedies comply with Aristotle's description – not even all Athenian ones. In *Modern Tragedy* (1966) Raymond Williams asks, 'What do we mean now by tragedy? What dramatic forms have expressed basic notions of the tragic in the past?' One half of the book sets out a very useful historical scheme demonstrating a variety of forms which embody changing cultural definitions of the tragic. Medieval tragedy allocates a role to Fortune, for instance, while Neoclassical tragedy is more secular; the understanding of what is involved in the 'fall of princes' changes as feudal society dissolves into a society of the mercantile city. But what, if not a single form, *is* the

tragic? Williams (p. 56) gives this universal definition: tragedy can be generalised as 'the bare irreparable fact'. Underlying the historical variation of
tragic forms is this deep shape: we leave the theatre having confronted and
survived a deep loss that cannot be reversed.

4.1.11 Action and aesthetic design

We have been arguing that some shapes of action have an intrinsic argument. This is sometimes mainly to do with *aesthetics*: the neatly closed
shape of a romantic comedy, especially if we are taken for a journey of
delightful confusions in its middle, offers us a feeling of safety and completion. We might feel the same about a vase.

In some cultural circumstances, aesthetic questions become a self-conscious part of dramaturgical design. German playwrights of the 'Classical
revival' around 1800 wanted to recall the sense of rational order they saw in
ancient Greece, an order they also saw embodied in its art. Schiller's *Mary
Stuart* (1800), for instance, has five acts in emulation of Classical precedent,
but the dramaturgical design is made ostentatiously 'Classical' through
symmetry.

Basic to the play is the clash between Mary Queen of Scots and Elizabeth I.
Acts 1 and 5 centre on Mary, Acts 2 and 4 on Elizabeth; the central, third act
stages their meeting (see 5.2.13). Schiller elegantly skews this symmetry by
having Mary at the centre of Act 5 but offstage: her execution happens in
neighbouring offstage space, creating a sense both of tension and of loss
(see 5.2.5). Other energies are at work in the play: an urgent emotional
register bursts out at times. The Classicism is also at work in the verse form
and in the mode of actor's body that Schiller presumes (see below, 4.2.3.2).
All such elements taken together communicate a sense of value and meaning to the audience quite independently of the story being told.

4.1.12 The arrangement of plots and action
sequences

All actions and events in *A Doll's House* contribute to the same action
sequence. While Doctor Rank, Mrs Linde and Krogstad all have their own
stories, and all experience change, their presence in the play is as counter-
points to and agents within the main story of Nora and Helmer. The play
has a single plot, and part of its power is its focus on this single thread.

King Lear consists of a plot and sub-plot. As we suggested above (4.1.4),
Lear's journey from belligerence in Act 1 to atonement in Act 5 is a single
action sequence which constitutes the main plot. Gloucester's somewhat
similar journey, less foregrounded by the play's design, is the sub-plot. Part
of the play's power comes from the juxtaposition and combination of these

two threads. As Pfister (1988: 219 ff.) agrees, the Gloucester sub-plot echoes and affirms the main Lear plot. The echoing structure suggests that a particular shape of experience (of unsettling and dangerous change; of the need for deep reassessment of our personal responsibilities) is all-pervasive, is a general truth of the times. Further, the doubling of the argument adds to the sense of weightiness: this 'truth' is a heavy burden.

Note how the two plots are interwoven: they occur in the same place and time-scheme. The action alternates between the two plots. Sometimes they collide. This interweaving silently invites us to compare the two plot lines. In the last paragraph we highlighted their similarities; but there are also important differences, of which we shall here consider two.

First, the two men learn different, but complementary, things. We might say, for instance, that while Lear learns pity, and the need for it given humanity's weakness before nature, Gloucester learns the need for fortitude and the possibility of grace. Recall the scene at Dover, where Poor Tom (Edgar disguised) fools Gloucester into thinking he is taking a suicidal leap over a cliff, whereas he simply falls to the level ground. After this, he values life. By virtue of their differences within a single frame of reference, a similar experience, the two plot lines perform a *mutual elaboration* of the **existential** situation Shakespeare might be seen to be exploring in the play as a whole. The idea of blindness and insight which echoes between the two plots helps invite this sort of experience of the play.

But second, the differences within the single frame of experience include a difference of character-type and generic reference (the sort of play we might think we are witnessing at any one moment: 6.4.4). Recall again the 'clifftop' scene. It is very bizarre and could, out of context, be a piece of clowning. And take Act 1 scene 2, in which Edmund fools Gloucester into believing Edgar plans to murder him. If we look freshly at it, without knowledge of the impending action, it has the shape of a comic scene, one as old as Roman Comedy. Gloucester is the old dupe, the *senex* or *veccho*; we are invited to take delight in his gullibility and the wit of the young trickster who manipulates him. Yet this is nothing to do with 'comic relief'. This early, there is nothing yet *to* relieve. Rather, we might speculate that the pressure is to *feel with* Lear, *look upon* Gloucester, as an object. Gloucester is set up as an 'objectified' version of Lear.

But then look at the scene of Gloucester's blinding (3.7). Bloody and terrifying events which in a Greek or Roman tragedy might be reported are here done on stage, and done with slow deliberation. The scene often evokes deep uneasiness and deep pity. But Gloucester is not a tragic hero; he is a bit of an old buffer. In a way, this makes his suffering all the more distressing. There is not space here fully to pursue this line of exploration, though you might want to do so yourself. For instance, the argument becomes more involved once we suggest that perhaps Lear too is a 'bit of an old buffer'. The shape emerging is of two character-plot *potentials* (possibilities and expectations about what they are and might become) being set up and then made to collide, interweave and reflect one another. The bizarre but truth-bearing discourse (see 3.1.5.4) the Fool brings to Lear – which includes pop-ular comic tales – is also brought onto the stage in the figure of the foolish Gloucester (who *also* reflects Lear himself). Consider, too, laughter as part of a tragic response.

We might also find thematic linkages – such as jealousy, lust and merit – between the plot strands in *A Midsummer Night's Dream*. But here the plots have roughly equal status; there is no hierarchical plot/sub-plot structure. Again, the plots interweave, and we have already noted the pleasure offered by their being skilfully juggled to mutual resolution. Indeed, the multiplic-ity of plots contributes to a sense of richness and variety; the play is like a big bag of toffees. In this case, then, a particular arrangement of plots sup-ports the aesthetic, pleasure-giving functioning of the play; it declares itself as delightful artifice.

We have so far used 'plot' and 'action sequence' as if interchangeable, and legitimately so. We might in some circumstances want to distinguish between them. Let us again take our example from Pfister, perhaps to invite some further reading (see especially his discussion of Jonson's *Volpone*, pp. 213–16). Ibsen's early play *Peer Gynt* (1876) has an 'episodic' structure in which the **eponymous** hero has several unrelated adventures in different parts of the world. Each adventure has its own logic of cause and effect, so each is a complete action sequence. But linking them is Peer, and his quest to 'find himself'. This overarching quest narrative might be seen to consti-tute the single plot.

Webster's tragedy *The Duchess of Malfi* (1614) owes some of its power to a neat use of action sequences in relation to plot. The central figure of the Duchess has two foils (see 2.2), Cariola and Julia. Cariola the waiting woman is given the theatrical function of a presenter – she helps to display the Duchess to us. Julia, the adulterous wife, is placed within an indepen-dent action sequence – she aims to satisfy ambition by taking as a new lover the Cardinal, who then kills her. This climax to the action sequence forms an ironic parallel to the main plot involving the Duchess. For even though Julia almost takes on a male role in organising her own life – she threatens Bosola with a gun so that he will have sex with her – she is still killed. But there is more than irony in the relationship between main plot and Julia's action sequence. Just before her death she is told that the Duchess has been murdered, and then she is forced to kiss a poisoned Bible. This violent use of old-fashioned ceremonial is the sort of thing that tormented the Duchess. The deliberately neat parallel is set up with obviousness. It may be grim, but it also has a theatrical panache.

Let us recap. Some plays, like *A Doll's House*, have a single plot. Others, with multiple plots, may treat these hierarchically (*Lear*) or afford them equal status (*Dream*). In *Malfi* there is an ironic interaction between plot and action sequence. Multiple action sequences may be interleaved, each action sequence corresponding roughly to a plot strand (*Lear*, *Dream*). Or they may be given in succession, sometimes contributing to a single plot (*Peer Gynt*). Variations on these possibilities help construct meaning and contribute to audience pleasure and, sometimes, to a declared sense of 'theatricality', where, as in *Malfi*, the stage declares itself as a stage.

Webster has his Duchess of Malfi die during the fourth act. We might see her courtship and marriage, conflict with her brothers, persecution and murder, as three action phases within an action sequence to be completed with Antonio's pursuit of revenge and the succession of their son as Duke as phases four and five. But with the Duchess's death the erstwhile melancholic misanthropist (and misogynist), Bosola, undergoes a fundamental change. He comes to see her worth and he, too, becomes her avenger. It is possible (we would invite such a view) to see Bosola as Webster's chief focus for the final acts of the play. His conversion and pursuit of revenge seem like a fresh action sequence, or a second phase in a two-phase sequence centred on him that only really emerges in the design of the play at this point. Although the Duchess dies, she does not learn through her suffering. But Bosola learns from it. It is as if he were a tragic hero by proxy. On this reading, Webster in fact gives the Duchess a subsidiary status in the play bearing her name.

While an inspection of plot (Duchess) and sub-plot (Julia) can help us to comment on Webster's thematic design and his management of events, a more thoroughgoing analysis may begin to lay bare the possibly unconscious ideological scheme (see 3.1.5.4) of the play: the male-centredness of a play named after a woman. Our use of Pfister's levels of action has helped us in this.

4.1.13 *Plays within plays, metatheatricality and levels of fiction*

Shakespeare's *Hamlet* and *A Midsummer Night's Dream* both use the device, fairly common since the Renaissance, of the play-within-a-play. The 'Mousetrap' play which Hamlet uses to trap Claudius into guilty reflection works on the king because its plot mirrors his own story. In terms of the plot of *Hamlet*, this is perhaps all we need to say about it.

But there is, of course, much more to say, too, in connection with themes and theatricality. It is, after all, a very *old-fashioned* piece of writing that the prince has these old-fashioned players perform. And he himself has much to say about playing and its effects on our emotions (2.2.544 ff.). Right at the crisis-point in this rather modern play, with its interest in psychological depth (2.7), comes a public pondering about the power of theatrical formulae which, though somehow outmoded, nevertheless persuade and move. Not only does Hamlet muse on this: we also witness the direct impact of what some might call 'crude' drama within the 'reality' of Hamlet's world. On a broader canvas, Phyllis Gorfain (1983) suggests that the play as a whole is deeply interested in the idea of *play* as inconsequential, or pretended, action. Thus Hamlet's playful stabbing through the arras which kills Polonius, his playing at madness which might as well be madness, the purposeful bit of play-acting he brings to court, and the playful duel which Claudius designs to be deadly, all contribute to this deeply embedded theme – of which the fact that *Hamlet* itself is just 'play' is a part.

This last point links with our concern with the self-conscious theatricality of some plays. *Hamlet* can be seen as a very showy, highbrow piece which Shakespeare's company, the King's Men, were using to show themselves and their chief playwright off as ground-breakers. It is a tragedy, yes. But it is also a play *about* plays, and not just at the 'Mousetrap' moment. Where plays comment on plays and theatricality, they are said to have a *metatheatrical* dimension. Clearly, the mechanicals' play of Pyramus and Thisby helps give the *Dream* such a dimension too – as well as providing the means for us to be pulled between the snobbiness of their court audience, the workers' own sincerity and our own desire to laugh at their incompetence.

The fictional world of a play-within-a-play is 'below' that of the play which contains it: we take it less seriously as a fiction. So, too, are dream sequences realised on stage. Some plays – notably in the early twentieth century – play with this hierarchy. Strindberg's *Dream Play* (1902) is a case in point.

Our discussion here has links with the discussion of 'worlds' in 5.2.12.

4.1.14 Story and plot

Sophocles fashioned the *plot* of *Oedipus Rex* out of a previously existing *story*. He could have made his play a different shape and still told the same story. Many other playwrights have told the same story, but in different ways. One of the means by which Shakespeare got to know about King Lear was probably the old play *Leir* (*c*.1590). Underlying both plays – which have different plots – is the same story. A dramatic plot, then, is the arrangement of a story for presentation on the stage (Pfister 1988: 197).

What that arrangement does, and the motivations we discern behind it, are every bit as important as the story itself. At this level of work, reading for the story is only a small part of our enterprise. Taking the hint from Aristotle, we can make the general observation that dramatic plots tend to condense the story, make it more linear and clarify or introduce structures of cause and effect. Often structures of coincidence, juxtaposition and irony are also introduced or developed. On such bases, thematic, moralistic, ethical or critical arguments may be built. As we have seen so far in this chapter, a particular shape of plot or arrangement of plots is arguably always meaningful in itself, and certainly contributes significantly to what this particular act of storytelling comes to mean to its audience.

Pfister (p. 196) tends to suggest that the story comes 'before' any plot. We have ourselves said that a story 'underlies' a plot. Temporal (before) and spatial (under) metaphors are useful, but we should be careful with them. Consider *A Doll's House*. Ibsen tells a story about a woman called Nora and her husband. We know from his diaries and letters that the character and her situation are loosely based on an actual woman he had heard about. Her real-life story and Nora's are similar, but not the same. We have seen how Ibsen was manipulating the conventions of the well-made play. Presumably, then, the events – such as discoveries and threats – and, indeed, characters (such as Krogstad and Mrs Linde) created in the fashioning of Nora's *story* out of the real woman's were determined by the sort of play Ibsen wanted to write. Nora's *story* depends on the plot-shape Ibsen had in mind. Once written, though, it can be told by other dramatic plots and in other media.

Stories only really exist as things told, that is, as real or imagined events given shape. Dramatic plots tend to tell stories, to embody them, in particular ways; they give a particular general shape to the world and the way we view it. For instance, they condense, and do not *usually* employ flashbacks, as novelistic plots quite frequently do. Different genres do the telling in their particular ways, and then individual plays have their own plot strategies. We need to think of every play we encounter as a *specific embodiment* of a story. Our object of enquiry is that embodiment – the story-and-shape – not the story 'underlying' or to be seen 'through' the play.

4.1.15 *The telling of stories*

During the 1980s the British theatre company Shared Experience became famous for their particular brand of 'storytelling' theatre. It is not that they narrated the events on stage as if speaking a novel. Rather, they acted plays – such as Shakespeare's *Cymbeline* – in such a way that they 'stepped back' from the action and characters, keeping their audience constantly and pleasurably aware that the actors had a story to communicate, a story to re-tell. They 'demonstrated' their characters, then, but not for Brechtian reasons of distanciation. The feel of their shows was, rather, that the audience were being introduced to a box of delights, intriguing, precious and beautifully fashioned. Delight was strengthened by the use of only minimal sets, costumes and props. This was theatre that was centred on imagination.

Part of the magic of those shows derived precisely from the fact that, for the most part, dramatic texts let the events narrate themselves. This, in turn, is one reason why plays tend not to use flashbacks, which in novels usually need the intervention of a narrative voice to place them in relation to the rest of the action. There is rarely a narrator-figure in drama, in contrast to the dominant practice in novels or short stories (see 2.2). A dramatic text is a script for a piece of collective storytelling, in the West since 1600 usually without a separable narrator.

We thrive on stories; we love to hear them. And *telling* stories is a deeply human activity. Each of us has a notion of the story of our own life, which helps us make sense of who we are; it is part of our identity. We make sense of the world by making or learning stories about the world, ordering our experiences into causes and effects. The practices of science and medicine depend on stories, as does commentary on the arts. We tell the history of the universe or evolution; connect in orderly fashion the nature of the virus, methods of infection, life habits, symptoms, the action of drugs (they change the situation), likely outcomes for individuals and the likely demographic scenario to come. And we sort artworks into movements or models of cultural production (Chap. 6), linking them to events at large.

Just as theatre and playing can become part of a play's concerns (metatheatricality), some plays script a concern with our need for and delight in telling stories, of setting out a narrative, of making the disorderly confusions of real life settle down into an acceptable or pleasurable pattern. Prospero's account to Miranda of their past history early on in *The Tempest* can be regarded *either* as a rather heavy-handed bit of exposition on Shakespeare's part, *or* as a bit of lengthy exposition which also *characterises* Prospero's driving desire to have the record put straight, the story properly told – and concluded. The events on the island which he controls are part of his making the story he wants to tell happen. Caliban has his own story to tell; it contests Prospero's.

4.1.16 *Live and narrated action*

Prospero's account to Miranda is the major piece of exposition in Shakespeare's *The Tempest*. It gets the story so far established, so that the action can meaningfully start. It helps simplify what has to be presented on the stage: exposition facilitates the condensing of the action (see 4.1.14 and 3.1.2, above).

But in this play, and most others, the situation after the opening is changed by events which happen offstage as well as on it. We learn about offstage happenings by hearing characters tell one another about them – or, in some plays, by being told by a narrator. In nearly every play we meet there is both *live action* and *narrated action* (see Pfister 1988: 204–11). Again, we can put the fact that things are made to happen offstage down to the condensing principle of drama: to have everything necessary to the action done on stage would often be confusing and would make for very long plays.

4.1.16.1 CONDENSATION, DECORUM, EMOTIONAL EFFECT AND AESTHETIC THRILL

When Hamlet is sent off to England it is a ruse. Rosencrantz and Guildenstern are instructed to murder him at sea. By his good fortune, he accidentally discovers the plot, kills them instead, and returns to Denmark finally to avenge his father. The episode is one of several making up his journey from feckless melancholy to death in vengeance. But it is an entirely narrated episode. Since all the live action takes place at Elsinore castle and its precincts, we might guess that the action is narrated for the sake of *condensation* of the plot. The focus is kept tight.

Playwrights have other reasons for choosing to have action narrated rather than witnessed directly. One is *decorum*. It may be decided that what needs to happen in the course of the action (say, a murder or a rape) should not be shown, lest it disgust, alarm or perhaps excite an audience – or lay open the players to abuse. The eighteenth-century London stages of Covent Garden and Drury Lane, while busy with comedy, farce and spectacle as well as the odd tragedy, were resolutely decorous in this sense. This decorum was part of the theatres' role of contributing to the **Town's** civility.

A second reason is *emotional effect*. A narrated event works directly on the hearer's imagination. Especially if the language in which it is narrated is vivid and evocative, an audience may become more emotionally disturbed than they would were the events staged instead – because the real thing can never be as weird as what we imagine.

This seeming paradox, that absent action can be brought somehow closer through words – that the insubstantial can give the effect of substance – can also deliver an *aesthetic thrill* to an audience. Right at the heart of conventional Western theatre is a paradox: *all* of the events before us, whether enacted or narrated, are both there (we witness them, believe what we see and are told) and not there (they are fiction). The aesthetic thrill depends on this paradox.

Several of the plays of the Roman writer Seneca (*c.*4 BCE–65) involve very bloody and terrifying deeds, but almost all of these are narrated rather than enacted. It is supposed that Seneca's plays were written to be read aloud rather than performed, but they were none the less one of the major influences on the Renaissance revenge drama, especially that sub-genre since called the 'tragedy of blood'. An important early example is Kyd's *The Spanish Tragedy* (1585–7), where we see Horatio killed and then see his father describing the corpse. Renaissance plays actually stage the blood and gore, but at the same time, as we suggested above, there is an aesthetic effect to be had by narrating action – this is not merely redundant description. Thus in Kyd's play, as in other Renaissance plays, there is an interest in the *interplay* between the direct experience of violent, live action and the narration of the violence and its effects.

West (1991) suggests that both the 'realist' David Garrick and later the 'classical' Sarah Siddons in the second half of the eighteenth century were appreciated for their *art* in consciously presenting their role while displaying true emotion. The actors were to be passionate but not to be overcome. This serenely poised management of emotionality was itself decorous – the actor was a model of both restraint and honesty, a model citizen. The narration or recall of extreme events provided effective moments in which to stage this ideal, and some plays – Hannah Cowley's *The Fate of Sparta* (1788) is one – were scripted specially to deliver that effect.

We might say that Brecht contests the dominant conventions of Western theatre by having all the action in some sense narrated even while it is enacted. The actors 'demonstrate' the action, put it at a distance from them and us (2.5.2). In Brecht's play *The Mother* (1932), the characters/actors stage a 'Report on the events of 1 May 1905' (scene 5). Here, not only do the performers 'demonstrate' the characters; those characters themselves also report significant past events in which their comrades died. The characters narrate the events as they act them out. The scene is very difficult to stage without making it sentimental and, indeed, 'epic' in a very un-Brechtian sense – it all too easily becomes monumentally moving in conventional terms. The combined emotional effect and aesthetic thrill of action *narrated* within the fictional frame is difficult to overcome.

4.1.16.2 STAGEABILITY, LIAISON, ARGUMENT AND PLEASURE

In Act 3 scene 2 of *The Tempest*, Ariel makes himself invisible and plays tricks on Stephano, Trinculo and Caliban to begin punishing them for attempting to usurp Prospero's authority. The local action ends with them following the sound of Ariel's music offstage. We next hear of them much later, at 4.1.171–84, when Ariel recounts to Prospero what we have already seen – and then briefly continues their story: they have been dragged through hedges and finally 'left . . . I'th'filthy-mantled pool' (l. 182) near to Prospero's cave. And then, almost immediately, they arrive on stage, '*all wet*' (l. 193 SD) to suffer even further manipulation.

Let us comment on this sequence of staged and narrated actions. What strikes us first? Perhaps it is indeed the *pleasure* the audience is set up to get from the appearance of the bedraggled bunch in Act 4. What delivers that pleasure? The moment is clearly one to be exploited for direct comic effect, signalled by the rare stage direction at l. 193. But there is also a structural pleasure scripted, which is again to do with the *interplay of presence and absence*. Crucial to this is the way in which what Ariel narrates is much wilder than what we witness in the first onstage action. We see something; it is elaborated in our mind's eye, though we lack direct contact with it. Finally we witness the results – we are rewarded by the 'true' presence on stage of the object of our delight. Note that the shape here is a **crescendo**.

A more banal – though also important – consideration is the question of *liaison*. The interplay of live and narrated action sustains the continuity of the servants' plot-line across its interruptions by other plot-lines. The audience are kept up to date, given sign-posts, reminded where they are in each story. But we can take this further. Prospero is also kept up to date. He needs to know what has happened. This is on the one hand a matter of plausibility – he is supposed to be in control, after all. But it is also a matter of what

Prospero represents: he is indeed 'the one who needs to know'. Recall our remarks about him in 4.1.15.

We have just described how a plot-line is sustained across its interruption by others. The other side to this coin is that those interruptions are made possible: the audience can concentrate securely on several matters at once. We have here an especially interesting case of interruption, since it is Prospero himself who halts the betrothal masque, having suddenly realised that 'I had forgot that foul conspiracy / Of the beast Caliban and his confederates / Against my life' (4.1.139–41). The interruption pits the 'light' of love, sex and marriage against the 'dark' of conspiracy. Yet what we get from the conspiracy sub-plot at precisely this moment is broad comedy. By the play's ending, Prospero has forgiven all. We might see the comic pleasures to be had in the servants' plot-line as part and parcel of this scheme of forgiveness.

Yet more banal – and this time, surely, not very important at all – is the question of *stageability*. It would be difficult to make a scene within the originally prevailing stage conventions which satisfactorily showed the physical punishment of the servant characters. It might also be difficult given the actual technical facilities. But surely much more important than either is the audience's delight in *cruelty at a safe distance*.

One of the ways in which *Richard 3* and its **eponymous** hero work their sinister charm at the opening is by having Richard, once his exposition is over, both say what he plans to do and then immediately *do* it. He tells us he plans 'To set my brother Clarence and the King/ In deadly hate the one against the other' (1.1.34–5). As Clemen (1986) notes, Shakespeare is here making use – perhaps ostentatiously and playfully – of the medieval 'planning monologue' usually delivered by the **Vice**. For our present purposes we might also call this, in more general terms, *anticipatory narrated action*. The rush of audience pleasure comes when Clarence immediately enters – and the duping begins; from the 'rhyme' of narrated and staged action – an action is described, and then it happens. And that pleasure is intensified by Richard's announcement of Clarence's entry: 'Here Clarence comes' (l. 41). He is in control, and so are we: rhymes make us feel secure. The pleasure puts us in a particular relationship with the duping of Clarence – one that is progressively to be disciplined as the action unfolds.

Pfister (1988) uses the terms 'scenic realisation' and 'narrative mediation' where we have used 'live action' and 'narrated action' respectively. While we have suggested that Shakespeare sets us a snare in the devilishly attractive Richard, Pfister sets out a sophisticated account of the trick played on Malvolio in Shakespeare's *Twelfth Night* (1602), involving both anticipatory *and* retrospective narrated action. We witness the tricksters plan, carry out and then reflect upon the deception. We take delight in the plan and execution on the terms just argued. But that reflection is a sobering experience for characters and audience alike, especially since it is prompted by the more serious, high-ranking characters (pp. 209–11). There is, then, a *moralising* potential in the interplay between staged and narrated action.

Pfister also makes a very good account of Leicester's soliloquy during Mary's execution in Schiller's *Mary Stuart* – a case of *simultaneous* narrated action (pp. 205–7).

4.1.16.3 CHARACTER PERSPECTIVES AND CHORIC FUNCTIONS

When Ariel reports his tricks on Stephano and the rest, he does so with a vividness that expresses his own pleasure. The same goes for his report of his management of the opening shipwreck: 'the fire and cracks / Of sulphurous roaring the most mighty Neptune / Seem to besiege' (1.2.203–5). This is not instruction to a scenographer, nor is it merely narration – the intensity of these lines comes from a *character perspective*. This is *his* point of view. Narrated action – or 'narrative mediation', in Pfister's terminology – is always potentially from the point of view of a character as much as a message being sent by the playwright. With this example we can go a step further. This particular perspective is one which the character is forced to present: Ariel is eager 'To answer thy [Prospero's] best pleasure' (1.2.190).

In Shakespeare's *Antony and Cleopatra* (1606/7), Enobarbus makes his famous barge speech (2.2.195 ff.). The events he describes predate the play's beginning, but strictly speaking, this is not exposition – it does not affect our understanding of events. Most regularly, the speech gets trundled out in commentaries as 'evidence' of Cleopatra's character or as 'evidence' of Antony's besottedness. But it is much more than either of these. Especially if we note Enobarbus's competition with the Roman officers, the speech tells us a great deal about Enobarbus himself. Played well, the speech is *simultaneously* deeply engaging for the audience and patently obvious as a piece of private enthusiasm.

When, in *Hamlet*, Gertrude describes Ophelia's death, she describes something that obviously neither she nor anyone else has witnessed. While this would be an impossibility or a deception in real life, Shakespeare's stage was not concerned with plausibilities of this sort. She appears here as *chorus*. The events need to be told. Again, while questions of stageability are perhaps pertinent, they are hardly of great importance. The events are all the more pathetic because distanced from the stage; Ophelia's presence is truly 'lost'. Perhaps also these words produce more pathos than words delivering onstage action, or silent action, possibly could. But most important of all, surely, is that it is *Gertrude* who is at the staged centre of pathos; she is here the subject of empathy, the one who truly and deeply feels. This does not 'mean' that she is guiltless. It contributes to the range of quite separate attitudes the play invites us to take to her.

4.1.16.4 SILENT NARRATION

Plays, for the most part, tell their own story without the aid of a narrator. The narration is done through the way the scenes succeed one another –

silent narration. We have seen how narrated action as well as staged action contribute fundamentally to this.

While admitting that what we see and hear on stage is a realisation of a script for performance by those who have 'interpreted' or 'produced' it, we can distinguish between staged and narrated action in an important way. The experience of an audience is generally that staged action is there for us to interpret; and we select what we concentrate on, shift our focus. By contrast, narrated action forces our focus in one direction; and it carries its own interpretation of the events reported. It is an account, it has a perspective (Pfister 1988: 204). This perspective can act on us without our knowing it. When it is apparent it can sometimes feel as if the author is making a direct intervention. Thus Cranmer's prophecy about the future Elizabeth I in *Henry 8* (1613) can be taken to be Shakespeare's compliment both to the memory of that queen and to the popular daughter of James I.

As an exercise: (a) Without detailing the staged action sequence concerning the aristocratic characters such as Alonso, trace all the staged and narrated action concerning the shipwreck and the fate of members of the crew and fleet in Shakespeare's *The Tempest*. Write an account of how this storyline is plotted and contributes to the pleasures and meanings generated by the play. Note, for instance, that the Bo'sun and Master appear in Act 5 – the moment is a reward to them, the audience and the aristocrats. (b) Explore the relationship between staged and narrated action in any one play you are studying. You may want to use only part of it.

4.1.17 *Character distribution*

Different plot lines in the same play will involve different sets of characters. These sets may cross over significantly, as is the case with the Gloucester and Lear plot lines in *King Lear*. Goneril, Regan, Cornwall, Albany, Kent and Edgar for a start are all significant players in each. Or the sets may be more or less discrete, with only one or two characters participating in more than one. Such, for instance, would be the case for Hal in *1 Henry 4*, if we say there are separate 'Falstaff' and 'Henry' plot lines as well as 'worlds' (see 5.2.12).

Clearly, a useful way to get hold of the plotting of a play is to look at the character distribution scene by scene. The upper table in Fig. 4.4 tabulates the distribution of characters from about midway in Shakespeare's *The Tempest*. Whether or not we decide to give separate (sub)plot status to Prospero's dealings with his daughter, the underlings and the shipwrecked aristocrats, the table helps us get a hold on the design of the play's action. At a glance we can see that either Prospero, Ariel or both are involved in every scene: Shakespeare structurally foregrounds their control of events.

	3.1	3.2	3.3	4.1	5.1	Epilogue
PROSPERO	X		X	X	X	X
ARIEL		X	X	X	X	
MIRANDA	X			X	X	
FERDINAND	X			X	X	
ALONSO			X		X	
SEBASTIAN			X		X	
ANTONIO			X		X	
GONZALO			X		X	
ADRIAN			X		X	
FRANCISCO			X		X	
OTHERS			X			
CALIBAN		X		X	X	
TRINCULO		X		X	X	
STEPHANO		X		X	X	
MASTER					X	
BOATSWAIN					X	
'IRIS'				X		
'CERES'				X		
'JUNO'				X		
'NYMPHS'				X		
'REAPERS'				X		
SPIRITS			X	X		

	3.1	3.2	3.3	4.1	5.1
Prospero/Ariel	X	X	X	X	X
Lovers	X			X	X
Servants		X		X	X
Aristocrats			X		X

Fig. 4.4 Character distribution by scene in Shakespeare, *The Tempest*, Acts 3–5 and Epilogue

The lower table is a condensation of the first and reveals the patterning of the action more clearly: see section 4.1.17.

Act 3 focuses first on the young lovers and then the servant class. Note who is the agent of control in each: Ariel deals with the underlings. Some sort of dramaturgical decorum seems to be in operation. Then in 3.3, both Prospero and Ariel deal with the aristocrats. In the single scene of Act 4, which contains the betrothal masque, Prospero has the spirits perform for Miranda and Ferdinand, but the servants also appear; perhaps there is some sort of contrast being scripted? And then in Act 5, all three groups are brought together.

The Tempest is tragi-comic – it stages the happy resolution of deadly conflict. It is also a Romance: the healing action takes place in an idealised or exotic world, and the play invites our celebration of it as pure invention. One of the ways it does this is by being so clearly *designed*. The plot-lines are not merely interwoven: they are woven together in a patterned way – lovers; servants; aristocrats; lovers and servants; all three groups. This patterning is illustrated in the lower table at Fig. 4.4.

If you know the play, or want now to read it, you might easily make further comments on the basis of Fig. 4.4. But we can also go further with this sort of mapping, as Fig. 4.5 will demonstrate. To get there, we need first to ask a question.

4.1.18 What is a scene?

The scene ends when the lights go down. The mother has died in the daughter's arms and '*the light fades to nothing*'. Or no, the scene ends when the curtains close. The colonel lies dead on the floor and the smoking gun is in the butler's hands: '*curtain*'. Or the king says, 'To battle!' and everyone leaves the stage. *Then* the lights go down or the curtain closes – or both. But what happens on the Elizabethan or Jacobean stage, where there are no front **tabs** or lighting board? What is a scene, and when?

The original texts of several Renaissance plays do not mark scene divisions; others do. A good rule of thumb for editors wanting to insert scene divisions and numbers is that a scene ends when the stage empties. In the Renaissance, you clear the stage so that the next bit of action can begin. The exits are part of the action.

We shall see in Chapter 5 (5.2.1) how the flat-and-relief system of shutters, developed after the introduction of scenery in the Restoration, tends to make the change of scene principally a change of location. And persons may be left or discovered on stage at the end or opening of any scene given in relief, upstage of the closing and opening shutters. The later practice of drawing a front curtain between scenes facilitates both scene changes and having the stage unemptied at the head and foot of *each* scene. Sophisticated lighting does the same job as the curtain. From the mid-nineteenth century onwards the scene might change before our very eyes, as part of the entertainment.

Any playtext we meet will observe conventions of scenic division that are tied up with the technical development of the stage. We should note these. Scene divisions are also, of course, an important part of any play's design, as we saw in 4.1.17. The scene changes when the feel as well as the logic of the action demand it. These breaks are part of what the audience is to experience: something has been established or accomplished; so the scene ends and we all set off to another situation, a fresh episode.

In all that we have so far said in this subsection, the change of scene is tied to a change of situation on stage. For playwrights, actors and audiences in seventeenth-century France, this sense of a new stage situation was felt to

	3.1			3.2		3.3						4.1							5.1							Epilogue
	a	b	c	a	b	a	b	c	d	e	f	a	b	c	d	e	f	g	a	b	c	d	e	f	g	a
PROSPERO		U	X				U	U	U			X	X	X	X	X	U	X	X	X	U	X	X	X	X	X
ARIEL		U			U			X								X	U	X	X		M					
MIRANDA		X										X	X	X	X								X	X	X	
FERDINAND	X	X										X	X	X	X								X	X	X	
CALIBAN				X													X								X	
TRINCULO				X	X												X								X	
STEPHANO				X	X												X								X	
ALONSO						X	X	X	X												M	X	X	X	X	
SEBASTIAN						X	X	X	X	X	X										M	X	X	X	X	
ANTONIO						X	X	X	X	X	X										M	M	X	X	X	
GONZALO						X	X	X	X	X	X										M	X	X	X	X	
ADRIAN						X	X	X	X	X	X										M	M	X	X	X	
FRANCISCO						X	X	X	X	X	X										M	M	X	X	X	
OTHERS						X	X	X	X	X	X															
'IRIS'														X												
'CERES'														X												
'JUNO'														X												
'NYMPHS'														X												
'REAPERS'														X												
SPIRITS						M	M									M										
MASTER																									X	X	
BOATSWAIN																									X	X	

Fig. 4.5 French scene analysis of Shakespeare, *The Tempest*, Acts 3–5 and Epilogue
Key: M – mute; U – onstage unseen by other characters.

3.1a	Ferdinand *solus* and the logs – 'most poor matters/Point to rich ends' (3–4)
3.1b	Prospero watches the lovers – 'Fair encounter/Of two most rare affections!' (74–5)
3.1c	Prospero *solus* – 'So glad of this are they I cannot be' (92) . . . 'For yet ere supper-time must I perform/Much business appertaining' (95–6)
3.2a	Usurping servants divided – Cal.: 'Let me lick thy shoe. I'll not serve him' (22/3)
3.2b	Ariel further divides them – 'Thou liest' (43); then once reunited leads them astray with music – Cal.: 'The isle is full of noises' (130 ff.)
3.3a	Aristocratic usurpers divided – Seb.: 'The next advantage/Will we take throughly' (13–14)
3.3b	The false banquet
3.3c	Ariel as Harpy – 'You are three men of sin' (53 ff.)
3.3d	Prospero takes stock – 'My high charms work' (83 ff.)
3.3e,f	Processional exit of the aristocrats – Alonso leaves distracted; his usurpers follow; Gonzalo and Adrian comment, 'All three of them are desperate' (104)
4.1a	Prospero blesses the union – 'as my gift, and thine own acquisition/Worthily purchas'd, take my daughter' (13–14)
4.1b	Prospero instructs Ariel ('What would my potent master', 34; 'Do you love me, no?' 48) and Ferdinand ('do not give dalliance/Too much the rein' 51–2)
4.1c	The betrothal masque
4.1d	Prospero cuts the masque short – 'I had forgot' . . . 'Our revels now are ended' . . . 'We are such stuff' (139 ff.)
4.1e	Ariel reports on the servant usurpers
4.1f	*Enter – all wet* and the washing-line gag
4.1g	Prospero takes stock ('At this hour/Lies at my mercy all mine enemies' 261–2) and promises Ariel freedom
5.1a	Prospero takes stock ('Now does my project gather to a head', 1) and decides that 'the rarer action is/In virtue than in vengeance' (27–8)
5.1b	Prospero *solus* – 'But this rough magic/I here abjure' (50–1)
5.1c	Aristocrats in the charmed circle; Prospero rehearses forgiveness; Ariel despatched to find the mariners
5.1d	Prospero accuses and forgives – 'Welcome, my friends all!' (125)
5.1e	Ferdinand and Miranda discovered: the game at chess – Mir.: 'Sweet lord, you play me false' (172); Seb.: 'A most high miracle!' (177)
5.1f	Ariel brings on Master and Bo'sun – Alons: 'there is in this business more than nature/Was ever conduct of' (243–4)
5.1g	Ariel brings on the servants – Pros.: 'this thing of darkness I/Acknowledge mine' (275–6); Ariel set free
Epil.	'Prospero' *solus* as character/servant-performer – 'Let your indulgence set me free' (20)

Fig. 4.6 *The Tempest*: tabulation of episodes identified by Fig. 4.5

occur with the entry or exit of a character – any character except perhaps servants. In the rather formal and statuesque proceedings of the **Neoclassical** stage, then, each new combination of characters is marked – and this includes the playscript – as a new scene.

We can take any dramatic text and divide it into 'french scenes'. It turns out to be a useful exercise. It is useful to production managers and directors in planning who to call for which rehearsal, for dividing the play up into manageable bits of action. Within the scope of this book, it is especially useful for getting a closer take on the patterning and design of a play's action.

4.1.19 French scene analysis

Fig. 4.5 presents a french scene analysis of the same portion of *The Tempest* as tabulated in Fig. 4.4. It is, then, a more thoroughgoing picture of character distribution. We now have the second half of the play divided up into about 25 episodes, or bits of action, and we can see at a glance who is involved in each.

The episodes we have identified are tabulated in Fig. 4.6. Note that we have given each french scene (or episode) a brief title or summary, and selected a key quotation – sometimes two – for each. This work of analysis, basic commentary and selection made us pay close attention to the whole of the text, and gave us a working focus (the french scene) at every moment. Nothing could pass us by. We now have an overview of the play's structure, a handlist of its episodes, and key quotations which we can put to use in an essay. Composing the titles and selecting the quotations started the work of detailed commentary on the play – we had to decide what was significant. For instance, for 4.1.a we have tried to encapsulate the contradictory nature of the episode – the union Prospero blesses is scripted also to be a trading in women between men. We have similarly foregrounded what looks like deliberate contradiction in 5.1.e. Would your choices have been the same as ours?

Fig. 4.5 is a bit dazzling at first sight. It makes little sense on its own – the tabulation of Fig. 4.6 helps open it up. But Figures 4.5 and 4.6 are of much less use to you than the tables you will make for yourself – for it is in the act of *making* a french scene analysis that we encounter a play's detailed action-design at close hand. The two tables took one of us about three hours to draw. In the course of doing that, enough notes were made to fill a chapter if they were written up. French scene analysis is good preparation for an essay, then! The next job would be to select what was useful to attempting the task set by the essay.

Rather than write such an essay here, let us develop just a few points – mostly about the play's design – and leave the rest for you to discover. For instance, we now have 4.1 divided up in such a way that we can see the order in which the two groups of lovers and servants appear. So should we say that there are really two scenes here, not one? Or that the sequence we noted in Fig. 4.4 of 'lovers; servants; aristocrats; *lovers and servants*; all three groups' should really go: lovers; servants; aristocrats; *lovers* (4.1.a–d); *servants* (4.1.f,g); all three groups? Not at all. It is indeed 'lovers *and* servants' (4.1.a–g) because the stage never empties; Prospero and Ariel remain on stage (4.1.e). The scene continues; the two episodes are held together. So the play is designed with even more exquisite playfulness than we had already established. There is a break but not a break. This works on the audience.

Note, too, the 'rhyme' between 3.2.a,b and 3.3.a,b: in each, we see a group of usurpers divided amongst themselves; and then a trick is played on them. We might from here develop a commentary on the sequencing, rhythm and build-up of the stage tricks and spectacles in the play.

In 4.1.c, the betrothal masque, we have a group of onstage spectators. But note also that within this group Prospero is then scripted to become the subject of Ferdinand and Miranda's gaze in 4.1.d. The audience's gaze is similarly led; and the audience are thus encouraged to look *at* Prospero and not *with* him.

We found it difficult at times to decide whether or not to start a fresh french scene – especially when Ariel left or entered the stage. While the play is divided very definitely into episodes, Ariel is scripted to flit in and out of them. Our 'difficulty', then, in fact leads us to an important feature of the play's design, which the last sentence encapsulates.

One place where we decided to make more french scenes than strictly necessary was at 3.3.d–f. The sequence in which the aristocrats leave the stage seemed to us important. And we have deliberately used the word 'processional' in our summary title (Fig. 4.6) to underline the formal nature of this play.

We have left the betrothal masque undivided for now. But it has its own rhythm, its own aesthetic, which the author is quoting – it is a pastiche of a real court entertainment, and recognisable to the original audience as such.

French scene analysis helps us to see more clearly the way in which the stage empties and fills (see 5.2.13). We can see, for instance, that the stage fills – with the spirits who deliver Prospero's masque – in the action phase concerning the lovers. Writing 'M' for 'mute' can be a revealing exercise. For instance, we might note while reading *A Midsummer Night's Dream* that all the humans are gathered together for the festivities of the last scene. If we are canny, we might also note the ungenerous way in which the aristocrats are made to poke fun at the mechanicals, introducing a 'minor key' into the romantic comedy ending. But a french scene analysis (in the absence of a walk-through) will quickly demonstrate that Helena and Hermia are scripted to be *mute* for this scene. Why? What shall we do with this in our production?

And just one more teaser. Note that in 4.1.c we have included 'Ceres' but not Ariel. In 4.1.e, Ariel says he wondered whether to remind Prospero about Caliban 'When I presented Ceres' (l. 167). One editor, Kermode (1964), asks, 'Why does Ariel mention this?' (p. 105 n.). Our work here surely helps us towards the answer he misses – the line is part of the stage trickery and wonder being worked on the audience. We as spectators learn that we have been watching Ariel without knowing it. Productions which choose to make Ariel *apparent* as a player in the masque miss this opportunity for playful wonder.

As an exercise: Make a french scene analysis of any one play – or part of it – that you are studying. Make a table of episodes and key quotations. Comment.

4.1.20 Bits, beats and musicality

There is an amusing story about the visit of Russians from Stanislavski's
school of theatre to the United States in the 1930s. Already in awe of these
emissaries from the great master, the Americans then listened in wonder as
the Russians talked about the 'beats' of a scene. Yes indeed, drama is like
music. It has its local rhythms, its *leitmotifs*, its movements and its changes
of key.

Then it turned out that the Russsians had really been talking about *bits*
of the scene, but in a Russian accent: 'let's look at thees beet'. They were
simply doing the same sort of job as we have suggested you do above in
section 1.20.

True or not, the story has two useful suggestions to make to us. First, it
really is useful to think of a play's shape and mood by using music as a
metaphor – just in the way suggested above. But second, let's not get too pretentious about it!

4.1.21 Agon and contradiction

By 'protagonist' we mean the main character in the play. But in fact the word
comes from the Greek *proto-* ('first') and *agonistes* ('actor' or 'combatant').
Aristotle and others tell us that Athenian tragedy evolved out of a religious
ritual in which a chorus narrated mythic events. Eventually, the convention
developed that one of the chorus would stand out and set up a dialogue with
the rest of the chorus. Later on, the protagonist began to impersonate people in the story. This is our real protagonist, the *first actor*.

But what of this idea of the agonist? Actor and combatant are, in ancient
Greek, embraced by the same word. Tied up with this word for actor is the
idea of struggle. The actor is not so much an impersonator as the one who
struggles.

It is very common to say that struggle, or *agon*, is at the heart of drama.
The hero struggles with his adversary, or Fate, or his inner nature. Many
plays can indeed be understood in this way. But we might also take the cue
from our short account above and say that at the heart of drama is dialogue
– not simply speeches, things said by characters, but *debate*, question and
answer. Plays struggle – explicitly or implicitly – with ideas and beliefs; one
of the most important things about characters is the differences between
them. And plays set up a dialogue with the audience, airing differences of
idea and belief.

We would be mistaken to think that all drama derives from ancient
Greek ritual, or any ritual at all (see Schechner 1988: 1–6). But we can usefully think of drama as something which deals in oppositions, in *contradiction*, difference. A good way into a play is to think about what it sets up
in opposition to what: within characters, between characters, between ideas,

between itself and the audience, between itself and other ways of telling stories.

A focus on contradiction will help us maintain a sense of plays as *dynamic* artworks, things that are moving because they are on the move.

4.1.22 Lines, differences and closures

What we have to say in this final subsection may be difficult to grasp. Getting hold of these ideas and their implications will be important for an under-graduate, but can be left alone by the school or junior college student. For this reason, we shall be brief.

Most of the dramatic texts we discuss in this book are *linear*. Even while there may be complication along the way (points of entanglement and cri-sis, which we may find fearful or funny), the play works its way through to what feels like its proper end. By design, the play concentrates on this one line of development – or maybe two.

Many of the dramatic texts we discuss also achieve *closure*. By the end, we feel that things have satisfactorily been resolved. Perhaps there is comic synthesis – the coming together for the wedding or feast. Perhaps there is the emotional release and the learning of tragedy. Or perhaps the secret has been discovered.

And throughout this book, we concern ourselves with *difference*. We make sense of the ways plays work by distinguishing one sort of play from another. And as we have just summarised in subsection 4.1.21, we suggest that plays can be thought of as 'difference machines' – things that are dri-ven along by difference.

There are strong arguments that texts and ways of thinking that concen-trate on difference, that are linear and attempt closure, have dominated Western culture for centuries, but need now to be challenged. Some femi-nists argue, for instance, that these are very much *male* ways of thinking and doing things. Whether or not there is indeed an essential difference between male and female culture, much feminist theatre has been based precisely on an attempt to escape from and challenge these very deep conventions (see Aston 1994).

Postmodern performance and film challenge theatre on much the same front (see Carlson 1996). From a post-colonial perspective, Western theatre is seen to have been one instrument among many by which Europe and North America have dominated other parts of the world (see Bharucha 1993).

4.2 The actor's body

When a group of people sit in chairs and read a play 'round the room', they shut out of their activity a key element that is scripted by the dramatic text

– the body. In this section we shall look at the scripting of the body, asking how the actor's body is told to move and how it is invested with significance. Second, we look at what assumptions are made by the dramatic text about the body: how different sorts of performance possess, and promote, different feelings about the actor's body.

4.2.1 Stage directions

We have already said early in the book that stage directions give instructions as to when, where and how the actor is to move. A typical direction might be: '*Sits R[ight], and with a pair of scissors seems busily engaged in trimming the flowers in pots on stand.*' This is an instruction for the actress playing Lady Audley in Hazlewood's *Lady Audley's Secret* (1863: 252); she has just been threatened with blackmail by the drunken gamekeeper who has seen her murder her first husband; now, as the husband's friend enters, she assumes her mask of innocence. With this context in mind we can see that the stage direction scripts a multi-layered picture: trimming flowers is, on the surface, a proper pastime for a Victorian lady, but the actress has to 'seem' to be doing it – we have to watch it as a polished performance of how to be a Victorian lady, done by a character who isn't one. Furthermore the requirement to be 'busily' engaged allows the actress to show hints of that violent energy that killed a husband: it's not just the scissors but also the meticulous concentration that suggest the murderous calculation. This quality, together with the skill of the performance and the decorative charm of the 'lady', all give special charisma to Lady Audley. So the stage directions can script much more than the mechanics of movement or emotional expression: they can give an aura of energy or specialness to an individual.

In the same way a stage group can be organised, not merely mechanically but also into relationships of power and energy. Take an incident in the second scene of D. H. Lawrence's *The Widowing of Mrs Holroyd* (1914): Mrs Holroyd's husband has come back from the pub with two women friends; as he goes to fetch them a drink a rat runs through the open scullery door into the kitchen where they are all sitting. The rat runs under the sofa, centre stage at back; one of the women gets onto the table, downstage and slightly to the left of the sofa; the other woman later scrambles onto the armchair near the table, clinging onto her friend's skirts as she does so; Mr Holroyd, moving upstage, begins to approach the sofa, on which his wife sits. She has this direction and line: '*bunched up on the sofa, with crossed hands holding her arms, fascinated, watches her husband as he approaches to stoop and attack the rat; she suddenly screams:* Don't, he'll fly at you' (p. 159). The group has been organised so that the two drunken women are slightly to one side, in undignified postures. This leaves the serious, central focus on Mr Holroyd's approach to the sofa and his wife. Her attitude is defensive, vulnerable; his is that of the hunter. For a moment there is silence as she watches in fascination. The stage directions have produced a statement about division of gender roles: male as hunter, female as vulnerable, defensive, but fascinated by the hunter. We know, however, that Mrs Holroyd resents and is unhappy with her husband: the actress is invited to time the suddenness with which she shouts out against the tension of the silence, for that shout can indicate not just a fear *for* the husband but an anxiety at having him so near. The mechanics of this everyday realistic incident are thus scripted by the stage directions, but so too they script a deeper statement about sexual antagonism between two characters within a context of 'natural' (as the play has it) gender roles.

> As an exercise: Analyse some stage directions from the play you're reading, first, to establish what movements etc. they script, and, second, to show what else they suggest.

4.2.2 Implicit stage directions

We said much earlier that many plays, especially Renaissance ones, contain implicit directions for actors. To remind us of that point, and to extend it a little, let us look at a moment in Middleton's *Women Beware Women* (?1621). Bianca has been tricked into a situation in which the Duke can sexually assault her. She reacts with shock to his sudden appearance and he says: 'Prithee tremble not./ I feel thy breast shake like a turtle [dove] panting/ Under a loving hand that makes much on't' (2.2.320–2). Clearly his hand is already on her breast, which he can feel panting – but it is more cruel than that, for he insists on making 'much on't', fondling it as one might stroke a captive bird. At the same time, in his speech, the syntax is smooth and untroubled, evoking its image of a turtle dove. The very fluency of the verse rhythm produces a breath pattern in the actor which displays bodily control. The mode of speaking thus also scripts the body, producing the power which compels Bianca's 'submission'.

The scripted action here portrays a turning-point in Bianca's story. But it is also useful to focus on how the bodies are scripted over a whole play. A good example is supplied by Shakespeare's *King Lear*. In the ceremonial opening scene the bodies are required to move with the public display and formal measure of a state occasion. Halfway through the play, the clothes are drenched with water, dirtied or torn off the bodies. One of the elderly bodies is bent over, in the stocks; another is imprisoned in a chair, while his eyes are gouged out. The movement across the stage is the uncertainty of the blind or speediness of the mad. At the end of the play bodies are left to litter the stage, their dead weight insisted upon in the image of a pietà (the dead Christ on the Virgin Mary's lap), from which this time there is no resurrection. We could say that the scripting requires that the actors' bodies

become steadily more clumsy and move irresistibly from stature of upright
dignity to being folded over and brought close to the ground. This scripted
action for the body clearly reinforces the play's bleak picture of human life.

As an exercise: From a passage of a play with few stage directions
reveal what is scripted for the body; try then taking an overview of the
action of the bodies in the whole play.

4.2.3 *What scripts assume about actors' bodies*

At the start of this book we glanced at the matter of conventions of performance, and said that in any one period there would be the dominant conventions, residual ones from a previous time and emergent ones. The
scripting for the actor's body may assume an already-existing convention for
playing, it may wish to challenge this convention or it may seek to develop
a new one. If one is merely reading stage directions it is not always possible
to visualise that familiar actions may be done according to very different
conventions, that standing and walking may entail different attitudes in different theatres. In some respects this understanding of the different conventions which are being scripted only comes from knowing a little about
various theories of performance, as we shall show later. But it is also possible, first, to see how the dialogue text assumes, and scripts, a particular sort
of bodily action.

4.2.3.1 THE BODIES ASSUMED BY DIALOGUE

In the scene from *The Widowing of Mrs Holroyd*, above, the script assumes
that Mrs Holroyd's line will be shouted as if it had been dragged out of her,
impulsively, by the crisis. The actress will have worked hard to produce a
sense of a person in the grip of circumstances. Contrast with this Lady
Bracknell's response, in Wilde's *The Importance of Being Earnest* (1895), on
hearing that Jack has lost both his parents: 'To lose one parent, Mr.
Worthing, may be regarded as a misfortune; to lose both looks like careless-
ness' (p. 360). Clearly this line is not trying to imitate realistic speech, nor
even to sustain characterisation. Its manner is derived, residually, from
comedies of wit, within which the performer herself displays conspicuous
skills in timing and verbal acrobatics (as contrasted with the physical skills
of clowns). Wilde's line assumes, and reinforces, a poised body, that holds
itself back through the network of pauses on the punctuation marks until
the punchline is delivered. The punchline is expected because of the balanced syntax; but it is also expected because the speech requires the performer's body to move between personal conversation, with 'Mr Worthing',
and public address. That public address is produced by the lifting of the

head and upper torso as the performer breathes in time with the syntax. It is this technique which Wertenbaker uses to show how Liz's body can be transformed from that of a convict into something more 'civilised' when Liz says: 'Your Excellency, I will endeavour to speak Mr Farquhar's lines with the elegance and clarity their own worth commands' (*Our Country's Good* 1988/1991: 83).

This sort of scripting to hold the body in equilibrium contrasts, deliberately, with the sudden distortions and extensions of the body required by melodrama: 'He is gone – gone! and no one was a witness to the deed!' (*Lady Audley's Secret* 1863: 248). To say the second 'gone' with the necessary additional emphasis the performer has to organise her muscles to produce the right sound, which, quite apart from any added gestures, creates the apparent size of melodrama. It was in a bid to limit that size, and the distorted body, that Robertson used the everyday furniture in *Caste* (1867), directing that an actor 'has been twisting about' with a chair during a speech (p.139): to have to act with the chair is to limit the size of the body's movements, and concentrate them on an everyday object. In a similar way Shakespeare ended the performance mode which Marlowe had scripted in *Tamburlaine* (1587), where the long sentences flowing across several verse lines require a great deal of breath, and breath control, having the effect of inflating the body (as for an opera-singer) and causing it to walk with a strutting movement: Hamlet, by contrast, has lines with numerous breaks in them.

As an exercise: Take a passage of dialogue or verse and explore what sort of body is scripted by it, paying attention to breath patterns and syntax.

4.2.3.2 BODIES SCRIPTED BY THEORIES OF PERFORMANCE

In 1803 the German theatre director Goethe developed rules for actors, which were based on the idea that graceful performance would be developed by the study of Classical statues (see Nagler 1959: 428–33). This body is assumed by the plays of Goethe's contemporary, Schiller: in a work such as *Mary Stuart* (1800) this Classical body is under threat from a newly emerging passion, the tension between the two inhabiting the performed text of the play and giving it its force.

In scene 4 of Brecht's *The Good Person of Setzuan* (1943), Shu Fu the barber ejects Wang the water-seller from his shop, and then strikes Wang's hand with his curling iron. When Wang asks others sitting outside to act as legal witnesses, '*all are . . . eating. No one looks up.*' They are deliberately ignoring him. Much in the way that we saw Desdemona composed into a formal picture in 1.1.2, Brecht here composes a clear picture of social attitudes. The Unemployed Man, Grandfather and Sister-in-Law selfishly fill their bellies while ignoring someone else in need. Brecht called such a picture a *gestus*. Willett (1977: 173) usefully glosses this word as referring at once to 'gesture', a physical attitude, and 'gist', an outline. The *gestus* of eating the rice physicalises a typical social attitude. Brecht wants us to ask where this attitude comes from. The class and employment status of the characters will matter.

Now, just before Wang asks for witnesses, two contrasting propositions are put to him. Shen Te says he should see a doctor, quick. But the Unemployed Man says, 'He doesn't want the doctor; he wants the magistrate! The barber's a rich man, and he ought to get compensation.' Both Mrs Shin and Wang think this is a very good idea. Wang enthusiastically says, 'It's already very swollen. Would it mean a pension for life?' Fearing that the swelling may be going down, but reassured by the others that it hasn't, '*Holding his hand very carefully and still looking at it, he hurries off*'. It is a moment of great comedy, a gift to the performer. But it is also, of course, a very fine *gestus*. Wang carries his hand *both* as a precious part of his body that has been wounded and hurts, *and* as a precious object that he can use to get cash. With great economy, Brecht physicalises the contradiction between going to a doctor for the sake of health and going to a judge for compensation – between the value of the hand in terms of its usefulness, and its exchange value, its price. For Brecht and other Marxists, capitalism reduces everything to its exchange value and prevents us from seeing the real use-value of things. This threatens our well-being and perhaps our survival. Wang is about to endanger/ruin his body for the sake of profit. In this comic gestus, Brecht not only uses the actor's (Wang's) body to deliver the *gestus*. The body is also the direct *subject* of the gestus. Marxism is about human survival.

There is another *gestus* on stage too. We saw in Chapter 2 how Brecht wants his actors to *demonstrate* the character they are showing. They take up an attitude to the character, and to the audience, and they do this for a reason. Brecht's theatre deliberately seeks out its social purpose. Underlying the *gestus* of Wang's hand is the *gestus* of the Brechtian performer. The performer makes clear in her or his attitude the social relationship that is being sought between stage and audience. Whenever we read or perform Brecht's plays, we need constantly to keep both these levels of *gestus* in mind.

|5|

Spaces

This chapter develops ways of thinking about the significance and use of space in the theatre, and especially how dramatic texts script space. A good reading of a dramatic text – whether for commentary or for production – needs to pay attention to this aspect as much as to character or dialogue.

We start by seeing how an emphasis on space can develop a commentary on *A Doll's House*, thereby teasing out some questions and concerns that we might apply to other plays. We then set out these and more considerations about space systematically, to provide a kind of checklist. Within this second section you will find examples and models that will contribute to an understanding of *historical* developments in the theatre. In the short final section we introduce one further historical playing arrangement and look at the idea of taking an historical overview.

5.1 Space and *A Doll's House*

5.1.1 *Spaces in the world and on the stage*

The opening stage direction provides a detailed description of a room. The room is similar to those lived in by many people in Ibsen's audience. The world of the stage directly mirrors the world of the audience. We can be more precise. That audience can tell, as soon as the curtain goes up, just what *sort* of middle-class people they are about to meet with on stage. These people are not rich, but they are somewhat comfortable and aim to rise.

In the course of the play, several of the items described will be used by characters, others not. The sofa will provide a place for intimate conversation between Nora and Christine; the piano will be played for Nora's dance of the tarantella. But also, these are people who can *afford* a piano and a sofa – as well as the displays of ornaments and leather-bound books which remain untouched during the performance.

The set is a replication of the world, but also a machine for acting. It represents a single room, but contains within it distinct areas in which the action will be focused. We have mentioned the sofa. Also, as George Bernard Shaw famously celebrated in 1913, the table becomes the place where Nora faces Helmer squarely in Act 3 to insist on an adult conversation. A lamp provides stage focus for it.

The lamp also perhaps signifies Nora's wish for clarity. And we may feel that the sober conversation mirrors the one Ibsen is conducting with his audience. It is as if he, too, were sitting seriously at a table.

There are four doors. They help plausibly replicate a bourgeois apartment; but two, perhaps three, are significant to our further understanding of this design as an acting machine. In the next two subsections we shall look in some detail at their scripted use.

If the single setting provides several foci for the action, it also changes during the play. The Christmas tree takes up a prominent position, is at first bright and cheerful, but suffers decay in tune with Nora's development. She also brings in parcels; fills the room with her children and shared laughter; fills it again with her desperate dancing. At times there are several people on stage at once, at others only one. While this has much to do with the logic of the action – who needs to encounter whom for the plot to work – the *feelings* of fullness and emptiness (see below at 5.2.13) are important to what the play comes to mean to its audience.

When, early in Act 1, Helmer admonishes Nora for wasting money, she crosses to the stove as if for comfort. Commentaries on the play often note this. If we are working well, we will also note that Nora has already been scripted to put her parcels down on the table next to it. Shopping and the warmth of a hearth are scripted to coincide – and in the precise context of Helmer's line, 'A home that is founded on debts and borrowing can never be a place of freedom and beauty' (p. 25). Moreover, Helmer is then scripted to follow her to the stove. Dialogue, as we said in Chapter 1, tends intrinsically to suggest blocking, who moves where and when. But in this act, for instance, Ibsen takes care to script Helmer's pursuit of Nora about the stage.

We have said that the world of the stage in this play is continuous with the world of the audience. Let us now also say that the lit stage is separated by a **proscenium arch** from the audience, who sit in relative darkness. They are segregated according to how much they can afford for a seat. The theatre in which they sit is a valued and central cultural institution, though one in which battles are being fought about what sort of play should be put before them. Plays – especially this one – have an afterlife in the press and in earnest debates in homes and cafés (see 6.1.2). They can be read as well as seen.

We started this subsection with the sentence, 'The opening stage direction provides a detailed description of a living room.' We then raised questions about the room the stage set represents, its relation to the audience and its status as a machine for acting. But we also need to note the following: it is a living room that is scripted (not a castle chamber, desert island or town square); and it *is* described, and in detail. To questions about the specific features of scripted space we can add useful ones about what *categories* of space are scripted, and about the *extent* to which they are scripted at all.

This brief beginning can help us develop a commentary on *A Doll's House* as a dramatic script, that is, as a set of instructions for producing activity on a stage. We can also use it to think more generally about what can be usefully noted about the scripted space in any dramatic text, the spatial conditions for which it is written, and the significance of the extent to which it explicitly scripts space at all.

Let us make a sketch summary of what we have raised so far with the spider diagram in Fig. 5.1. You may want to make your own version.

Remember that the diagram sketches the way we have raised the issue of space just here. It is not by any means the only diagram possible. As you continue with the chapter, you will find that there is more you can add. You will also probably find that a single two-dimensional diagram cannot do justice to all of the questions you will come to ask about space. But you will find it useful – especially when you come to plan a piece of writing or a presentation – to make this sort of sketch as a way of thinking through those questions and planning a route through them. And do argue with and contest the diagrams we present.

Let us now look a little more closely at *A Doll's House* to develop our understanding of space and to see how this can help us arrive at a commentary on the play as a whole.

5.1.2 *The door slams*

When Nora leaves the doll's house for the uncertainties of an independent life, she does so offstage. Ibsen is scripting the use of the stage space here with some precision. Nora says 'Goodbye' and '*goes out through the hall*'. Helmer sinks down in a chair by the door; looks round and gets up, realising fully that 'She's gone!'; and then '*A hope strikes him*' that, after all, a 'miracle of miracles' might save their marriage. Then, '*The street door is slammed shut downstairs*' (p. 104). What can we say about this use of space?

Let us start with the fact that Nora leaves twice. She leaves the room, then the house. In the time between, Helmer is given a moment of remorse and hope. But if this is a signal of his reformation, it has come – for the time being, at least – too late. The sound of the door, its very hardness communicating a sense of brutal finality, cancels his hope.

Or we might shift our focus and consider Nora herself. The sound of the door slamming suggests that she has crossed a space of potential indecision.

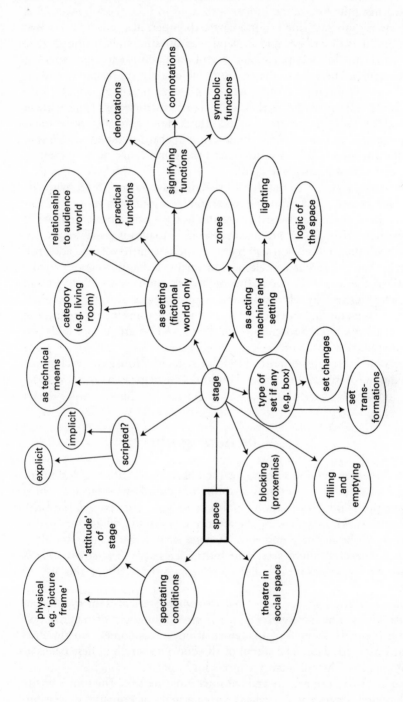

Fig. 5.1 Starting to unpick space

The Christmas tree directly means that it is Christmas: this is its *denotative* meaning. It has associations with festivity: this is its *connotative* meaning. The lamp at the table may stand for Nora's wish to illuminate the situation: this is its *symbolic* meaning.

Both the hardness of the sound and the fact that it signals a second act of departure speak her resolve.

Either of the last two paragraphs might have been prompted by a description in a novel. But if we imagine ourselves sitting in an auditorium, there is a basic effect to be noted, quite apart from our engagement with the story. *We* are being left. Dialogue has frozen and the stage is emptying. We cannot see Nora's important final act. We as spectators are cut off from it.

The stage conditions for which the play was written are significant here. In a darkened auditorium before a lit stage, audience members can some-times feel very alone, and at others very together. The impact of an offstage sound effect in these conditions is likely to be intensified.

Let us also consider audience expectations (see 6.4.4). We have learnt that Ibsen is manipulating the established conventions of the 'well-made play', to an extent depending on this formula but also disrupting it to provoke thought. A conventional happy ending might have Nora return from the hall, to be clasped in Helmer's arms as they weep and resolve to find their mira-cle together. The period between Nora's stage exit and the offstage sound effect of the slamming door is the time – we might even call it thinking-space – in which that audience expectation is raised, in order to be dashed.

Our account here so far has tended to suggest that Nora's exit is unplea-surable for the audience. Expectations of a conventional happy ending are dashed. The stage cools and empties before us. We are left in Helmer's sad company. Against this we have written one paragraph concentrating on Nora's resolve. Yet some in that original audience, and certainly many in audiences since, will have taken sufficient pleasure in Nora's resolve as to override any sense of difficulty or loss at the play's ending. Who is in the auditorium matters, as do possible differences between them (see 6.4). Some, indeed, might see Helmer at this point indulging himself again in self-dramatisation (see 1.1.2). We might decide to *play* it that way, in any case. Nora heads for a new reality while Helmer indulges in his one-man play – a slightly different way of thinking about his being scripted to be left alone onstage.

The sound of the door slamming has a finality about it, and the play, indeed, ends with it. But where can Nora go? How might she survive? Is Ibsen contriving to ignore this very real question, as some have argued? Or does he script things so that such a question is begged? Can our discussion so far help with this question?

Our attention to this one organisation and use of stage space has raised some questions of interpretation. Or, to put that a better way, we have found that our interpretation of the play's ending needs to include attention to the scripting of stage space. The question is not what happened in the story or what the characters are feeling, but rather, what is scripted to happen on a stage in a theatre. At the most basic level, Ibsen has scripted an effect, a '*coup de théâtre*'. The double exit, and especially the offstage sound effect, constitute a basic structure which will move, startle or interest an audience irrespective of the fictional situation. We need, then, to think about the way this works *with* the fiction.

While we might come to some conclusions about the ways in which Ibsen was aiming to work on his audience, we would then in any case need to accept that what is scripted seems designed to produce contradictory responses in individuals or between individuals (see 6.4.3.3). A useful essay would develop this sense of contradiction.

Last, we have again raised the question of Ibsen's manipulation of audience expectation. A spectator who becomes conscious of this will experience the fiction as if it were in inverted commas, something quoted from somewhere. Another way of saying this is that it is 'distanced'. We might sometimes find it useful to use our category of 'space' in this sort of metaphorical way, too.

> As an exercise: Read the closing moments of *A Doll's House* and review the argument above. Draw up two columns and list positive and negative feelings that might be aroused by Nora's leaving, and what produces them. You can, of course, refer back to the rest of the play – but be specific about the dramatic script and its work on the audience.

5.1.3 *Living rooms and the logic of spaces*

There is only one set in *A Doll's House*. It represents a living room, the space which Raymond Williams (1980) has identified as characteristic of plays from the Naturalist movement which Ibsen helped inaugurate. Williams suggests that the living room is a significant setting for two reasons. First, Naturalism was typically concerned with the problems of the bourgeois family, and the living room is the place in which significant interactions between husbands and wives, parents and children, family and servants can be played out. Second, Naturalism was deeply and often pessimistically concerned with the notion of 'determinism'. That is to say, the plays mostly express the feeling that our past actions, genetic inheritance and environment all conspire to limit our ability to take control of our situation and change it – or ourselves. The living room, then – especially when realised as the **box-set** developed in the nineteenth century to depict domestic interiors realistically – is also symbolically a trap.

In this early Naturalist play, Nora and the audience come to see the living room – and hence her marriage of which it is the centre – as such a trap. It looks like an ordinary middle-class home, but in fact it works more like a doll's house. Her cultural environment blocks her self-realisation as a person, reducing her to the status of an object. At the end of the play, she leaves this restrictive environment. The audience are never taken anywhere else.

There is, then, a basic *logic of space* at work in the play. There is a single and limiting space from which the protagonist finally breaks free.

Let us now pursue this idea in more detail. When Nora exits to the hall at the end of the play she enters a space we can glimpse through one of the upstage doors. Through the other upstage door – on the other side of the piano – is Helmer's study. Let us think briefly about her passage through each of these doors.

At the opening of the play, we have something like the reverse of its ending. The stage is empty. An empty stage feels dead. The entry of actors will animate it, bringing 'presence' to the stage. We hear a doorbell and a door being opened. Our expectations of stage presence are then fulfilled when Nora enters: through the open hall door we see servants whom she controls. The hinterland space between the living room and the outside world is active, bright, visible to us, and in Nora's control. She moves with ease and confidence, and we can see, and therefore sense, an ease of access between this domestic world and the outside.

Contrast her relationship to the door to Helmer's study. Ibsen might have scripted her to arrive home to be greeted by Helmer in the living room; but, with great economy, he scripts space to set up the logic of their relationship from the start. Having entered the domestic space with bright ease, Nora then *'tiptoes across'* to the study door, *'listens'* and then remarks, 'Yes, he's here.' They then conduct an affectionate conversation through the door. She does not open it. Eventually, Helmer comes out of his study to join her (p. 24).

Nora never, in the course of the play, opens the door to Helmer's study. It is easy to remark that this is the way things were in those days. But in order to think and write adequately about this as a piece of drama, let us note how Ibsen specifically embodies this social fact on his stage. Here at the start, Nora makes a *verbal* crossing of the barrier she cannot cross physically. She knows what lies beyond the door and confidently pitches her voice through it. But she will not do this again. From this point on, the space works to entrap her – or perhaps to confirm the entrapment of which she had been oblivious or which she had hoped to deny.

If Nora is progressively trapped in the room, then Helmer moves with ease between it and its hinterlands, including his study. We quickly come to see his seemingly free and natural movement from space to space as a privileged use of private space. There is some poetic justice, then, in having him left trapped alone in his nest at the end.

Note that while poetic justice is a matter of the audience's moral and ethical sensibility – they may feel it is just that he should be abandoned – it is also an aesthetic matter: Helmer's isolation mirrors Nora's earlier entrapment. The feelings evoked are not just to do with what has happened; they are also to do with the play's *design*.

5.1.4 Meetings, perspectives and entrapments

If the living room is the typically preferred location of Naturalism for the reasons Williams states, it is also simply a plausible place in which a variety of people might meet. Neoclassical drama of the seventeenth and eighteenth centuries similarly used town squares. Especially if we make use of 'french-scene' analysis (4.1.19), we quickly see that Ibsen has a succession of individuals interact with Nora in this first act: Helmer, Mrs Linde, Krogstad and Doctor Rank. Their movements into and out of the main playing space are an important part of the play's local design – especially if we think about Nora and space.

After Helmer goes back to his study, Mrs Linde is announced and a conversation ensues in which there is some exposition – we hear about Christine herself, and get hints of Nora's secret. But note especially in this context that Mrs Linde also talks about a life beyond Nora's. This is a woman of the world, one with a perspective on life. It is not a comfortable one. Nora's perspective on life at the beginning is that things will turn out right. By the end of the play she looks towards an unknown future in which she seeks self-fulfilment. But here Ibsen sets up a perspective beyond the doll's house which is painful: as if he sets these two perspectives up in dialogue with one another. In some later plays, he scripts space so that there is a *physical* perspective, a 'beyond' to the present action (see 5.2.6.2, below).

Krogstad's entry into the room is also from the hall door, but contrasts with Mrs Linde's. His arrival disturbs both women. Note how Nora pushes him back out into the hall, taking control with some desperation, for him to enter Helmer's study from there. She is defending her space.

So we learn that Helmer's study has two doors – one into the hall, and the other into the living room. Why? Clearly, there is a technical convenience for Ibsen here. For instance, Doctor Rank, who pops out when Krogstad joins Helmer, must have entered the study directly from the hall. There is no special dramatic reason for this. The succession of meetings with Nora is simply thus made more plausible.

The concrete arrangement of the Helmers' flat in the fictional world is that both study and living room give off a hallway, and that there is a connecting door between them. But in terms of their marriage, and in terms of the theatre, this is not a symmetrical arrangement. Helmer has use of the interconnecting door while Nora does not. Moreover, we in the auditorium are trapped in the living room with Nora. Helmer's study is out of Nora's reach and ours. His space connects independently with the outside world as well as with Nora's. Entries into the stage space disturb or impinge upon her. There is no orderly procession through the hall door. Rather, just as there might be in a farce, there are multiple unannounced comings and goings involving three doors. The technical solution is exploited dramatically.

If the short flurry of comings and goings creates a sense of unease, Nora recovers by playing with her children. Note how she again takes control of the space by making a mess in it, using furniture to hide under and laughing. But when Krogstad enters again, Nora's response is to send her children back into the room offstage left. Persuaded by the arguments of her husband and Krogstad that her secret actions mark her as a moral reprobate and hence a danger to her children, she sends them there to protect them from herself as much as from Krogstad. She isolates *herself* in the room. She (and this does not *necessarily* mean Ibsen) fears that the sins of the parent pass on to the child: she shares a deterministic attitude.

From this point on until her departure, the hinterland spaces of the study and hallway will take on a threatening aspect for Nora, accentuating her entrapment.

> As an exercise: (a) On the basis of the opening stage direction, sketch a stage plan for *A Doll's House*. (b) Work through one act of the play and comment on how Ibsen scripts the space to be used and what this communicates.
>
> Note: If you are not already, get familiar with making such sketches (see Fig. 5.2). They need not be elaborate. Remember that stage rooms rarely use right-angles.

5.2 A systematic approach to space

In this section we list and explore a number of considerations which can keep us alert to the ways in which space functions in the theatre, and how these functions are scripted or assumed by the dramatic text. We shall be concerned with three intersecting notions of space – the *fictional space* (the

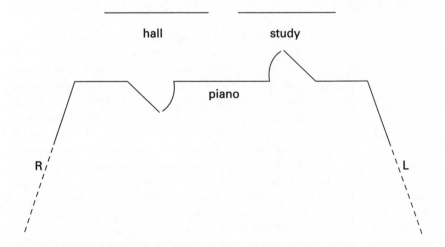

Fig. 5.2 Sketching the box-set

place of the action), the *theatrical scene* (what is put on stage to represent this, the set) and the *stage* itself. We begin with an important question:

5.2.1 What sort of stage are we on?

In the last section we saw how the set Ibsen scripts for *A Doll's House* not only (a) represents something but also (b) works as a machine for acting and (c) engenders feelings such as claustrophobia in the audience. The same three aspects – (a) *signifying*, (b) *mechanical* and (c) *aesthetic functions* – will be pertinent to any set we encounter.

Rather than read the dramatic text 'transparently', looking for the story, we need constantly to hold in mind, as we say in Chapter 1, that plays are scripts for activity on a stage. The *way* in which the fictional location is represented – a **box-set**, say – depends upon the type of theatre the play is written for and the technical means developed within it. The type of set also constrains what sort of acting machine it can be. The box-set invites use of hinterland spaces, for instance. And both the type of set and the relationship between stage and auditorium help shape what sorts of aesthetic effects are possible. Those aesthetic effects – the feelings evoked in the audience – are closely tied up with the way in which the audience are placed to view the stage, which we shall call the *spectating relations*. A lit stage separated from a darkened auditorium by a 'picture frame' invites an attitude of easy ownership of what is looked upon, like a picture on the sitting-room wall.

Let us look briefly at a stage arrangement likely to be as yet unfamiliar to a majority of readers of this book, in order to demonstrate further the importance of relating the type of theatre a play is written for to a consideration of the mechanical and aesthetic functions of the set (if there is a set at all) – functions which are fundamental to the play's meaning in performance.

If you pick up a copy of *The Colleen Bawn* (1860), an Irish melodrama by Dion Boucicault, and glance at the locations of the three scenes in Act 1, you will see that it opens outside Mrs Cregan's country-house residence; then the scene is '*The Gap of Dunloe (1st grooves)*'; and then '*Interior of Eily's Cottage*'. The first and third scenes require some depth of stage – in the first, someone comes on from rocks at the back, and later we look across the lake to a light signal from the distant headland; in the third we are inside a cottage room on the headland. But the scene between them only requires a two-dimensional landscape painted on two large shutters (or flats) which can be pushed on from the wings either side, guided by grooves in the stage; these grooves are the ones nearest the audience, the first of several. The second scene is thus called a 'flat scene', and it contrasts with the 'set' or 'relief' scenes, where three-dimensional furniture is set and landscape is created by using free-standing pieces to give the appearance of depth or relief rather than flatness. The shutters needed to be closed after the first scene so that the third one could be set up in its place. This basic mechanical arrangement governed the organisation of stage space for about 200 years. But the interplay of 'flat' and 'set' scenes was usually much more than a mere technical necessity. Very early on in its introduction, in the Restoration, the interplay was invested with significance. Thus in the precise middle of Etherege's *The Man of Mode* (1676) the stage is opened out to its deepest, to show the open-air pleasure grounds of The Mall. For the central character this is the moment at which he loses his control on the action, which is imaged as his losing control on the space. Our sense of him changes as he is moved from playing on the front of the stage, close to the audience and more or less at one with them, to being tucked away several metres back, peeping round bushes. The interplay of 'flat' and 'set' scenes makes the depth rather than the width of the stage important; the spectating relations are shaped, first, by the audience's proximity to or distance from the action and characters and, second, by the different feelings produced by looking *at* a platform lit by the same light as the audience or looking *into* a separated world.

5.2.2 A simplified historical scheme

There is no need to absorb an entire history of Western stages before continuing with this chapter; and this is not the place or opportunity to write one. You will, however, find it rewarding to become progressively familiar with such a history as you read more plays. Good histories include Glynne Wickham's (1985); Leacroft (1988) is an excellent source of detailed architectural drawings; and the story Richard Southern tells in *Seven Ages of the Theatre* (1962) remains very suggestive.

In fact, let us pick up on Southern now, in order to lay out a map useful to our immediate purposes. Please refer to Fig. 5.3 as you read. Southern helped design several of Britain's regional repertory theatres in the 1960s and 1970s, and wanted to get away from the restrictions of the **proscenium-arch** theatre and *back* to the openness and accessibility of the Renaissance stage. The audience are thus, for instance, again wrapped around the stage. But the technical advances of four centuries also allow such a modern stage to be used very flexibly – scenery might fly in and out, multiple levels be built, or the space be left relatively bare. We shall assume you have some familiarity with the box-set–proscenium-arch arrangement, the Renaissance open stage (such as at the Globe) and modern flexible stages.

Scenery arrived on the English commercial stage in the Restoration, after theatres reopened in 1660. Its use had already been developed at court, for masques. These elaborate performances of song and dance, performed by members of the court itself, celebrated the monarch as fount of wisdom, authority and justice. He or she sat in a central position before the spectacle. The discovery of perspective techniques in painting – where the flat canvas looks as if it has depth, and the viewer feels as if they are looking into a

Fig. 5.3 The development of Western playing spaces

(i) the late medieval/early Renaissance booth stage mainly consisted of a temporary platform erected in a public space – playing was both on the platform and on the ground before it; (ii) the Elizabethan open-air amphitheatre developed the booth stage idea in a permanent structure, with the audience on three sides at several levels and musicians in a gallery above the stage; (iii) the Elizabethan hall theatre had a similar stage design within a covered room, with most of the audience end-on (apart from a few sitting on the edge of the stage itself); (iv) in the Restoration theatre the space was divided into three sections, with audience at one end, the 'scene' at the other, and between them a forestage or proscenium with audience on either side of it; (v) in the second half of the eighteenth century the pit, in front of the stage, took over some of the area occupied by the proscenium and became the focal point of the auditorium; (vi) by the late nineteenth century there was no proscenium space shared with the auditorium, the action happened behind the proscenium arch; (vii) theatres of the mid- to late twentieth century were designed to offer a facility again for playing both in front of and behind the proscenium arch.

Illustrations by Mick Wallis, based on Leacroft (1988) and Southern (1962).

distance – had been developed in Italy and the technique emulated in theatre scenery there. The English court masque adopted it, and then the new theatres after 1660 picked up on the fashion. The introduction of scenery on the English stage introduces a change in spectating relations, and new theatres were built to accommodate it. The audience feel centrally placed to look in on the action – and, indeed, spectacle – and often through it to vistas beyond.

The theatre borrowed perspectival painting itself, producing the illusion of depth on flat canvas. But depth was also suggested by painted flats or shutters run in grooves from the wings, narrowing down into upstage space.

5.2.3 Two aspects of the theatrical scene: backdrop and environment

'Scene' now means two things: a division in the text, like an act; or what the ancient Greeks called *skena*, the thing acted in front of, on a stage. The Restoration theatrical scene (*skena*) was originally a backdrop to the action, which was played downstage. Notwithstanding the stage–auditorium division, the scene was in one space (upstage), actors and audience in another (downstage). The upstage cloths and flats were usually painted so as to give a generic indication of location – a view of an Italian city, for instance. Thus the same scene might do for several plays. A single theatrical scene might also be perfectly acceptable as backdrop for several locations within the one play – it merely indicates the generalised place. Where a cloth *and* flats are used, the scene is potentially a three-dimensional place: thus instead of acting *in front of* it, the gradually developing practice of moving upstage to act *within* the scene, especially in tragedy, culminated in the theatrical scene being understood as an environment for the action.

From here we can trace a double movement: the progressive retreat of actors and action away from the space of the audience, coupled with the envelopment of the action by the scene. It is the culmination of this process with the box-set which Southern found so limiting. The flat-and-relief staging with which we opened this section occupies a substantial part – some 200 years – of this process of change.

Our historical sketch has distinguished between two aspects of the theatrical scene, as:

- *backdrop* to the action, or
- *environment* for the action.

Yet even acting within the scene can retain a sense of the scene as backdrop. In specifying the set for *A Doll's House* in so much detail, Ibsen firmly establishes it as environment, in contrast to the domestic box-sets that his theatre could easily have furnished from stock (perhaps with shelves painted on the walls). Thus our backdrop/environment **binary** has historical significance;

but it is also a useful tool for thinking about any theatrical scene we encounter.

Use of the scene as environment is not confined to Naturalism. Consider Act 3 scene 1 of Lorca's *Blood Wedding* (1933), set in a forest which we suggest below (5.2.8.2) might also symbolise psychic or bodily interiors. German Expressionism provides similar examples. Even though the effect is managed literally through the use of backdrops, consider how Mathias in *The Bells* (1871; see 5.2.6.2, below) becomes 'enveloped' within the courtroom. The way a scenic device works depends on the context of its use. Again, in Sheridan's *Pizzaro*, done at Drury Lane in 1799, there was a famous theatrical *coup* when the hero escaped from his captors: having left the stage, he reappeared high up on a fragile bridge over a cascading torrent. This was no mere perspective backdrop to the action – it now shaped it, making it more perilous, helping to establish the development towards an increasingly spectacular stage practice. And that rather extraordinary form, British Pantomime, often switches quickly between scene as backdrop and scene as environment. We might see this as part of the form's self-conscious and pleasurable 'theatricality'.

5.2.4 Space and the persistence of its meaning

The last three subsections are all very well, but plays survive their original conditions of performance. We regularly see Renaissance plays designed for an open stage with minimal scenic apparatus done in proscenium-arch theatres and on modern flexible stages. Surely we need to get back to the story and the characters, and not get bogged down with details of stage history, details we cannot reproduce? Well, we certainly do need to find ways of remaking old plays for modern conditions. But a central part of the play's meaning is the way it was originally designed to work on stage. We do not necessarily have to replicate this, as if we were in a museum; but the mechanical and aesthetic functions we can see at work in the text are *part of the play's production of meaning* and so are a fundamental part of the materials we are working on when we restage plays from the past. The French term for the way in which a play is staged is *mise en scène*. A good challenge for modern directors and designers is not simply to find a *mise en scène* for the action and characters of a classic, but to find one for its originally intended *mise en scène*. The last three subsections are important!

As an exercise: Especially if you have a suitable anthology to hand, turn to three plays from distinct periods, say from the Renaissance, the Restoration and the period of Naturalism. Consider how you would demonstrate to someone else how each bears signs of the sort of space it is written for.

5.2.5 Three regions of fictional space

We can distinguish between:

- *onstage* fictional space: the space of immediate action, directly represented onstage
  (e.g. the Helmers' living room)
- *neighbouring offstage* fictional space: implied as in direct continuity with this, immediately offstage
  (e.g. the room offstage left where the children go)
- *distant offstage* fictional space referred to elsewhere in the world of dramatic reference
  (e.g. the bank or Christine Linde's shop and school)

We have also used the term *virtual* space to denote locations implied or referred to but not seen.

5.2.6 Logic and status of the onstage fictional space

In this long subsection we follow a journey through a number of scripted theatrical sets and stage arrangements, to pick out significant general shapes and to see how these are made to work on an audience. Its aim is to stimulate similar investigations of your own. Our main focus is on the onstage fictional space. But we also look outwards to offstage space; and we look at moments where the stage ceases its function as representing a fictional location to become, literally, a stage. Thus, we begin with questions about the *logic* of the theatrical scene – its basic design and how it works – and go on to look at occasions when the *status* of the stage as fictional space is made to collapse.

5.2.6.1 FOCUS AND TENSION

We noted above how Ibsen creates a number of different *foci* for the action within a single stage set. This variety helps hold interest and assists plausibility, but these concerns are perhaps subsidiary to the main project of limiting the action to a single oppressive environment.

For much of Jonson's *Volpone* (1606), the protagonist's bed is focus for the action. If we consider the original production conditions, we can see how strong a focus it is, being set on a bare stage. It is also of course Volpone's lair (see 5.2.6.3, below), and the 'stage' upon which he acts the dying man.

A scene may set up a *tension* between two or more foci, so that our attention moves between, say, a plinth in the middle of the stage, a window high up, and a downstage commentator. These are the arrangements for the penultimate scene of Arden's *Serjeant Musgrave's Dance* (1959), where the plinth is a combination of clock tower, lamp post and market cross. Various different figures speak from this platform, beginning with civic dignitaries. Acting as an onstage audience and commentator is the cynical figure of the Bargee, placed downstage. Whenever we are drawn to concentrate on Musgrave, our attention is likely to be distracted by this other focus, the Bargee: and his gaze is also fixed on Musgrave, but with a consistently sceptical attitude.

After the civic dignitaries have left it, Musgrave moves onto the plinth, from where he begins to conduct what appears to be an army recruitment meeting, until he suddenly displays the skeleton, dressed in red uniform, of a comrade killed on army service overseas. When this is identified as the remains of Billy Hicks, a native of the town, the only woman on stage gets up in alarm and then leaves. Not long after, she appears at the upper storey window with Annie, the woman who loved Billy. Up to now our focus has been moving between the passion of Musgrave and the cynicism of the Bargee. But now our sudden movement to a new focus, the window, produces a forceful and significant extension of the spaces of the stage. For looking down from that high window onto an all-male scene are two women. The *axis* of tension has shifted; and a realisation of how the stage has been gendered is produced by this sudden shift in the **focal economy**.

With this shift the sense of the whole scene changes. Up to now, we have moved between Musgrave's religious passion and a cynical reaction to it; but when Annie appears the Bargee takes a ladder from the plinth to the window. Then shortly afterwards he joins Musgrave on the plinth, and Annie begins to climb down the ladder. The window is not forgotten, for the other woman later throws a bundle from it to Annie. The bundle, as Annie reveals, is another uniform of a dead soldier, its red colour duplicating the colour draping the skeleton on the plinth. Not only is the tension now between two sorts of passion, male and female, but also the centrality of the plinth with its red uniform is undermined by the repetition of that colour elsewhere. For the first time in the scene Musgrave's passionate singleness of purpose is confronted – as it were, *de*-centred – by another passion. Thus the tension between foci organises, in a persuasive way, representations of gender and religious zeal – even without our needing to hear any dialogue.

In *The Dumb Waiter* (1960) Pinter plays games with dramatic tension by having the lift device, set at the margin of the onstage fictional space, periodically erupt into noisy action and so shift the attention of characters and audience to the sinister virtual space. This repeated tension between onstage and offstage space, together with the lack of any significant clarification of the situation offstage (the controlling environment in which the two men find themselves), puts deliberate strain on dramatic plausibility. Thus the physical tension also creates a tension between the 'transparency' of the events onstage – their acceptability as a representation of real life – and their status as pure invention.

5.2.6.2 PERSPECTIVES

Offstage virtual space in *A Doll's House* is established by the set (doors) and by the dialogue. Since the Restoration, upstage painted scenes and back-cloths have not only helped establish the onstage fictional space but often also presented vistas into the distance. We might usefully call this type of offstage virtual space *perspectival* space.

A perspective might merely enrich the specification of the location: park-land stretches out below the mansion window. But it will often have a sym-bolic function too. All four acts of Ibsen's *The Pillars of Society* (1877) are set in the garden room of a house. An upstage vista presents the garden, a gated fence and beyond this a row of brightly coloured houses in the town. People move about and chat in the distance. The play is concerned both with the confinement of women and with 'floating coffins' – unseaworthy ships, cynically used for the sake of profit. The vista might at first suggest a com-munal spaciousness, the easy connection between families. More abstractly, it might also suggest a space beyond present confinement. Yet, especially as the fourth and final act is set in gloomy twilight, the houses beyond finally suggest merely another wall. This town, this culture, is enclosing, petty and mean. It blunts perspective. But it also looks back at the protagonist in just, but ironically unwitting, accusation. Karsten Bernick is a cheat. In the final act, the town is illuminated and a huge transparency dominates the vista, proclaiming Bernick as a 'Pillar of Society' (p. 108); and this emblazoned trust in him is more than he can bear.

As Oswald drifts into syphilitic dementia at the close of Ibsen's *Ghosts* (1882), '*The sun rises. The glacier and the snow-capped peaks in the back-ground glitter in the morning light*' (p. 97). There are suggestions perhaps not only of nature's implacable law but also of a desire to reach out beyond the confines of present life.

The idea of reaching out beyond the confines of the present is staged with a grim – if spectacular – concreteness in the final act of the 1871 melodrama *The Bells*. Mathias is about to go to bed; he pauses to celebrate his triumph in escaping any exposure of the murder he committed several years before. He exits and puts out the light. Then suddenly, out of the darkness, where once the bedroom wall had been, a courtroom crowded with officials stretches out in front of us: Mathias is sitting on a stool in its centre. This sudden new perspective was managed by having the bedroom wall painted realistically on a gauze screen. Behind the screen was a black curtain and behind that the courtroom was set. When the black curtain is raised, we can see through the gauze, as if through a haze, into the courtroom. This haze, combined with all the new colour, the shadowy crowd, the new steely light and – especially – the new depth of the stage, is like a dream. The perspec-tive effect has done two things. First, it has moved us from everyday reality into psychic dream-space; second, it has changed the audience's relation-ship with the stage – the familiar dimensions of the domestic interior have suddenly and inexplicably extended, the clearly defined stage picture has given way to something hazy and indistinct; while we still watch Mathias we are *also* in his head. So when stage perspective opens before us, it can suggest much more than literal distance; furthermore, it can alter our sense of our relationship with the stage.

5.2.6.3 CHARACTER LAIRS

What makes this moment so unnerving in the narrative of *The Bells* is that Mathias' bedroom, his private territory, becomes hugely public. A stage area that gives a character special status may be called a *character lair*; it is an area that literally belongs to them and to no-one else. No other character in *Volpone* lies in the bed, for instance; Nora does not enter Helmer's study.

Such a connection between an area and a character can be apparent even when the stage space is less concretely defined. For instance, Brendan Behan's play *The Hostage* (1958) has as its central situation the imprisonment by republicans of a British soldier in a room of an old lodging-house in Dublin. At the opening of Act 2 the house is in darkness, the soldier is confined to the room and two IRA men are on guard duty outside. We become aware, however, that all the other occupants of the house are concealed in the shadows looking for an opportunity to slip past the guards and get into the soldier's room, to look at him and take him gifts. These attempts to get into the room will continue, with varying degrees of success and comedy, for the rest of the play. The soldier's room exerts a fascination on the occupants of the house.

For the soldier, the room is a prison: left on his own for the first time, he runs round it searching for possible escape routes. When he asks to go to the lavatory, he is marched out of the room and then back again. Soon after this, however, there are sounds of a parade outside: all the other occupants of the lodging-house suddenly appear, and they crowd at the windows to watch the parade go by. As it passes, they read out what is on the banners. Now these windows are imaginary. What the audience actually see is two groups of people standing at the front of the stage looking out into the auditorium and acting as if they are peering out of windows. Where they are standing is, apparently, a passageway in front of the room where the hostage is – but there are no walls between the passage and the room. As the occupants continue to watch the parade the soldier-hostage comes down to the front of the stage and explains to the audience the political circumstances giving rise to the parade and the banners. He is ignored by everybody else. Then he returns to his room and shortly afterwards four of the occupants manage to slip past one of the guards and get into the room, where they crowd round the soldier and paw him. Back in his room, his 'lair', he acquires a sexual attraction.

5.2.6.4 LEVELS

The area around the soldier in *The Hostage* is apparently charged with special attractiveness because people are generally desperate to get into it, but there is otherwise very little that concretely defines it. We shall return to this particular use of the stage later (see 5.2.6.7, below). For now, however, let us move back a little to look at a physical tension between two foci, and especially how the stage may be organised so that we are compelled to watch the *contrast* between one special space and another. A very familiar example of this involves another confined character, Juliet, who can only have a conversation with her lover Romeo by talking to him from her balcony. The contrast between these two spaces, and the tragic separation between them, is forcibly suggested by the use of different *levels*. She is high up, he is down below.

The stage Shakespeare used did not have the facilities for large scenic constructions. Built into its basic architecture, however, there were two distinct performing spaces – the open stage and, above it, the minstrels' gallery. Difference of level was thus a forceful way of suggesting not just separation, but difference between two situations. For example, in *Troilus and Cressida* (*c*.1600), Cressida observes the Trojan soldiers returning from battle from above, in her balcony. Her descriptions of them are witty, but she is nevertheless physically separated from the public world in which the men move. She talks, they fight. The contrast in levels suggests two aspects of Cressida: an innate intelligence on the one hand; a vulnerable, ornamental, status as a woman in a male world on the other. Similarly, we might say that the narrow space of Juliet's balcony, which also frames her as a static image, contrasts with Romeo's freedom of movement and activity on the open stage below, a contrast which defines the supposed difference between their genders.

This use of levels can still be found in the more complex scenic constructions of the modern stage. We have already noted one such use in *Serjeant Musgrave's Dance*. A more famous example is Arthur Miller's 1949 play *Death of a Salesman*. The opening stage direction describes a '*small, fragile-seeming home*' – almost dream-like – over which towers a '*solid vault of apartment houses*' (p. 7). Much of the narrative is clinched in this one contrast of levels: the traditional American Dream faces extinction in the face of modern capitalist development.

The home itself is presented schematically. We see three rooms at once, each set on a different level; there are no realistic walls between them. In Act 1, as Happy and Biff talk in their bedroom (a raised platform), they and the audience hear their father Willy mumbling to himself in the unseen parlour below. The parlour is the bedroom's understage: it is as if his embarrassing presence undermines them. After some time, light fades from the bedroom and rises on the kitchen, set at stage level and downstage of the bedroom, into which Willy has now emerged. He continues his private musings. The use of levels helps us observe divisions between sons and father, shared and solitary space; it also facilitates a cinematic cross-fading between spaces.

But this schematisation of spaces and use of levels rather than more realistic walls also means that the actors can use the same stage space in contrasting ways. The long opening stage direction includes the instruction that '*Whenever the action is in the present the actors observe the imaginary wall-lines, entering the house only through the door at the left. But in the scenes of the past these boundaries are broken, and characters enter or leave a room by stepping "through" a wall on to the forestage.*' The forestage serves both as backyard and as '*the locale of all Willy's imaginings*' (p. 7). Thus, Willy's reminiscent musings become at first a conversation with his absent and merely imagined sons in younger times. But then the young Biff and Happy actually appear on stage, and we move into Willy's mind. We have established two ways in which the levels act as a contrasting device. Here we see that they also contribute to a *fluidity*. In the fantasy mode, walls melt. In the play as a whole, the division between concrete reality and Willy's fantasy also melts.

During the play, space can be real or imagined, present or past, but the character is not necessarily in control of the shifts between one and another. Past events can emerge, unbidden, as a sound cuts across speech or a new area of stage is suddenly illuminated. Respect for fixed boundaries makes the present feel claustrophobic. But the fluidity of the past can feel as much threatening as joyous. Because their focus on, and use of, the levels and areas seem to be led by the lighting, the characters appear to be in the grip of something larger than themselves, not so much entering spaces as being drawn into them. The characters are positioned in time as much as space by the levels, just as the home itself, the 'dream', is positioned by the property development that towers over it.

5.2.6.5 SIMULTANEOUS ACTION

When the levels represent different rooms, it is possible to show two apparently unconnected sets of activity which happen at the same time – to stage *simultaneous action*. This was present, in a sense, when Cressida talked about the soldiers below her. But a much more startling example is the rape scene from Thomas Middleton's *Women Beware Women* (?1621). While the owner of the house Livia plays chess with Bianca's mother-in-law below, Bianca herself is taken upstairs supposedly to look at paintings but in fact to be seduced by the Duke – or raped if she fails to comply. Livia knows all this; the mother-in-law does not. As audience we watch both areas of action simultaneously, and the scene gains its ironic strength from this simultaneity. The game at chess is a distracting ploy used by Livia. As a game of strategy, tactics, power and capture, it also acts as an ironic image for what is going on without the mother-in-law's knowledge. But more than this, the two women's *pursuit* of the game, their cool absorption in it, becomes an even stronger metaphor for the amoral manipulation of women's bodies and emotions as a means to advancement within a social hierarchy. Here, simultaneous action works to produce an attitude in the audience towards something much bigger, and more intangible, than the spaces themselves – it is an attitude of ironic recognition of the mechanisms of male-controlled society.

If we move to a more modern play, with very different technical resources, we can again see the arrangements for simultaneous action, and note a rather different attitude produced in the audience. In 1881 George Sims, the author of *The Lights o'London*, used lighting to direct the audience's attention to three locations at once: '*The lights have been lit in the Hall and the Lodge by this time so that the triple action can be seen by the audience*' (p. 115). In the Lodge, Bess prays for the success of Harold's interview with his father; in the Hall, Harold's father looks over his dead wife's letters and resolves to pity Harold for her sake; between the two, on the lawn, Harold, who has just quarrelled with his father, faces his future as an outcast. This 'triple action' has, again, an ironic effect, since the audience know more than any one of the characters. But that effect also produces an attitude toward the relationship between person and place – the audience feel that if the characters were not so irretrievably locked into their specific places, they could solve the problem. The staging makes us long for a movement between places, for things to be un-fixed rather than fixed. The clear separation between Lodge, Hall and lawn feels as if it belongs to an unnecessarily constrained old order, whereas what the audience is enabled to see – with the newest stage technology – is the possibility of a modern world which, in its very fluidity and interrelationship, could resolve the crisis.

If we now recall *Salesman*, we can compare very different feelings about fluidity in relation to historical change at different moments in history.

5.2.6.6 UNSTABLE SPACE

Simultaneous action is, literally, action in two or more places at once. We began with 'character lair', where we focus on the relationship between character and a fixed point in space. Then we looked at 'levels', where two or more characters are connected across contrasting spaces. And we arrived at 'simultaneous action', where the spaces are contrasted but the characters are not explicitly connected. In this case our feelings about one space – say, that of the hostess's chess game – can change drastically once the action begins elsewhere: it gets less cosy when a rape starts happening upstairs. The chess game that had seemed so hospitable comes to seem treacherous: it may be said to occupy *unstable space*.

A play can make space unstable without setting up simultaneous action. For instance, in the third act of *The Duchess of Malfi* (1614), we see the Duchess in her bedchamber chattering to her husband and her maid-servant while she arranges her hair. The activity requires the stage properties, brushes and mirror, associated with private space and leisure time. But this is more than mere privacy: it is also the space of self-definition which she has claimed at the play's beginning. Her companions leave her as a joke and then, unseen by her while she chatters on, her murderously jealous brother Ferdinand enters, carrying a dagger. This unannounced penetration of the privacy changes our feelings about the space: it seems vulnerable, entrapping, dangerously cut off from public space. By exploiting the onstage–offstage boundary, Webster stages a struggle between the Duchess's attempts to create gentle order and attack on it from without. That attack comes from her brothers, who in their turn see her project as disorderly: it does not fit with their plans for her to marry in the interests of their dynasty. The stage oscillates between gentle orderliness, tyrannical control and a frenzied brutality. At the play's end, the stage is littered with bodies.

5.2.6.7 CARNIVAL

We have already noted in our discussion of *Death of a Salesman* (1949) that the same spaces could shift between past and present; they acquire different values in different time-schemes. But there are nevertheless, as we noted, certain rules to be observed by the actors in relation to space and time. The potential instability is limited by these rules. In circumstances where there are no such rules space can become very unstable. We can also phrase that back to front: where space seems very unstable, there appear to be no rules. These are the circumstances of *carnival*. Carnival is the time in the religious year when the usual rules about moderation and restraint of appetite are in abeyance. In medieval Europe carnival was supposedly a time when all normal social hierarchy was turned topsy-turvy, when transgressions were licensed and order disintegrated into sensuality and laughter. In such a rule-bound art form as drama, it is rare to find carnival on stage, especially in scripted form. Nevertheless we have already bumped into an example, and we are now going to return to it, since it forms an appropriate final sequence to our consideration here of fictional space.

When we looked at *The Hostage* earlier we noted the soldier's prison/lair. In doing so we began to suggest the fluidity of the stage space – the lack of walls, the mimed windows. This fluidity is particularly apparent when the parade goes by. The occupants of the lodging-house stand in a passageway watching a parade that supposedly passes through where the audience are sitting. While they do it the soldier walks from his room, through an imagined wall, and talks, through another imagined wall, to what he sees not as a street but as a real audience. But he talks with reference to a parade which occupies the same area as the audience. Used in two different ways simultaneously, the stage space retains its fictional dimensions even while these are revealed as unreal. This is more than a matter of the space temporarily becoming what anybody decides to treat it as – which would be the case on the Shakespearean stage. Here it is always two things at once, superimposed on top of one another, never properly separable: a lodging-house in Dublin, and a stage here and now. This doubleness also affects the show's original pianist, Kate: her piano is half on-, half offstage; she is only a musician, not a character in the lodging-house; she is literally present when people are fictionally 'alone' on stage; she is asked to supply music for songs, and also to lend money to buy cigarettes; a half-off-stage piano is a place where people hide from an IRA guard. The fictional space is unstable, but so is the division between fiction and immediate reality.

Simultaneous and contradictory use of the stage as fictional location and as literal stage smashes the conventional rule by which we customarily keep these two functions of the stage apart. The stage becomes crazy; it challenges our sense of the serious. The carnivalised stage can be seen as an undercutting of the self-seriousness of dominant forms not only of representation but also of belief. This can be a pure gesture of refusal to be serious: Behan was certainly something of a joker. But it can also be a rhetorical gesture suggesting that getting to or near the truth is not a simple matter. Getting at the reality of things – such as the common history of Britain and Ireland – is risky, confusing and contradictory. No presently existing maps and rules are of use.

5.2.6.8 HINTERLANDS

We looked in the beginning of this chapter at *buffer zones* or hinterlands to the main space of the action, such as the Helmers' hallway. They mediate between the onstage fictional and offstage virtual spaces, but are rarely there just for the sake of plausibility. They most likely contribute significantly to the action.

One example of this sort of contribution can be observed in the second act of Sean O'Casey's *The Plough and the Stars* (1926). The scene is a pub, with a counter coming down the depth of the stage on audience left and windows onto the street at the back. Outside in the street a political meeting is being held: this is Dublin late in 1915, with Irish republicans and nationalists about to rise up against British rule. We can occasionally see the speaker at this meeting as a silhouette against the window. At a point almost halfway through the act there are two groups of people, at either end of the bar, arguing at one another. One group consists, loosely, of nationalists; the other group (of two) consists of the pro-British Bessie Bridges and the vaguely Marxist Covey. The woman in each group is not only very vocal, but her anger is particularly focused on the other woman, whose conduct and propriety are criticised.

Their argument is suddenly interrupted, and silenced, '*when the tall, dark figure is again silhouetted against the window, and the voice of the speaker is heard speaking passionately*' (p. 169). When this brief nationalist speech is finished, the silhouette goes, and onstage the argument between the two women begins with renewed force, gets to shouting pitch and threatens to become a fight. The speech, coming from that hinterland space silhouetted in the window, clearly has a major impact on these people's lives. But by putting the political activist into the hinterland and the 'ordinary' tenement dwellers onto the stage proper, O'Casey is proposing to us a relationship between, on one hand, the concrete, three-dimensional, lived – but unselfconscious – activities of everyday life, and on the other, the dogma of politics which, however two-dimensional, controls people's consciousness.

This relationship is restated with more force, and more difficulty, towards the end of the act. The stage empties of all except the barman, and in come three uniformed men, fired by the speeches, talking quickly, and carrying two flags. Suddenly there is colour, noise, up-tempo rhythm – energy: qualities which make the onstage space very vibrant, and hence attractive. The men pause, to listen to the silhouetted speaker. And then they all quickly leave. The stage empties; a pause; then re-enter Rosie the prostitute with her semi-drunk and embarrassed client. Suddenly the hinterland feels, by contrast, like a space which is not only two-dimensional and dangerous, but also colourful, energetic and unreachable. The audience themselves become tempted by the hinterland space.

5.2.6.9 SIGNIFICANT OBJECTS

In the scene that we described earlier from *Serjeant Musgrave's Dance* the central plinth is an object that makes meaning, signifies, in its own right. As a sort of market cross-cum-clock tower-cum-lamp post, it is the sort of thing you might see in any small town square. And it is used as such by the civic dignitaries – the first person to speak from it is the Mayor. It continues in this sort of function, albeit with a quiet irony about the connections between civic and military institutions, when Musgrave uses it as a recruiting platform. But when a skeleton is suddenly suspended from it, the object turns into a gallows – without, of course, ceasing to be a part of the civic authorities. When guns are produced it turns into a defensive position, especially with the arrival of dragoons to arrest Musgrave. At the very end of the scene, when the military action is finished, Annie occupies the plinth with the skeleton of her lover on her knees, like the image of the Virgin Mary and dead Christ. After its civic and violent significations, the object is now the place of a pietà, a suffering after violence. That movement from male to female occupation, with the changing significations, is also suggested by careful control of shape and consequent movement. The plinth structure, upward-pointing to Musgrave's heaven, is individual, authoritative, phallic – the sense of height actually grows when the skeleton is hung from it. To give themselves authority, the men mount it. Annie comes into the action by coming down a ladder from a high opening – and ends by bringing the skeleton down to her. The very shape of the movement made necessary by the significant object itself fundamentally structures the logic of the scene.

5.2.6.10 SKETCHING THE SET, MAKING CHECKLISTS AND MAKING A COMMENTARY

Playwrights who specify set are very likely to be constructing such zones, foci, lairs, hinterlands and tensions, and conferring some objects with a special significance. A proper account of a play needs take them into account, which makes a sketch of the scenic space a must when reading a play. The list we have made here is by no means exhaustive: its purpose is to stimulate your own activity of investigating the logic of the stage space. You will doubtless come to carry your own checklist around in your head. Sketching it down occasionally will help you develop your skills of analysis and commentary. Any checklist we make is likely to change – at least in emphasis – as we move from one stage practice to another. What might it look like in the case of Bertolt Brecht's epic theatre, for instance?

Note that even on the relatively bare and open stage of the Renaissance, where no theatrical scene is specified or assumed, the plain distinction between onstage and offstage space affords Webster a powerful structure for articulating Ferdinand's brutality (see 5.2.6.6, above) – and perhaps also for making his audience feel complicit with it. The excitement of the radical shifts in *The Hostage* depends on the convention that the stage represents a completely fictional world out of which the performers never step. But this idea only came into existence properly in the middle of the nineteenth century, when theatre architecture gradually removed the acting area in front of the **proscenium arch** – the forestage – and pushed the action back into the 'scene'. The forestage had been lit by the same chandeliers that lit the auditorium, had shared the same space as the audience. Once the action was pushed back, and the proscenium arch painted to look like a picture-frame, the audience grew accustomed to looking into a fictional space that was clearly separated from their own world of the auditorium. But almost as soon as the apparently solid, fixed location became the norm for stage setting, long before Behan was writing, dramatists and designers began to explore ways of exploiting this new convention by breaking it. The logic of any one fictional stage space is related to the prevailing conventions of spectating, and these are deeply connected to theatre architecture.

Miller's use of levels and areas in *Salesman* might be likened to Behan's in *The Hostage*, in that there is fluid movement between different areas and periods of simultaneous staging. But note what the movement is between – past and present of the same family in *Salesman*, fictional Dublin and the real stage now in *Hostage* – two very different sorts of contrast. Once we spot such things as simultaneous staging we then need to ask what its *particular* use suggests about people, history, place and time. We hope that, once you have observed the arrangements, you will go on to ask what sorts of attitude are produced in the audience, and what sorts of insight are being formulated. The relationship between people and space ends up suggesting relationships between people and gender, society, time and history.

As an exercise: Select three moments from one or more plays at which you think the set or general stage arrangements are being used with particular force by the playwright. For each, sketch down a checklist (levels, tensions, etc.) and play with diagrams (of the space; but also, say, spider diagrams derived from your checklist) to tease out the logic of the space and how this is being exploited at your selected moments. Write 1–500 words about each.

5.2.7 How fictional space is established

In the *theatre* fictional space is created by two means, which Pfister (1988: 267 ff.) denotes as *verbal techniques* (dialogue) and *non-verbal techniques* (e.g. scenography, props and the movement of characters). Consider that a ship at sea might be established by a character carrying a telescope on a bare stage. The location would be secured more by scanning the horizon with the telescope; by body mime (the ship rolls and pitches); by sound effects; by a sailor-suit. Examples of non-verbal techniques thus include the visual techniques of mime and costume and audio techniques. Howard Goorney quotes how, in their production of *Johnny Noble* (1945), Joan Littlewood's company made the audience feel seasick through body mime and lights.

In the *dramatic text* Pfister again identifies two means, *word scenery* and *stage directions*. Word scenery typically works through existential presupposition (3.3.5). Titania invites Bottom to 'sit thee down upon this flow'ry bed' (*A Midsummer Night's Dream*, 4.1.1). No original stage direction specifies the scene. Contrast, for example, the detailed stage direction that heads *A Doll's House*.

What can we make of this difference? First, Shakespeare's script assumes a bare stage in which the establishment of locations is principally by means of verbal technique. Second, those locations are generic: it does not matter precisely what sort of flowers are there, for instance. Third, neither the original script nor its versions published at the time assume production by others than Shakespeare's own company. Any stage object that might be used could be specified directly. The original script – divided into 'parts' – simply told the actors what to say. So the balance between stage directions and word scenery tells us something about the original production conditions.

Word scenery need not be purely for the sake of information. It can be a source of pleasure and display, most notably in verse drama. Spanish drama of the sixteenth century incorporated the poetic form of *gongorismo*, the florid and lengthy description of, say, a city. The flourish might simply contribute to the poetic 'register' of the stage presentation as a whole, but it might also be associable directly with the character delivering it. Thus, in Lope da Vega's *Fuente Ovejuna* (1612–14), the army captain Flores paints a magnificent picture of the scene in which Commander

Gomez sits 'upon a sturdy / Stallion the colour of crystallised honey, / With jet-black mane and tail' (p. 42) before the royal city he aims to capture. In some 50 lines like this, Flores stuns the villagers of Fuenteovejuna into admiration of their master. But Lope simultaneously stuns his audience with this display of word-power.

We have already mentioned Enobarbus' barge speech (4.1.16.3). Part of what he is doing is creating a virtual space. Partly also the speech is a display of composition on Shakespeare's part. But significantly too, this is Enobarbus' picture of Cleopatra, which he is presenting to Agrippa and Maecenas. It is his *character perspective*: too often it is taken as an 'objective' description of the Egyptian queen and her lover Antony. Flourish or no, word scenery – precisely because it is delivered by characters – always has the potential to allow us into character perspective.

It can also act as thematic carrier. For example, there is repeated knocking at an offstage gate in the porter scene (2.3) of *Macbeth* (1606). As he makes his way to the gate the porter imagines himself admitting various sinners to hell. Since the real gate is not seen, the word scenery transforms it into a sort of hell-gate – which, in a sense, it is, since Macbeth has just murdered the king.

As an exercise: Inspect carefully how fictional space is established by one or more dramatic texts you are studying. Consider how the play-text scripts or invites the establishment of fictional space in production.

5.2.8 *Signifying and aesthetic aspects of the theatrical scene*

We have distinguished between signifying, mechanical and aesthetic functions of the theatrical scene (5.2.1, above). Here we look a little more closely at signification and aesthetics.

5.2.8.1 DENOTATION AND CONNOTATION

A set that stands on stage has a direct representational meaning; but meaning is never purely denotative. There are always connotations, and much theatre depends upon them. Osborne sets *Look Back in Anger* (1956) in a flat within a Victorian house. The original audience might easily connote mild discomfort and shabbiness with such surroundings, but of more thematic importance are connotations of Victorian strictness and old-fashionedness. Jimmy is physically surrounded by reminders of what he is rebelling against.

By careful attention to detail, Lawrence makes it clear to his audience that the protagonist of *The Daughter-in-Law* (1912) has aspirations to rise above her class. The set denotes a working-class room, but one with middle-class pretensions. Connotations as to her character flow from this.

5.2.8.2 METAPHOR AND SYMBOL

A set may have metaphorical or symbolic significance. The scene Lorca specifies in Act 3 scene 1 of *Blood Wedding* denotes a forest; but its context in the play, what happens there and his short but also precise description – '*A forest. It is night. Great moist tree trunks. A gloomy atmosphere*' (p.74) – produces such strong connotations of psychic and bodily interiors that the forest scene easily comes to *stand for* either or both of these worlds.

We have here used metaphor and symbol as loosely equivalent terms. Symbol usually carries the sense of an 'outward sign' of something. The bulldog supposed to stand for British strength and determination is emblazoned on clothes, flags, mugs and official programmes. These all suggest that it is emblazoned on Britain itself. **Semioticians** use symbol in a less precise way, as we shall now see.

5.2.8.3 ICON, INDEX AND SYMBOL

The philosopher Charles S. Peirce proposed that there are three basic sorts of sign. Theatre semioticians have found this proposal suggestive and useful.

An *icon* is a likeness. Russian *ikons* are painted likenesses of saints. The backcloth painted perspectively to represent a wood is an icon. Indeed, most theatrical signs including scenic ones are iconic: the set looks like what it represents. But some representations are more schematic than others. The tree Beckett specifies for *Waiting for Godot* is not like a real tree in nature, but more like a diagram of one, just as the map of the London Underground is a diagram rather than a picture of the actual tangle of lines. Peirce distinguishes between two sorts of icons: *diagrams* and *images*.

An *index* points to something: our index finger is the one we point with. Smoke indicates that there is fire. An offstage bang indicates that a door has been slammed; a wash of blue light indicates that the moon has risen.

A *symbol* is arbitrary, treating one thing as another with which it has no real connection. A paper banknote stands in the stead of gold, goods or labour. A fish or a lamb stands for Christ.

Like all simple schemes, this one gets complicated once you start to think about it. But the complications become interesting, and can again help us think and write about theatre. Consider two things. First, theatre is fundamentally symbolic in Peirce's terms, since it treats all manner of things as if they were others: the stage is not the world. Second, a pine table on stage standing for a gilt table in a queen's chamber is standing for something it is not, but is still a table. It is not only like the thing it is not, but is also the same sort of thing, a table. Much theatre works through *iconic identity*.

So, as Keir Elam (1980: 21 ff.) suggests, Peirce's three categories are best thought of as *aspects* of theatrical signs we meet, rather than distinct species of sign. And it is as aspects that we can most usefully deploy them in our commentaries.

While we shall get most mileage out of Peirce's categories when commenting on actually realised designs, dramatic scripts may none the less specify, imply or assume degrees of iconicity. Naturalism values image over diagram. The rationalist Brecht and his designer Caspar Neher favoured diagrammatic stages with a strong indexical impetus: clear abstracted representations point to class struggle and imperialism, for instance.

Note that indices in particular activate the neighbouring offstage space. The knock at the door announces someone's imminent presence. This is the opportunity for dramatic mistakings: misreading the signs is part of the basic stuff of drama.

5.2.8.4 AESTHETICS, PLEASURE AND MEANING

Aesthetics is often taken to mean concern with beauty and value, but is more strictly understood as a concern with feelings and responses. An aesthetic effect can be purely pleasurable, but it can also help convey meaning. We need to be alert to both possibilities as we read.

It matters whether a setting is given as dark or light, blue or yellow, shabby or sleek. Aesthetic details stimulate connotative meanings and help set the tone of the scenes played within the setting. They not only affect the meaning of individual scenes, but also contribute to the rhythm of the stage and argument of spaces (see 5.2.12 and 5.2.13, below). The enlarged stages of Covent Garden and Drury Lane theatres helped serve a public taste for spectacle from the late eighteenth century. Partly this is a case of pure pleasure-taking; but wanting to be overwhelmed in the theatre in 1790 was also part of a feeling that life can put us in contact with the 'sublime', the mysterious grandeur of nature which humanity may only glimpse.

Brecht set his face against what he called 'culinary' theatre – art which serves itself up as a feast for consumption. But some of his detractors claimed that his spartan aesthetic was itself just pure artiness. Some influential designers at the Royal Shakespeare and National Theatres in Britain during the 1970s and 1980s, who tended towards minimalist white- or black-box stage spaces, have been accused of radical chic, of being 'Brechtian' because it looks cool. Such designs simultaneously connote radicalism and give a direct aesthetic pleasure. As it happens, Brecht was not against enjoyment in the theatre. That is another story, but the *sorts* of pleasures he wanted his audience to have mattered to him politically. Our own analysis needs always to be alert to how an audience is given and denied pleasure as much as to how it gains information. The setting, conditions of spectating, stage rhythm, and features such as transformations all contribute towards this. They work *by means of* pleasure.

5.2.8.5 INTERTEXTUALITY

Things have their meaning in relation to others. A sock is not a shoe or a glove. *A Doll's House* is not a well-made play. Consciously or not, we compare any book we read, play or movie we watch with others. The general notion that texts have their meaning principally in relation to other texts is called *intertextuality*. Some texts directly call attention to other texts or textual systems in order to make their own meaning. Gwynne Edwards (1987) observes how the colours Lorca specifies for *Blood Wedding* mirror those of peasant ceramics. The play relates itself self-consciously *as an artwork* to rural life and culture.

> As an exercise: Starting with the idea of denotations and connotations, draw out the signifying and aesthetic aspects of the theatrical scenes in any one play.

5.2.9 Metaphoric use of the stage and the flexibility of the theatrical sign

The politician who talks about 'the ship of state' is speaking metaphorically. A metaphor treats one thing (a ship) as if it were another (the state or what sustains it). Many plays have metaphoric dimensions. The ship which founders in the first scene of Shakespeare's *The Tempest* (1610/11) could itself be understood as 'a ship of state' – the aristocrats are notably incompetent in understanding or managing it. The scene is acting as a *metaphor*.

But consider now how that scene might be staged. Nowadays we might expect some elaborate scenic arrangement, but the first performances were probably done with none. In either case, actors staggering around the stage floor as if it were the moving deck of a ship are treating one thing (the stage floor) as if it were another (a deck). A famous routine of the Peking Opera involves a sustained body mime in which the performer punts an imaginary boat across the stage as if it were a river. Theatre, then, regularly makes a *metaphoric use of the stage*, even when it is not necessarily making metaphoric figures.

The setting for the original production of Caryl Churchill's *Fen* (1983) was an agricultural field on which were placed various domestic items (a chair, an ironing board) when the scene was an interior. The stage floor moves from one to another, but the field is never – metaphorically – out of the rooms of those who work on it. In the final scene this movement between places is duplicated by a movement across time. The dead Val has reappeared, talking to figures from the past as well as the present. Others from the play's cast come on, in the present, including Nell, walking on stilts, like a fenlander from the seventeenth century; there's also a scarecrow boy there, from centuries ago. The same stage space is treated as if it is inside and out, past and present, living and dead, simultaneously.

That the stage floor can change its referential meaning from moment to moment – now a stone floor, next a muddy field – is a particular instance of a general principle that theatre semioticians have foregrounded, the *transformability or flexibility of the theatrical sign* (see Elam 1980: 12 ff.). We are prepared by convention to accept two pieces of wood nailed together as a sword, or maybe as a golden crucifix. The ease with which we accept one thing (bits of wood) as another (a sword or crucifix) enables performers and designers to make one sign (wood as sword) transform to another (wood as crucifix) in an instant. The sign itself is flexible. This also means that a stage object can stand for two things even at the same time. The stage is thus a very *associative* space: it easily brings various referents into relation with one another.

While these are mostly questions of design and direction during a production process, some playscripts clearly make use of this potential.

5.2.10 *Theatre as a syncretic system*

A novel works by virtue of the printed word alone. A newspaper cartoon uses words and pictures. In **semiotic** terms, a novel uses one signifying system (written language), whereas a cartoon uses two. A playtext uses one signifying system – again, the printed word. But it is a script for an activity which is itself a sort of text – the theatrical text (see 1.1.3) – which employs a large number of signifying systems. These include, for instance, spoken language, costume, lighting, sounds, gestures, movements and scenography. Each of these can make sense on their own: think back, for instance, to the various *different* ways in which a seaborne location can be signified as discussed above at 5.2.7. Theatre can be thought of as one huge signifying system which contains several others. Semioticians refer to such a system as a *syncretic system*.

Some playwrights – especially in the twentieth century – exploit this fact. A playtext may, for instance, script a transformation which depends on changes in some signifying systems on stage, while others remain constant. At the opening of Howard Brenton's *The Churchill Play* (1974) a catafalque stands on stage, bathed in light shone through a stained glass window. Silence helps establish the scene as Churchill's sombre and dignified lying in state. But then while the scenic object remains, lighting, sound and action around it change radically and we are in the company of prisoners who have no respect for the dead man, rehearsing to present an entertainment for official visitors. The catafalque remains a catafalque, but changes its situation and meaning in an instant. The transformation of the scene of which it is a part from state ceremony to inappropriate play-acting brings nationalist ideology and myth-making into sharp collision with ordinary broken lives. The eloquence of the effect involves both the persistence of the denotative meaning of the object and its shifting connotative function.

Transformations can be subtle: the cloak that Nora throws about her shoulders as she contemplates suicide is transformed into a costume element in the world of melodrama she is stepping into. An essay properly attentive to the play as dramatic script would note this. We develop the idea of dramatic worlds below (see 5.2.12).

5.2.11 *Logics and conventions of the stage*

The notion of 'upstaging' someone is part of common parlance. You have taken 'centre stage' in a conversation, for instance, and I say something which undercuts you as the point of interest for your audience. Let's take this back to an actual stage. Centre stage is a strong position. So too is downstage centre. Upstage is less strong; but an upstage entry can disrupt an audience's point of focus from a strong position.

Are there other strong positions? Some hold that downstage left is strong – perhaps for right-handed spectators, or because Westerners read from left to right. Certainly, a downstage marginal position is a strong one from which to comment on the action on the rest of the stage. A disruptive upstage entry probably achieves its effect not only because it is behind another's back but also because it takes up the perspectival position.

Strong positions depend not only on position itself, but also on the spectating conditions. Note that our remarks so far are most pertinent to a picture-frame stage; and consider even within this arrangement how the use of **limelight** affects spectatorship. The strength of various positions also depends on what is done at them and what other possible points of focus are being occupied onstage – and on the sequence of their occupation.

Augusto Boal (1992: 150–55) has a game, in which the players successively take up a position of 'authority', that is worth playing as a way of vividly concretising your sense of all five of these factors. Our concerns here link with the issues of groupings and stage action raised in 4.1.17.

Different stage conventions focus action in different stage areas and assume different forms of movement about the stage. Some give areas of the stage a symbolic significance. We need to attend to the *assumptions* a dramatic script makes about stage space as well as what it manifestly scripts.

Restoration comedies play downstage in intimate contact with the audiences they ridicule. The players tend to 'cross' the stage, moving from left to right and back again as they speak. While scene remains backdrop, entry to the stage is through the stage doors close to the audience; the character enters the action but the actor 'makes an entrance' too – and perhaps, moreover, the actor is playing a show-off character.

The Elizabethans treated the understage as hell; the innovator Shakespeare has fun with this by having the Ghost of Hamlet's father call up from the 'cellarage' and Hamlet stamp on the stage to attract his attention. The canopy over the Globe's stage was painted to represent the heavens. Up and down have similar associations on secular stages, too.

As we shall see later (5.3.1, below), medieval players frequently had direct contact with their audience. The *platea* is simultaneously audience and fictional space. But in the conditions dominating throughout most of the twentieth century, invasion of audience space by the action could feel threatening or exhilarating. Spectating arrangements are intimately tied up with social norms. Twentieth-century spectators tended to conceive of themselves in general life as private individuals. Invasions of audience space challenged this assumption; but, of course, challenging the assumption can only go on so long as the convention of individual privacy remains dominant.

5.2.12 Fictional worlds and the argument of spaces

We noted two ways in which the setting of *A Doll's House* is significant. First, the fictional world mirrors the world of the audience. Second, the particular fictional space presented does not change, and this argues something.

Bevington (1987) calls attention to the argument of spaces in his edition of Shakespeare's *1 Henry 4*. Scenes roughly alternate between the tavern world and the world of the court, and a significant shape of the action is Price Hal's shift of loyalty from the first world to the second. A key feature of the argument of spaces is the value conferred upon each. Hal's movement from the corrupt world of the tavern to the responsible world of the court is a positive one. Bevington points out that there are moments when the tavern scenes are reminiscent of (and even make reference to) medieval depictions of hell and its temptations. Like the hero of a **morality play**, Hal comes to his salvation.

Bevington also demonstrates how Shakespeare complicates this scheme. The tavern world is irresponsible, but also full of warmth; the court is responsible, but personally unrewarding. There are positive and negative aspects to each space. Further, these aspects are associated especially with two characters, Falstaff and the King. Hal's movement to the world of the court and adult responsibility involves rejection of the worst and retention of the best of both worlds and of both father figures. The play argues that Henry 5 – who Hal is to become – is the ideal synthesis of kingly authority and personal generosity.

Note that particular characters are associated with each world within the play, while others – like Hal – move between them. This is a significant part of the play's design, best discovered by means of french scene analysis (see 4.1.19).

Significant, too, is the relationship of the audience to each of these worlds. While this is more complicated than for our opening example of *A Doll's House*, it is worth thinking about when commenting on the play. As a start, we could note that the world of courts is remote from most people, but that the Elizabethan chroniclers (like Holinshed) in particular offered a sense of intimate knowledge of historical royal actions and motivations; that taverns are familiar places to most; and that most in the original audience would be familiar with tavern *scenes* in the by-then 'old-fashioned' morality plays concerned with temptations of the flesh. Each of these relationships is potentially exploited by the play and so contributes to its meaning.

Within each world there may be a number of scenic locations; in *1 Henry 4* the scenes of highway robbery clearly belong to the tavern world. While we may personally be able to think of school, college or work as one world and home as another, we are less likely to distinguish in this way between the kitchen and the bedroom. Similarly, in many plays individual scenic locations may have particular associations, while not being distinct enough for us to want to call them 'worlds'. Yet they can still contribute on their own account to an argument of spaces. At times in our lives the bedroom may well come to feel like a different world, rather than just another part of home; the line between location and 'world' is blurred. Two things follow. First, we should not worry too much about getting the distinction between mere location and world 'right'. Second, you may find it useful as you get familiar with this work to spot how locations 'become' worlds in the course of a play. Would you say this is true of the Helmers' living room?

The audience will have a relationship to the world of the play as a whole, and this, as much as the subsidiary relationships, will change according to the conditions of production. Shakespeare's audience were witnessing the history of their monarchy: monarchs still mattered. Audiences now probably rather get a sense of English 'heritage' – the world of the stage is to a large extent 'Shakespeare'.

The worlds presented by a play need not all be presented directly onstage. They may be 'virtual' spaces, referred to by characters but not visited by the action. In Chekhov's *Three Sisters* (1901), the young women long to live in Moscow rather than their small provincial town: how they value Moscow and how the audience are made to evaluate this valuing are central to the play's design. Similarly, a world might only have its existence in the mind of a particular character, whom others see as deluded. We have seen how Nora seems at first to live in a world of romance and melodrama. The loftspace in which Old Ekdal keeps his collection of animals in Ibsen's *The Wild Duck* (1885) is visible onstage; but those around him see Ekdal's dedication to this space as a form of delusion, an escape from hard reality.

Clearly, the argument of spaces is tied up with the plot-shape of a play. But they are not the same thing. Consider, for instance, that while Lear and

Gloucester in Shakespeare's *King Lear* occupy plot and sub-plot, they are in the same world or set of worlds.

The *relationship* between plot-shape and argument of spaces can be a useful way into a play. *A Midsummer Night's Dream* presents four sets of characters: the fairies; the mechanicals; the lovers; and parents and court. The plot-lines specific to the first three groups are made to intertwine in the wood, a world most especially associated with the fairies. The wood is a place of mistakings and magical transformations, a necessary place of processing between the divisions in civil space with which the play opens and the unitings in royal space with which it closes. We might usefully deploy an actantial analysis of the play here (see 2.4.2). Our attention to the argument of spaces might go further by noting that, at a social level, the world of the mechanicals is greatly distanced from that of the court *and* of any likely audience. The last scene works on this embarrassment. Our notion of 'worlds' is a flexible one, usefully extended, sometimes, from scenic location to world-view. Also, the wood is not only a fairy world, it is also very much a theatrical one: the play self-consciously displays its ability to juggle plots, to our confusion and delight.

We noted how each of the two worlds presented in *1 Henry 4* had contradictory aspects. It is often noted that the 'Absurdist' plays of the mid-twentieth century are designed to make the world of the action seem deeply contradictory to the audience. On the one hand, scene, character type and the superficials of dialogue are very close to the world of the audience. But the dialogue itself, and the existential presuppositions it makes (3.3.5), suggest something very different.

As an exercise: Take two or more plays you know, preferably from different periods. For each play, decide (a) How many worlds are there? (b) What are the key qualities of each? (c) Are characters distributed significantly between them? (d) What relationships do you think the original audience might have had with these worlds? Now consider (e) what the argument of spaces is for each play; (f) how this might change according to when and where the play is produced. Lastly, is there anything to comment on in the similarities and differences between the examples you have chosen? Do they have any significance?

5.2.13 *Rhythms of the stage*

Closely associated with the argument of spaces is the way in which the stage is scripted to feel enclosed or open, empty or full at various moments. What the play comes to mean to an audience and the way that it feels are influenced by this. When reading a play we therefore need to attend both to the number of bodies on stage and to the shape and dimensions of the theatrical set if one is specified.

Shakespeare's *Othello* (1602–4) begins with successive and successively large fillings of the stage with people, culminating in the clash between Brabantio's men and Othello's. His calming of the throng quickly establishes his noble status. The **crescendo** of bodies helps accentuate his ability to command. The opening scenes of *Hamlet* (1601) are contrasted not merely by location, but also by body-count. From the desolate and relatively empty ramparts of the castle we move to Claudius's self-presentation to his court, which fills the stage.

Act 3 of Schiller's *Mary Stuart* (1800) is the famous 'opening-out' scene, set in parkland, where the stage itself is scripted to become much more spacious than it has been so far. This is the moment when Mary briefly experiences the bliss of freedom from imprisonment. The scene is neither merely an appropriate place for her to be, nor merely a representation of Mary's feelings. It embodies that feeling, exhilarates the audience directly by **kinaesthetic** means. And physical space in the first half of Chekhov's *Three Sisters* becomes progressively restrictive, culminating in the young women being packed into a bedroom while a fire rages outside. The last act opens out as the military prepare to leave for Moscow, an expansiveness which has connotations of loss and desolation in connection with the sisters.

Usually, the sense of the stage filling is pleasurable in itself. The *entry* of the Danish court in *Hamlet* furnishes a direct source of pleasure for the audience, whether or not it is staged with any pageantry. Similarly, as we noted in connection with *A Doll's House*, an emptying stage usually feels sad or cold. *King Lear* ends with the stage direction '*Exeunt with a dead march*' (5.3.326 SD). We have also, however, just noted an occasion when several bodies are chaotically on stage and another when a throng suggests orderliness. In both cases the number of bodies matters, but for different reasons.

Clearly these physical rhythms of the stage are intimately tied up with the rhythms of the action, the pace of scenic divisions, the argument of spaces and logic of space. Attention to one consideration calls up others. By swapping our attention from one consideration to another, we enrich our reading of the play.

As an exercise: Refer back to the plays you examined for the last exercise and consider the physical rhythms of the stage. Be attentive to the shape of the whole play and to local moments of significant change or contrast. Comment.

5.3 Models and maps of theatrical space

The last section developed various models which can help us analyse how space works on the stage and in theatres. Some worked very locally, others took more of an overview. Using the models depends upon some historical understanding, and we started to develop some historical maps to assist in this.

This last section hints at perspectives you might come to develop at university degree level, by turning again to the larger frame. Are there maps or models that can help us categorise wholesale conventions of space? In order to develop this question, we need first to set out one more important convention.

5.3.1 *Locus and platea*

'*Locus* and *platea*' describes a regular arrangement used by Christian plays from the later middle ages. *The Castle of Perseverance* (*c.*1440) is a famous example. Players and audience all occupy a circular outdoor space, at the margins of which are erected simple wood and canvas structures called scaffolds. This play has one in the middle of the area, too.

The area within the ring of scaffolds is known as the 'place'. Some scaffolds in some plays may be used by the audience, but they more usually walk within the place and sit around its edge. Each scaffold usually represents a significant location, such as heaven, hell or a palace. *Locus* and *platea* are the Latin for 'location' and 'open space', which correspond to scaffold and place respectively. The arrangement is also called 'place and scaffold'.

The action happens both on the scaffolds and between them, in the place. The place is a space of journeying between significant locations which are loaded with symbolic significance. It is also the space of intimate and often playful interaction with the audience. Scaffolds are to be looked

Fig. 5.4 Locus and platea (place and scaffold) staging
Illustration by Mick Wallis, based on Southern (1962).

up at with some wonder. A figure descending from a scaffold carries a special charge.

5.3.2 Locus *and* platea *as a general model*

In a famous book, Weimann (1987) showed how Renaissance plays still often work within the terms of the *locus–platea* binary even though the stage arrangement is very different. The underlying sense of space and its significance persists because the underlying assumptions of Christian belief persist, too. Believers have a spatial sense of their relationship to the Godhead: God is above, deep within or all around. Recently, Colin Counsell (1996) has attempted to develop Weimann's work into a generalisable tool for analysing Western performance, from Naturalism, Brecht and Beckett to postmodern performance. Even in a predominantly secular culture, there persists a sense of a higher and fixed order of things, and the stage remains a platform on which we encounter this. Counsell's readings into Western stage practice tease out the interplay between a 'symbolic order' and illusion (*locus*) on the one hand and democratic free play and the concrete (*platea*) on the other.

Those readings are very suggestive. But they involve something of a simplification of what is really going on in medieval place and scaffold playing. The whole arena, not just the scaffolds, is 'God's space'. God was felt as an immediate presence; moral values were felt to be concrete, not abstract things. The very distinction between concrete and abstract is difficult to apply to medieval Christian belief. This sense of the real immediate presence of the Godhead in everyday life has been called 'theological Realism'.

Models are useful; but we need to use them with care. They can help us tease out the significant features of specific moments of cultural production like playmaking: but they can also distract us from important detail. Still, we understand no thing without bringing some sort of model to it, consciously or not – so we need to get used to the *activity* of modelling, trying and testing a number of models at once.

5.3.3 *An abstract and a historical scheme*

Let us look at just one abstract model that Pfister (1988: 262–4) introduces in his exhaustive catalogue of methods for dramatic analysis. Considering the scenic embodiment of the fictional locale, he distinguishes between

- *Neutrality* as in the bare stage of Classical antiquity and the Renaissance
- *Stylisation* as in the diagrammatic scenic representations of the Restoration
- *Realisation* as in the detailed sets of Naturalism

Pfister rightly warns that although our examples fall neatly into chronological order, his three categories must not be taken to suggest a linear historical development. Stylisation and neutrality, for instance, have been regular features of the twentieth-century stage.

Pfister's work in general and our discussions in this book might still help us make and develop a scheme relating significant features of playing arrangements to more general historical features. We could start with:

- *God's universe and concrete experience, theological Realism*
   Medieval *locus* and *platea*;
- *theatre as civilised public institution, rational humanism*
   public square in heroic tragedy;
   Neoclassical unity of time, place and action;
- *rapid process of change*
   Renaissance flexible variety of space;
   reference to many worlds;
- *secular and individualist concerns, determinism*
   detailed specificity of Naturalism;
   enclosure.

Our list is concerned with categories of space and the social function of drama. It will not be a neat list, and the important one is the one you come to draw for yourself.

As an exercise: Flick back through this chapter and make a list of the models and approaches you have so far found most useful or suggestive when it comes to confronting a printed playtext. Make a second list of historical items of information or outlines that are new to and of interest to you.

|6|

Culture and interpretation

When Ibsen's *A Doll's House* was first performed in England the occasion felt very special. Much of this specialness came from the novelty of Ibsen's work, together with his reputation for saying uncomfortable things. But the feeling around the event did not derive from novelty alone: the performance of the play took on the aspect of a deliberate challenge to the status quo. It took on this aspect because the performance was done as a private staging at a commercial theatre, with an audience that included some famous critics of the dominant culture. So although the play's messages might not have shocked its immediate audience, the performance was done in conditions that implied that it had a combative, shocking relationship with the rest of society. It would have had a very different relationship if it had been done in a smart West End theatre in front of royalty. Thus the text of Ibsen's play was structurally positioned within contemporary London by its particular theatrical location, its performers and its audience.

The location, the performers and the audience are not things that might immediately strike you when you start reading a play, because as you start reading you enter the fictional world of the play. Nevertheless, in a performance, that fictional world is being represented by one group of real people to another, also real, group. Many playwrights have taken these groups for granted and have written with them in mind: their plays make their meanings within, and because of, this particular context. For us who read plays at some considerable historical and social distance from their moment of writing, it is difficult to identify how this real context helped in making the play's original meaning. Difficult as it is, however, it is still part of the work of exploring how to study a play. The sections which follow give some suggestions about the various issues you might think about as you open the play, and our examples illustrate how meanings derive from and are created by the status of the writer, by location, performers and audience.

6.1 Writers

6.1.1 *The house dramatist*

One of the reasons why Ibsen had a special status in the eyes of contemporary English theatre people was his apparent artistic independence. His plays seemed to express his own serious thoughts about society. This picture of the dramatic writer appealed to those in the English theatre who felt that dramatists were too much under the control of managers. Although a Society of Dramatic Authors had been founded in 1832, to campaign for proper financial payments and professional standing, for most of the nineteenth century writers had very little economic independence. There was no widespread or fair system of royalty payments, nor much protection by copyright. One of the most secure forms of employment was as 'house dramatist', where the writer was part of the production team at a theatre. He or she provided the sort of plays that were required – which might mean anything between pirating a text that had worked well at another theatre, doing an adaptation of the most popular story to hit town that month, producing yet another version of the shows for which the theatre had a reputation and providing a vehicle for the theatre's latest star acquisition (which could well be an acrobat or a performing dog). Clearly, in these circumstances, the question 'What is the writer trying to say in this text?' is an irrelevance.

It is not just for nineteenth-century plays that the question above is an irrelevance. For most of the history of the theatre, the writer's role tends to be insignificant in terms of their status in the production of plays. Clearly the writer was valued in terms of their particular skill, much as a good stage carpenter or theatre musician might be valued. But there were very few occasions when a writer could insist on her or his creative 'vision' and integrity against the wishes of managers or leading actors. To put the situation like this, however, is to assume that conflict was regular. This assumption is based on a romantic image of the embattled artist fighting desperately to protect her or his vision against the economically motivated forces of commerce. But in fact the separation between artist and businessman is not clear-cut. Shakespeare was a shareholder in his theatre company. His money came from his cut of the profits rather than the separate sale of his playtexts (like many Renaissance dramatists, he did not seek to publish his plays, because to do so would be to make them available to rival companies). It was always within the context of his theatre company that his plays were developed – as we shall suggest later, it is highly probable that the range of talents and interests around him would have had its effect on the sort of thing Shakespeare scripted for them. Furthermore, the company, as a company, had a sense of its own artistic reputation, which it sustained by the sorts of plays that were put on. Shakespeare declares his awareness of the competition between different theatres when he makes Hamlet have a conversation about the fashionable boy actors over the river, a reference which Hamlet's audience would have understood as applying to the Blackfriars theatre, just over the river from the Globe.

6.1.2 The play gets printed

When Shakespeare's collected plays were officially published for the first time he had been dead for several years: the publication was both a testimony to his memory and a commercial venture by the company. When the collected plays of Beaumont and Fletcher were published the theatres had been closed for five years; the volume was a memorial to a culture destroyed by the Revolution. These two examples suggest that when plays become books they have a separate life *outside* the theatre. Even when individual plays began regularly to be published to coincide with performances, it was not a book as such that the actors and production team worked from inside the theatre. The actors were only given their individual parts, with relevant cues; the prompt copy was a whole text, but not a completely coherent one – alterations, cuts and cues would be written into it. When plays started to become texts for reading, their initial function was as a sort of advertisement for the author or the show. This could only work amongst the literate – there was much less point in making plays that appealed to popular, illiterate audiences into books. Towards the end of the nineteenth century the play began to be read more frequently as a book, as a substitute for seeing the show (see 1.2.4). This appealed to the writers of minority intellectual drama. Once the next step was taken, and plays began to be material for school and university study, then the book apparently became more important than the show. Now students often read the book and then see how far the show matches up to it. The play, once a thing being worked on by a group of people in continual process, is now fixed in print.

6.1.3 The independent author

The printing of plays had beneficial effects for authors: their work could be separated out from the other creative activities in the theatre and published on its own. When this started to happen regularly in the Restoration, however, the writers already had a status which derived from their social class. Restoration theatre was mainly the domain of a fairly small social élite – actors, writers, critics, audiences moved in the same social circles, addressing one another and making jokes with each other in the plays they performed for themselves. Any individual writer's text functions as a part of this social grouping: the writer may have an independent income, and claim individual responsibility for the text, but s/he is nevertheless structurally positioned by the group. This was particularly true of the woman who sought to achieve independence as an author while being treated as secondary to men. Aphra Behn makes an image of this situation in her play *The Rover* (1677): the high-class whore, Angellica, talks to her maid on a balcony while down below, outside her house, a picture of her advertises her beauty to customers; men stop and comment on the picture, and then quarrel over it. The men only respond to the picture, the publicised fiction of Angellica, whereas the real woman has a mind of her own; but the real woman is separated from the public world of men (2.1).

Even the attempt to make the writer's creative role especially important does not necessarily mean that it is the solitary voice of the writer that we hear in the play book. The Royal Court theatre has defined itself, most noticeably in the 1970s, as a 'writers'' theatre, showcasing the work of new and challenging dramatists. But alongside this there developed a 'Royal Court aesthetic', a way of designing and lighting shows, a mode of acting; and together with this there grew up a Royal Court audience, expecting radical issues to be addressed, expecting stage language and images that would challenge propriety. Writing with the Royal Court in mind, the playwright has a sense of a particular audience and a particular way of doing plays. A play written in the 1990s for the Royal Court Theatre Upstairs, a showcase for young writing talent, is usually imagined and scripted according to conventions mainly learnt from television drama. To put it rather enigmatically, we could say that the theatre (or television) is already in the play – because it is in the mind of the playwright – before the play gets into the theatre.

The conclusion we might draw from all this is that our original question, 'What is the writer trying to say here?' is often an irrelevance as it stands, but could be rephrased more usefully to ask, 'What is the theatre trying to say here?' and 'To whom is the theatre trying to say it?' In short: what does the playtext suggest is being *shared* between theatre and audience? So in our attempt to get closer to what the playtext might be saying, what it might mean, we need to ask about the location of the theatre, the status of actors and the composition of the audience.

6.2 Location

Where is the performance situated in relation to the community who might watch it? A moment's reflection on performances in modern Western societies will lead to a rather various list, which might include the town's repertory theatre, a circus tent on the outskirts of town, the back room of a pub, a nearby theme park, a concert hall, a place of worship. Since we are confining our attention to scripted plays, we don't need to bother with most of these – but we still might need to distinguish between the theatre in the smart end of town, where the other 'night spots' are; the performance space in an arts centre; the college theatre; the amateur dramatics club; the community hall in an inner-city residential area – and, in the summer, the main market place in town and the municipal park. Let's take a brief journey through some of the issues around performance location before we look at the impact they have on the playtext.

The various venues listed above differ from one another in two main ways: *where* each venue is and *what* it is.

6.2.1 *Where the venue is*

The location of the performance space in relation to the rest of the town tends to influence what it offers to audiences, and what it might be expected to offer. While the theatre at the smart end of town might put on well-made plays, ballets and detective mysteries, the arts centre may show pieces involving physical theatre, video projection and nudity. In each of these cases it is the *cultural* rather than geographical location which matters – theatre as a night spot for a 'good night out', theatre as self-consciously artistic. But at a time when public transport was less readily available, the *geographical* location might itself suggest something about the range of plays, the dramatic culture. Thus, in the early decades of the nineteenth century, theatres on the south side of the river Thames in London – the 'Surrey side' – had a reputation for roughness, because they were situated much more closely to working-class housing areas than to the rich, fashionable part of town. This roughness amounted not only to large-scale and loud effects, but also to stories centred upon working people.

In 1900 a music-hall performer called Ella Shield created a hit with her song 'Burlington Bertie from Bow': this song was a parody of the song 'Burlington Bertie', sung by Vesta Tilley cross-dressed as a fashionable man-about-town. Burlington Arcade is near Bond Street in the wealthy West End of London; Bow is in the working-class East. The Shield song gains its force by articulating a mockery by the lower class of those above them. As we shall demonstrate in our examples below, texts are often designed to respond to, and develop, a sense of location – cultural and geographic – in their audiences; all sorts of character types, situations and jokes gain meaning when we understand this location.

6.2.2 *What the venue is*

In the late Middle Ages the townspeople of York could, once a year, watch the religious Corpus Christi plays as they processed through the streets of the city. Only a very few of those same people might be invited to gather in the banquet hall of a local manor house to watch a dramatic entertainment. In the hall the acoustics meant that voices could be used without the limitations that come from addressing a street, so different sorts of line could be written; and the assumption of a more socially homogeneous audience made possible jokes based on shared knowledge and values (see Harris 1992).

6.2.2.1 WHAT SORT OF PLACE IS IT?

The distinction between streets and hall thus impacts upon the sort of audience and the sort of play that is performed. In the same way, in Shakespeare's London, the large open-air theatres charged much cheaper entry prices, because they had plenty of space, than did the so-called hall theatres located in domestic buildings; so one venue felt very much more select, in social terms, than did the other – the hall theatre was a venue for the wealthy. And if you ever were to get in to the royal banqueting house to watch a masque you needed to be something like a minister of state. So even the most basic questions about the performance place – is it open and free to all? is it open with paying entry? is it a large custom-made building? is it part of another building? – carry implications about the sort of audience and play. The dramatist would be well aware of these implications.

> As an exercise: Take the questions above and ask them of the play you are studying, together with finding out about the venue (where and what).

6.2.2.2 WHAT ARE ITS INTERNAL ARRANGEMENTS?

Throughout theatre history, plays have generally been written by people who had close associations with particular companies and their theatre buildings – the act of creating a play often has a specific theatre in mind. So the detailed internal arrangements of a theatre building often take a key part in how that play is imagined, how it works, how it makes meaning. A dramatist writing in the Restoration period (1660–90) knew that in each of the two available theatres the area immediately in front of the stage – the pit – was frequented by the most fashionable men-about-town, who showed off not only their clothes but their charisma in witty ripostes to the stage. The front of that stage had, on each side of it, tiers of boxes – so an actor on the front of the stage was, in effect, in the auditorium, with sections of audience in front and at the sides (see 5.2.11). Those sections had different sight-lines: so when, for instance, a foppish gentleman on stage was playing to the fashionable wits in the pit, the whole player–watcher interaction was itself a spectacle for those at the sides. Given that the pit was predominantly male, and that women sat in boxes, the interaction of pit and stage becomes an enactment of gender positions, a demonstration of that regular thematic concern of Restoration comedy – the working of masculine privilege.

By the early nineteenth century the pit had become the territory no longer of the rich but of artisans. Over the ensuing years theatre managements tried to attract middle-class audiences back into the theatre. They did so by making alterations to the seating arrangements and furnishings (see Shepherd and Womack 1996). The pit with its shared benches was abolished, and replaced by stalls seats, which could be individually numbered and allocated. These seats were covered to look rather like armchairs, carpets were laid, and the auditorium walls acquired little lamps and lampshades and wall hangings, so that the whole thing began to mimic a wealthy middle-class sitting room. The appearance of a sitting room suggested, and enforced, sitting-room behaviour: rather than shouting and throwing objects at the stage, audiences moved with decorum and talked in hushed voices. And, as this new auditorium appeared, dramatists supplied it with plays in which characters moved with decorum appropriate to the onstage furnishings, the tables and chairs, cups and saucers. In Tom Robertson's play *Caste* (1867), conflict between characters is expressed not through shouting or weapons, but through the handling of crockery. On this stage, and for this audience, the passionately expressive mode of melodrama felt like a joke, an embarrassment. In 1885, when the seats closest to the stage were now regularly stuffed full with the most expensive people, a music-hall singer – Nelly Power – could make a point by studiously ignoring those in front of her, looking over their heads right back to the cheapest seats high up and singing, 'The boy I love is up in the gallery'.

6.2.2.3 WHAT DOES 'GOING TO THE THEATRE' FEEL LIKE?

Our account of the internal arrangements has concentrated on the auditorium. For most people, however, their feeling about the visit to the theatre, and hence their attitude to what they are going to watch, begins to be shaped before they get that far. As we have suggested, the location of the performance place and the sort of thing it is already do their work on an audience. Then there is the moment of entry – up steps, down steps, carpeted floor, concrete, doormen and ushers, a trestle table with tickets, mirrors and chandeliers, a bookstall, a coffee bar with paintings, beer in plastic glasses, gourmet ice cream. You might regard all of these as entirely irrelevant to the play you are studying. But even playtext readers carry in their heads an image of the theatre space – usually based on their own experience – so that they too make assumptions about the play which depend on their sense of what it means to 'go to the theatre'.

That phrase can imply something different if you are, say, on the annual outing with the gardening club, if you are a professional reviewer, if you are studying the play for an exam, if you are taking your new lover on a treat. Being in the theatre can feel like a magical playground, a workplace, a shop. And then we have to conjecture what it might have felt like in the past – in different spaces, with different relationships with the town. Again, readers make assumptions about 'old' theatres – what it was like seeing Shakespeare,

Ibsen, Osborne, Orton. What it feels like can, in its turn, establish how someone watches: enjoying the presence of glamour, looking for subversive implications, observing the lighting design, noting details of interpretation. And assumptions about what it feels – and felt – like can establish how someone reads. Without knowing it, our attitude to watching is the first step towards looking for a meaning in what we watch: the meaning we find is usually the sort of thing we began looking for. Thus the first audiences of Wertenbaker's play *Our Country's Good* (1988) may well have been influenced by the ambience of liberalism at the Royal Court theatre, just as readers may well be influenced by the letters from prisoners which preface the play, to take it that the play is arguing that, through drama, people may achieve a new sense of self-worth. By contrast, in a different setting, we might see that the play offers a cynical argument as to how the upper class may more subtly maintain its control of the lower class by teaching them to find enjoyment in the drama that was developed for the upper class (rather than enabling them to find their own lower-class 'voice').

6.2.3 Examples

Much of the direct evidence of location is difficult to find in the written texts that you study. What is invisible is not, however, absent, and you often will need to glance at a theatre history book to check out what the performing place is, where it is in the town or village, what its internal arrangements are. Here are some examples to show the different ways in which location constructs meaning.

6.2.3.1 MEDIEVAL

In York the staging of the plays in the Corpus Christi cycle, which told the Biblical story from Creation to Last Judgement, was an annual civic event. The plays were processed around the town on wagons, which stopped and performed several times, following a known route, from dawn to dusk. Audiences gathered at each stopping-point to watch something which was very well-known but also special, because it only happened once a year. The backdrop to each play was the familiar, real streets of York, but they were streets emptied of their usual everyday business. For the duration of the plays the fabric of the city is both concretely apparent and yet transported into some domain which is outside daily life, connecting back across the years to each other moment of the cycle's performance. The written text of these plays contains deliberate anachronisms, references to events and phenomena that postdate the supposed time of the Bible story. Far from being disruptive, these verbal references fall into place within, and underline, the sense of double location – the here-and-now city which is simultaneously part of God's eternal scheme.

6.2.3.2 RENAISSANCE

Between 1600 and 1609 Shakespeare's company of performers was working in their own custom-built theatre, the rebuilt Globe, in Southwark on the south bank of the river Thames in London. It was a sign of their artistic and financial success that they had been able to build this theatre – and although it was an open-air theatre, with entry prices accessible to a wide spectrum of social groups, an opening show – *Julius Caesar*, *c.* 1599 – had signalled a disdain for the taste of the more ignorant. Theatres on the south bank were commonly assumed to offer the clowning and jigs, songs and patriotic history that supposedly appealed to the popular appetite – one of them doubled as an animal-baiting arena. By contrast, when Shakespeare wrote *King Lear* (1605/6) he took an ancient British story, and then removed almost all the history-telling element out of it; he provided a clown, but made the clown's contributions more inscrutable than entertaining; his songs became obscure rhymes. These artistic decisions can be seen as attempts by the company to resist or develop their location. They were, nevertheless, still trapped by it. For when a satirical play – Beaumont's *Knight of the Burning Pestle* – opened at the fashionable Blackfriars theatre in 1607, among its catalogue of jokes was the figure of an old man, Merrythought, who is half-crazy and infuriates his family, very like the mad Lear. The principal characters, and targets, of this play are a pair of shop-keeping citizens who fancy themselves as educated playgoers. They are set up as an audience to the play within the play. Where they sit as audience is on stools on the actual stage; since this is the place where really only the fashionable men sat, their inappropriateness is established by their auditorium location. In the eyes of the Blackfriars dramatist these citizens are precisely the people for whom the Globe caters. The Globe's company only escaped from this typecasting by location when they bought the Blackfriars theatre two years later.

6.2.3.3 NINETEENTH CENTURY

In 1829 a play opened at the Surrey theatre, on 'Surrey-side', south of the Thames, called *Black-Ey'd Susan*. Its hero, William, is a naval rating; he is almost executed for striking down his captain, who tried to assault William's fiancée, Susan. Very many of the audience at the theatre would have been employed on and around the river; it was among these people too that the naval press-gangs operated, forcibly abducting men to serve on ships (an activity depicted in another Surrey play, *My Poll and my Partner Joe*: 1835). The play's division of sympathy between ratings and officers tends to reflect the majority class position of its audience. If well-dressed middle-class people went to this theatre they had to sit in seats stained by workers' clothes. Nearly 40 years later, in a theatre north of the river, it is the officer (this time in the army) who is the hero of *Caste* (1867). Of the two working-class men in the play, the skilled one, Sam Gerridge, is viewed with patronising affection as he dreams of setting up his shop for sale of gas and plumbing appliances; the other, Eccles, is unskilled, drunken, greedy, and is sent off at the end, with the full approval of the audience, to drink himself to death. The stage on which this is enacted is that of the flagship middle-class theatre newly established by Marie Wilton with her partner Squire Bancroft; they had bought a rough venue nicknamed 'The Dust Hole' (in Tottenham Street, in the West End) and transformed it into a smart theatre which they called 'The Prince of Wales'. Here the furnishings implied what the fictional narratives also stated, that the middle class could watch in secure comfort.

6.3 Performers

Marie Wilton and Squire Bancroft were able to make their innovations in the theatre because they had economic power: they were not just performers, they were also managers, employers rather than employees. This gave them an economic status similar to the audiences they wanted to attract. Over a century later, in England it is accepted practice that some leading performers are rewarded by knighthoods, while many go to Hollywood to develop the superstar lifestyles which feature in the popular press as examples of elegant living. In Shakespeare's time, by contrast, actors were defined in law as 'masterless men', people with the same status as vagabonds. This is one reason why the actors sought respectability and protection for themselves by obtaining patronage from high-ranking aristocrats.

The Elizabethan state felt that it needed to keep a close check on, to licence in advance, the plays that actors were intending to perform. For it suspected that these masterless men were liable to make performances which were subversive, critical of the masters. But as some of these actors gained a reputation for their work, they were invited to perform at the royal court – where what was seen to be on display was artistry rather than subversion. So it seems that expectations about, and response to, the performed play depend to some extent on what is assumed about the status of the performers – in relation to the rest of society, to other actors, to their art. Once again, we shall find that these considerations lead us back to our responses to the written text.

6.3.1 *Performers and society*

To define performers as vagabonds is to imply that they have no fixed place in society, that they are outsiders. To give them knighthoods is to recognise that they belong among the élite circles of those who more or less own society.

6.3.1.1 LAWYERS

While throughout theatre history there are examples of successful people who buy into the upper class – usually by acquiring a country house and an art collection – it is the economic arrangements of the profession in general that affect how people perceive the status of performers. Indeed, to call it a 'profession' is a sign of a modern attitude: the professionalisation of acting happened alongside the expansion of other middle-class professions (most notably the civil service) in the later nineteenth century (as depicted in Pinero's play *Trelawny of the 'Wells'*: 1898). The Royal Academy of Dramatic Art was founded in the early twentieth century, and thereafter acting schools became a recognised route to the stage, a specialised training similar to (if more trivial than) that followed by lawyers, financiers or even doctors.

6.3.1.2 PROSTITUTES

Prior to this date, the profession most commonly associated with acting was prostitution. From the late seventeenth through to the early nineteenth century there are stories (true and false) of actresses who also worked as prostitutes. Seen in this light, acting's social place amounts to illicit or improper work, part of the 'hidden' economy, catering for the baser cravings to which undisciplined people succumb. Now a lot more could be written about the social place of acting, but we need to confine our attention to the impact it has on the written texts of plays – on both the status of the play as art, and its assumed influence on audiences. A play performed by people similar to lawyers may be treated rather differently from a play performed by people similar to prostitutes. The former may be seen as contributing to serious public discussion – alongside parliamentary speeches, newspaper editorials and scholarly essays – of issues affecting society. That is certainly how the new professionals of theatre in the 1880s wanted plays to be considered. A student with this in mind will be on the look-out for the devices that emphasise the shape of *argument* in the text. By contrast, the 'prostitutes' play is part of the leisure activity of society, an entertainment for public figures who are off-duty. It is seen as a threat to proper work (taking Elizabethan apprentices away from their workshops) and a part of the idle life of the decadent rich (the playground of Restoration fops). More importantly, where acting is like prostitution, a play could be said to have the effect of stimulating the sensual desires of its audience, a form of seduction. Elizabethan opponents of acting said that plays made their audiences undisciplined, sexually aroused, unmanly. If this is your view of how plays work, you will be attentive to the seductive devices in the text. And certainly, some awareness of this issue can help to explain why so many Renaissance plays want to explore the audience–performance relationship in their plays-within-plays.

6.3.1.3 OUTSIDERS

The original Renaissance definition of actors as vagabonds suggests something other than prostitution. It suggests that the professional actors don't really have a place, even an illicit one, within society, but that they are outsiders. What lies behind this notion is the touring troupe – the *commedia dell'arte* clowns, the mummers, minstrels and acrobats, who went from one settlement to another. They worked on village greens, in town market-places, in the halls of great houses, always moving on after each show. Although they may carry their staging with them, they are performing on someone else's territory. For the population of a village, the arrival of the players meant a temporary break with the usual daily routine, and, since it was being done by those who had no fixed social place, for the duration of the performance one was outside of all normal social institutions. This feeling about the performance was strengthened when the routines of clowns deliberately broke with social and sexual taboos and made disorderly topsy-turvy a great deal more fun than orderly propriety. The arrival of the performing outsiders allowed those things which you might only jest about to be actually enacted in public.

Very few scripts as such come down to us from medieval and Renaissance travelling troupes. But there are many more scripts from the actors who toured between the early 1930s and the mid-1980s. If you are reading one of these scripts, you need to bear in mind the image of the outsiders whose performance enables the disallowed to be done in public. The author of the lesbian play *Any Woman Can* (1975), Jill Posener, remembers the excitement of playing to female audiences outside London: 'women would literally come up to us and say "I've never met another one"' (p. 24). The play is structured around autobiographical narratives by its central character. She opens the play by categorising herself as an outsider: 'You are looking at a screaming lesbian' (p. 15), but as the play goes on we get to know and empathise with her through her narratives. The form of the play invites women to identify with the outsider and, in doing so, to find a new sort of community, and power, as outsiders. The effect is to liberate them from being captive inside alien lifestyles.

So if you are studying a script performed by touring players you might be looking out for the ways it invites its audience to become and enjoy being outsiders – by turning normally authoritative figures into cartoons, by telling 'real' stories, by disrupting sober realism for a song, by calling attention to the genuinely 'deviant' identities of the actors. It is these qualities, rather than realistic character development, which are at the heart of the play's significance for its audience.

As an exercise: Find out who first performed the play you are studying. What bearing do you think this had on its performance?

6.3.2 Performers as stars

As we have said above, some performers in every period manage to attain a pre-eminence that apparently puts them in a class of their own. That separateness is often marked concretely by their wealthy lifestyle: the actor becomes a star. Once again, much could be written about stars, but we need to concentrate on the impact that stardom has on a written text.

Many plays are written with a specific company of actors in mind. All Shakespeare's plays were destined to be performed by the acting company in which he was a shareholder: he thus knew, in advance of writing, the physical characteristics and performing styles of the various actors. It is very difficult to establish what direct effects this had on the writing, although it is possible to suggest that his use of clowns was dictated by the talent currently available: Robert Armin did less knockabout than other clowns, so the fool in *Twelfth Night* (1602) is much less slapstick than, say, Launcelot Gobbo in *The Merchant of Venice* (1596/8).

One of the key differences between actors in a company is that each individual may specialise in a particular sort of role. To an extent this is still true today, but it was much more apparent, and necessary, when the same group of performers worked together on a long-term basis. In part this was a way of dividing the labour to ensure that a small group could cope with any new text, but it also allowed for a speedy learning of a new text; in that, say, the woman who specialised in virtuous heroines would know in advance the general range of sentiments and actions that any heroine would express. An audience learns to associate particular actors with particular character types, and a performer becomes popular not for being individualistic or surprising but for conforming to expectations, doing what the audience want to see him or her do. A writer who is preparing a text for a particular star will arrange the action so that it conforms with the expectations about that star: in the Restoration Nell Gwynn and Charles Hart usually represented characters who fell in love with one another, so, whatever the relationship between their characters at the start of the play, by the end the predicted romantic attachment will have emerged (see Dryden's *An Evening's Love* 1668). The writer can go a step further than this, and construct scenes designed explicitly to display the particular skills of the star – for instance, screenplays for Jean-Claude van Damme will incorporate quite a lot of display of muscular body and deft physical action, but very little philosophical soliloquy. The particular shape of a text we are studying may thus derive not just from the specialism, but also from the starring status, of its performers.

To identify a text as a 'star vehicle' is often to imply that it is moved more by commercial interest than artistic integrity. While this may be so, it does not follow that the text is uninteresting or, indeed, lightweight. Much of its shape and pleasure may be explained by the star's presence. The second part of Marlowe's *Tamburlaine the Great* (?1587) looks like a substantial repetition of the formula of the first play, with its hero going from one conquest to another, without much interesting opposition or character development. It was designed for Edward Alleyne, who scored such a hit with the first play. His forte was, as a later writer said, strutting and bellowing – particular forms of physical and vocal organisation that called attention to the quality of movement and sound, the orchestration of muscles and breath patterns, that made the performer's body larger than life, not bound by the conventions and proprieties of daily activity (see 4.2.3.1). To be present at this sort of performance is to be excited by something other than plot or character: for people whose daily lives are spent in fairly routine humdrum activities, Alleyne here – and the same goes for dancers or gymnasts – shows a different way that the human being can occupy space, being centred and powerful rather than just a functionary. To see the star aboard his vehicle is to be thrillingly in the very presence of human potency. This is an aspect of performance which is unique to the medium. Try considering this as one possible explanation for passages of written text that otherwise seem to have little function.

A particular twist on the relationship between star and writing is the case where the writing deliberately subverts expectations about fictional characters which are based on assumptions about the performer. It is now fairly common for film stars to be cast 'against type' – Arnold Schwarzenegger as a comic parent rather than a robotic action hero. But in the film industry this sort of casting can be little more than an attempt to demonstrate the flexibility of the star, and his continued availability for work when robotic action-hero roles have gone out of fashion. By contrast, the casting against type can also work politically, producing a new insight into something that had been taken for granted. When Isabel Mattocks was used for the part of Fiametta in Holcroft's *A Tale of Mystery* (1802) she already had a reputation for playing comically garrulous old women; but in this play Fiametta is the only person who is convinced of the innocence of the hero, a position she maintains even while being put down by her master as a garrulous old woman. Isabel Mattocks' audience this time might realise something about the sexist and ageist assumptions that had inhabited their previous laughter at old women.

As an exercise: Find out if there were star performers in the play you are studying, and then see if this has any impact on the way the play is written.

6.3.3 *What do we think actors do?*

Many modern students of acting assume that the good actor's job is to create a fictional character who is as convincing and life-like as possible – in other words, the actor has to make fiction seem to be non-fiction. This notion governs the actor's attitude to the written text, and the audience's attitude to the performance. But it has not always been like this. As we said above, members of a nineteenth-century company would specialise in stock types – an audience would take pleasure in seeing both the familiar materials and the new elaborations in the role of, say, the elderly mother, much as an audience of jazz or heavy metal like to hear again the already-known, even while enjoying the variants that make it not completely known. There are stories of nineteenth-century audiences protesting when the death of the villain was insufficiently acrobatic; we know he has to die, but the dying has to be a 'turn' – as in the concept of music-hall turn, comic turn – in its own right. Although the written text might look fairly thin at this point, the stage would be full of activity.

Actors who specialise in stock types can supplement or build on a written text because they have their own personal repertoire of routines – the range of gestures, facial and physical attitudes, vocal mannerisms that constitute 'business'. Stage business is activity that does not have the status of action (see Chap. 4); it can nevertheless be deeply pleasurable because of its skill and idiosyncrasy. In many ways the invention of 'business' links back to the *commedia dell'arte* clown's use of *lazzi* (see Rudlin 1994). These are units of activity in which the clown allows herself to be absorbed by the physical logic inherent in particular given circumstances; the clown follows through that logic, in all its potential absurdities, to the extent that it continues to 'work' as a stage event. Thus, say, putting your hat on and suddenly finding that it doesn't fit is a situation from which much perplexedly absorbing activity might follow. *Lazzi* can be very pleasurable to watch, because they stage the human body's precarious relationship to a potentially chaotic world of objects. For performers used to *lazzi*, a written text merely needs to set up the basic elements: for those of us reading such a play, we can only spot the possibilities by being alert to the props in a scene, especially those props that seem to move around. In a theatre where actors are trained to be convincing real people, a dramatist who wants *lazzi* has to script them in considerable detail: the opening act of *Trelawny of the 'Wells'* is wholly given over to a large farewell dinner; the waiter attending at the table finds, early in the act, that he has brought two left gloves by mistake; he starts by trying to get the spare glove onto his right hand, but the glove, deprived of its true place in life, ends up in all sorts of wrong places. Also, of course, we could look at the careful scripting of clown double-act business in *Waiting for Godot* (1955).

> As an example: See if you can identify any opportunities scripted for business or *lazzi* in the text you are studying. How do they work?

6.3.4 Examples

6.3.4.1 MEDIEVAL

The performers of the Corpus Christi plays in York were not professional actors. They were members of craft guilds (manufacturers of nails, grocers, paint-makers, etc.). Each guild took responsibility for a particular play in the series. The performance of the play became an 'advertisement' for the guild – not only in the sense that it was appropriate that the water-drawers did the play of Noah and the Flood, but also in that the guild's wealth could be displayed, as the York mercers did in the elaborate decorations and machinery of the Last Judgement. The players, as guild members, were known individuals in the community. This sense of communal familiarity is supported by the everyday contemporary language and anachronistic social references of the plays. Within this context of the 'communal', the religion is the more strongly emphasised, because in their serious performing of holiness the familiar figures seem to be at an unfamiliar distance from their audience, removed by their religious absorption to a higher level of spiritual specialness. Thus the amateur performers of the plays create a double image whereby the community plays to itself and at the same time enacts its capacity to be a sacred body.

By contrast, the mummers in the manor house make a virtue of apparently breaking in from the 'outside', entering through the hall, pushing past people, and taking payment for their show midway through it. In a house owned by someone else, they create topsy-turvy. These performers, not guild members but travelling players, are of unfixed social place: the professionals do a show that depends on 'shape'-changing, doubling of roles. The most virtuous figure in *Mankind* (*c*.1470), Mercy, and the devil, Titivillus, were probably doubled by the same actor. This is not the double image of the Corpus Christi plays, but is instead a tricksy effect that implies, but never states, the blurring of moral distinctions between good and evil.

6.3.4.2 RENAISSANCE

The leading actors in *King Lear* were shareholders in their company; *Knight of the Burning Pestle* was performed entirely by boys, who were all employees. In the eyes of the fashionable hall theatre, what was wrong with audiences at the open-air theatres was that they allowed themselves to be imaginatively carried away by the illusion. A major effect of having boys perform is that all the spectacular grandeur – the sheer size – becomes literally impossible; it can be quoted, but in doing so they bring it, so to speak, down to size. So a primary effect of the boys' play is that the theatre displays itself as satiric vehicle – that is its social function.

By contrast, in *King Lear* the audience is offered, and drawn into, a serious and coherent fictional world. The actor who took the lead role, Richard

Burbage, was famous for 'becoming' his parts; he made difficult what the boys' theatre made easy, the audience's ability to separate actor from role. This assisted in creating the sense of fictional world. So, too, in rendering the fool difficult and then removing him, the text denies the audience access to a commentary figure who is an intermediary between real world and play world. In making it possible for the audience not only to take seriously but to empathise with the fictional world, the actors of *Lear* absorb and reverse one of the major criticisms of acting. Their story of an old man who becomes physically embarrassing, who goes mad and in his madness sees visions of copulation, is one that might reinforce the contemporary connections between performance and irrational, unmanning sensuality. But for the audience of *Lear*, the play's ability to deal with these issues is testimony to the power and importance of drama.

6.3.4.3 NINETEENTH CENTURY

The text of *Black-Ey'd Susan* turned its leading performer into a household name. William the sailor was played by T. P. Cooke, who thereafter specialised in nautical parts. The written script is organised into units that display Cooke's skills: there are moments of dexterous physical combat, storytelling, pathos; the handsome actor was presented as a combination of physical vigour and emotional softness. William's scenes are perhaps better thought of as collections of 'turns' – display pieces for Cooke – as much as developments of the plot. Thus his first entry is with a band of sailors, arriving joyfully to find nobody there to meet them; when the women turn up, William thinks he can see Susan, but she isn't there; when news is brought of Susan the conversation alternates between reassurances and bad news. Increasingly fast emotional reversals are called for. In the next scene William moves from a tearful reunion with Susan into a fight with smugglers into a verbal attack on Susan's villainous uncle. The mode of performance changes in relation to the character(s) addressed. Part of the pleasure in the display pieces, the turns, comes from the rapid transitions between them.

> As an exercise: Try to find out which stars performed the play you are studying, and what they were famous for. Do you see opportunities scripted for their star display?

6.4 Audiences

Through our account of playwrights, locations and performers we have continually made reference to audiences. We have, for example, talked about Restoration playwrights as part of a distinct social élite, about working-class spectators at the Surrey theatre, about the citizens of York and their religious plays. Each time we are suggesting that the audience approaches the performance with perceptions in their heads about their relationship to writers, to the location of the performance and to the performers. These perceptions form the basis, often unconsciously, of how the audience understand the play and the significances they attach to it. All this we have already suggested through our series of examples.

6.4.1 *The audience's view of itself*

What we have not looked at is the audience's perception of itself. This might seem to be as remote as we can possibly get from the study of the written text, and certainly texts don't appear to tell you anything about this. Nevertheless texts are written with an understanding as much about audiences as about performance locations. The audience in the streets of York for the Corpus Christi plays knew that these were special festive occasions during which all normal business was suspended. Furthermore they knew that these were *their* plays, done by members of guilds which had a particular place within the hierarchy and government of the town. When a modern student of these plays is invited to consider the links between them, it can seem like a rather abstract literary exercise. If you were a medieval citizen of York these plays would link up not only because the Bible story is a coherent whole, but because the plays themselves are a sort of metaphor for the wholeness of the town as a community. Through celebrating Corpus Christi, the body of Christ, the town celebrates its own civic body.

By contrast, the activity of going to a fashionable theatre such as the Blackfriars in 1607, or either of the Restoration London theatres, was a way of displaying your membership of a wealthy élite. You went to the theatre as much to be seen as to see. Part of the performance of being seen is to demonstrate not only your acquaintance with important members of the audience, but also your wit and cultural expertise. A student of *Knight of the Burning Pestle* may spend a lot of their time wading through footnotes which identify sources of parody and double meanings. The Renaissance wit would find the parody and puns a delightful opportunity to show off his ability to spot references and pick up allusions. This is especially enjoyable because this play supplies a fictional onstage audience who don't really understand all of what is going on – they are culturally incompetent, and they are of the wrong social class. The fashionable audience's laughter – their display of their own *cultural competence* – is a weapon in a battle between social classes.

Within the general heading of the audience's perception of itself we have encountered two different elements: *the occasion of watching* and *awareness of social difference*.

6.4.2 *The occasion of watching*

The occasion of the medieval Corpus Christi plays was important, since it happened once a year; the Renaissance Blackfriars theatre was open throughout the season, but it was socially different from other theatres. The *occasion of watching* can be more or less strongly marked: an annual festivity is strongly marked, an office outing much less so; going to see a play as an alternative to going to a film or restaurant is barely marked as significant. The written text can help to promote a sense of occasion, creating opportunities for solemnity or celebration, but it cannot, in general, invent the occasion (though there have been experiments, most famously by Jerzy Grotowski, where the text is worked on in such a way as to furnish a sense of special occasion, with a special venue and highly restricted audience numbers).

As an exercise: Discover what was the original occasion of watching for the play you are studying.

6.4.3 *Awareness of social difference*

This again may be more or less strongly marked. Least strong is that of the audience for a television play who, sitting in their own home, are in totally familiar territory with no strangers present. More marked is the awareness of an audience at a 'popular' show – a West End musical, a well-known stand-up comic – since, though they may be a pretty mixed range of people, they are all out for a good time, they are people who like entertainment. The strongest awareness of social difference is that of people who know themselves to be a distinct social grouping before they ever enter the theatre – the Restoration wits, the political activists, the lesbian audience. The written text of a play can promote, indeed create, this awareness much more effectively than in the case of promoting occasion.

As an exercise: Is the play you are studying written to be watched by a specific or similar audience? Describe it.

6.4.3.1 DECLARING AN INTEREST

The promotion of this awareness by the audience of its own specialness can take three main forms in the written text. First, the play may announce that it is coming from a particular position, *declaring an interest*, rather than assuming it speaks from a position of disinterested objectivity. It may declare itself, for instance, as a gay play (or a play with gay performers). When watched by a gay audience, there is a sense of common language being spoken between stage and spectators. This has the effect of making an otherwise fairly disparate collection of people, who just happen to be gay, feel unified through a shared common quality, their sexuality (see Freeman 1996; Lucas 1994). In the case of political plays, which unite an audience in mockery of political targets, this is often dismissively referred to as 'preaching to the converted'. What is actually going on is that the 'converted' are being brought to an awareness of themselves as a coherent group, distinguished by the fact of their being converts to the cause. This awareness is produced during *The Cheviot, the Stag and the Black, Black Oil* (1973), a play concerned with English exploitation of the Scottish highlands and toured to Scottish villages by the 7:84 theatre company. The play is structured on the model of a Highland entertainment, the ceilidh, and at points the characters speak in Gaelic; the oppressors only ever talk English. When Doli sings in Gaelic the *'company and audience join in the chorus'* (p. 9): at this point someone who knew no Gaelic would be unable to join in, and those who do decide to join in are consciously using the language which the play sets in opposition to Englishness and oppression. It is through this awareness of themselves as a coherent group, their solidarity, that an audience gains strength to pursue their cause. In this way the play does its political work.

> As an exercise: Look at the play you are studying/reading to see whether it declares an interest. See what you can find out about its original performers and audience: do these correspond with the declared interest?

6.4.3.2 CREATING UNITY

Second, the play may indeed be assuming that it addresses a mixed audience, the 'unconverted'. The work that the text then does is to make the audience feel unity by sharing responses. This can be done in two ways: first, by producing an object for which everyone can feel a similar affection or hatred – as in the case of the aristocratic villain in a melodrama, or the boasting Herod in a medieval mystery play (or, in what might be described as a 'national drama', the experience of unity in response to the death of Princess Diana in 1997). Second, there is the use of humour to establish a shared sense of 'us' (who are normal and reasonable) against a strange outsider: thus when the Prince of Morocco arrives as a suitor to Portia in *The Merchant of Venice* he is felt to be inappropriate for her, and so strongly shared is this sense that few people quibble with the overt racism of Portia's remark about his 'complexion' (2.7.79). A slightly different case is that of

Kent's apparently unprovoked attack on Oswald in *King Lear* (2.2): in siding with Kent, we take up the position of the yeoman who assumes that courtiers are always the enemy.

As an exercise: Look at the jokes and points of assumed sympathy or dislike in the play you are studying; how do the jokes or sympathy/dislike work? Who are the outsiders? What positions are laughed at or sympathised with?

6.4.3.3 . . . AND DISUNITY

Often an audience will assume they are among people like themselves, that there is a basic sense of 'togetherness'. Some performers and plays aim to split up this feeling of unity. Many of us have seen the comedian who makes fun of latecomers or who picks on a group of people in the stalls. This splitting apart of an audience can, however, have political effect. Act 2 of Trevor Griffiths' play *Comedians* (1975) is set in a working-men's club, which uses the real audience as the club audience. Three of the turns shape their material to try to please a talent scout, and they start to tell sexist and racist jokes. Much of the play so far has been concerned with the 'politics' of humour. As the jokes continue, some in the real audience stop laughing at what they consider offensive material, while others continue to laugh. At this moment the real political differences in the audience have been brought to the surface.

6.4.3.4 CULTURAL COMPETENCE

Third, at a very basic level, and often without trying to make any points about unity, the play assumes a certain amount of shared knowledge on the part of the audience. We referred above to 'cultural competence' in the audience. This competence takes the form of recognising references, allusions, artistic shapes, familiar plot-lines. When the mechanicals are rehearsing their play in *A Midsummer Night's Dream*, they get into difficulty because they are not sure how to represent a lion without frightening the ladies in the audience. The real audience finds this funny because they know that theatre audiences realise that plays are pretend rather than real. In making their mistake about the rules of watching and performing drama, the mechanicals show themselves to be culturally incompetent. This incompetence is represented by Puck as a sort of ignorance of one's surroundings: 'What hempen homespuns have we swaggering here/So near the cradle of the Fairy Queen?' (3.1.70–71).

Unlike the mechanicals, many readers of this book are fairly competent in cultural terms. If the lines above were quoted out of any context and you were asked about the author, you might suggest Shakespeare (or at least say it was from that period): the language is not modern English, it is shaped into short rhythmic lines – we know in general that Shakespeare wrote plays in verse. We could probably go further, if asked, and suggest that this is taken from one of the comedies – you don't get fairy queens in tragedy. And, if asked what the plot might involve, you might suggest magic, romance and happy endings – things associated with fairies. Finally, it could be that you can guess at the play itself, since *A Midsummer Night's Dream* is commonly known as the Shakespeare play with fairies in it.

6.4.4 Genre

In spotting that this is poetry, comedy and romance you are recognising certain familiar features. In making that recognition you are identifying *genre*: it is poetry not prose, comedy not tragedy. Genre is a word of Latin origin meaning 'kind' – as in grouping, family, species, that kind of thing. To put a work of art into a genre is often a short-hand way of suggesting what its content is: thus in a guide to films on television you will find them categorised as, say, 'thriller', 'comedy', 'horror'. Although the viewer may well not have seen the particular film before, they will know what sort of characterisation, language and setting to expect once they know it is said to be a thriller. In the case of Puck's lines here, you know that they have to be from a comedy because tragedies have rules and shapes that make them distinct from comedies (they don't have fairy queens). In recognising the kind of thing it is, the genre, you make assumptions about how it will work and how it is to be watched, you have expectations about its content.

In the case of the guide to television films mentioned above, someone else gives the films their genre label. Quite a lot of commentary about different sorts of artwork depends on the process of putting individual works into categories; it is a process that helps to describe, explain or even evaluate the individual work, and it operates by referring individual works to a general type. While this can be seen as an academic imposition, it is also the case that some artworks deliberately advertise their genre category – a television programme might do it through its opening credits or its theme music (and, at a time of increased channel-hopping, it will set itself up very fast); a play might open with a particular sort of image, as for example a man standing with a skull while courtiers process across the stage, which is the opening to the aptly named *Revenger's Tragedy* (1606). Many artworks declare their genre because audiences derive pleasure from being able to recognise familiar features and from having their expectations fulfilled (see 5.1.2). Frequently people's experience of real life is that events happen unpredictably, without reason or rule, in a bewildering fashion. Watching a play or film that, for all its twists and turns, follows a basic predicted pattern feels, by contrast, reassuring. Going to see something in a familiar genre, or indeed seeing the same thing twice, is a way of experiencing a world in which what is expected to happen does happen, where you can be given what you desire.

> As an exercise: Look at the opening of the play you are studying: how does its title and opening image suggest its genre? How does it sustain or return to the basic structure of its genre? What expectations does the opening set up for you? How are those expectations satisfied?

Some plays aim to deny the audience the pleasure of having their expectations fulfilled: they are plays which might wish to challenge assumptions about people and values, so a genre category might be suggested, and then deviated from. So, in Shakespeare's *Twelfth Night*, we expect that a situation in which a woman in disguise as a man loves a man who loves a different woman (who in turn loves the disguised woman) will be resolved as soon as the twin brother of the disguised woman appears – the men and women will all pair off in mixed-sex couples in a final, happy last scene. But Shakespeare has not given the twins the same qualities: the brother is much more violent; and the ending has several threads left hanging loose – the brother is loved by a male companion who is then abandoned, the disguised woman never appears in women's clothes, and the happy pairing-up is interrupted by an angry Malvolio who threatens to be revenged on all of them in the future. So our expectations about what makes proper pairing-up, and how it solves problems, are unsettled.

> As an exercise: Does the play you are studying set up genre expectations and then thwart them? How does this process happen? What values are being questioned?

6.5 Interpretation

In looking at genre and its possible pleasures for an audience, we said that a play often needs to be *predictable*, at some basic level, for an audience to feel happy with it. Even where they are not always happy, this predictability is something which is *managed* by the play: it draws on an audience's cultural competence, offers them things they can recognise, and know, and feel secure with – and then makes surprising changes. This assertion of ours implies that predictability and surprise depend on one another for effect: the surprise is shocking because an audience has been led to expect something different, the renewed sense of security is the more profound because the familiar shape is rediscovered after it has been distorted. The surprise of Malvolio's final entry gains from its contrast with the signs of a predictable happy end. So, too, at the end of the movie *Carrie* (1976) the feeling of finality attached to a graveyard is challenged by the sudden appearance of a hand.

6.5.1 *Value judgements*

In discussions of drama, you can most often hear the word 'predictable' used as a value-judgement: 'predictable' drama is bad, surprising is good. This use of these words tends to ignore the fact that they depend on one another for effect in the way we suggest above. It may be that we have to look again at the language we use for assessing plays. For we use a series of opposed terms in the same way as we use 'predictable'/surprising: for example, caricature/character; flat/round; exaggerated or melodramatic or over-the-top or overacted/realistic; entertaining or escapist/serious. Do these pairs have a similar connection between the apparently opposed terms?

On the matter of caricature *vs.* character, we can note that Hamlet seems to have more inner depth when put alongside Claudius as a *type* of villain; we get engaged with Serjeant Musgrave's complicated inner turmoil because it feels more real – despite its wordiness – than the cartoon figures of civic dignitaries. By making Claudius and civic dignitaries into types (see 2.4.1.3) or cartoons, we attend to them as representatives of positions within a power structure rather than as free-floating individuals. The contrast of caricature and character is, again, *managed* by the text to produce both sense of depth and understanding of structural positions. The same might be said of the relationship between flat and round.

If we take exaggerated etc./realistic, we can again see a relationship of mutual dependence. The mechanicals' play at the end of *Midsummer Night's Dream* is comical because the acting is too large, the verse too simple, and the courtly audience mocks it. But most real audiences find the courtiers' wit too obscure to be amusing, and they come across as snobs, alongside whom the mechanicals are fun. The contrast is not only managed, but it often works to produce enjoyment of the exaggeration rather than the sober realism. In a play called *The Workhouse Donkey* (1963) John Arden made a political point out of the contrast between exaggeration and realism. In the final scene an art gallery is being opened by civic officials and politicians; a commotion is caused by rioters outside; during the commotion a disgraced councillor enters, sits on the table with the buffet on it, pulls down a paper chain to put round his neck and puts the decorative flowers on his head; he then delivers a speech which is based on the Book of Psalms. This presentation alludes to a model of theatre as carnival, as excess; it contrasts with the sober, and hypocritical, realism of the town politicians.

A value judgement that prefers realism to exaggeration is here shown to be one that not only supports hypocrisy, but that makes a political alignment: the sober, and realist, dignitaries want to get rid of their disgraced but theatrical colleague. At this point the audience, or the reader, of Arden's play comes to realise that their value judgement has consequences. These consequences have bearing not just on politics, but on the work of theatre: should theatre involve mess and anarchy, or should it restrict itself to tidy and clear meanings?

6.5.2 *Learning not to ask what it means*

This question is unresolved by *The Workhouse Donkey*, deliberately. The job of work done by the play is to disturb the audience's sense of easy definitions and clear separations. To try to fix its 'meaning' – to pinpoint in a couple of phrases what the play is saying – is to force the play to become much more simplistic than it is. The strength of *Workhouse Donkey* is precisely that it refuses to allow itself to be pushed around by the question 'What does the play *mean*?' Instead it forces us to ask a different question, which we can phrase in different ways: What does the play start us quarrelling about? What scheme of values does it disturb? What does it set up for debate? So, far from the play yielding up a clear-cut single meaning, it asks *us* questions. Where do we stand with regard to mess and tidiness, carnival and sobriety, exaggeration and realism?

This point about *Workhouse Donkey* could be made about all plays. Not all plays want to start a fierce quarrel, but most of them refuse to allow themselves to be pinned down to simple singular meanings. If their authors wanted to write such things as this they would have been newspaper editors and journalists, not playwrights. Consequently, we make life hard for ourselves by approaching plays the wrong way. If you come to a play requiring that it tells you what it means, in a neat and tidy way, you will be frustrated and disappointed. It won't ever quite fit; there will be bits you can't account for.

6.5.3 *Two simple, and better, questions*

The most useful way to begin your approach to a play is to ask the simple question: 'What have we got here?' 'What is this object like?' This will lead you into a description of the sort of thing it is. That description will, we hope, be more easily done using some of the language and approaches which we have introduced to you in this book. Don't try at this point to interpret it, to fix on a coherent meaning – just describe, as accurately as you can.

Once we have described what is in front of us, we can then ask the second question: 'How does this thing work?' Again we have tried to offer you some examples for thinking about how the activities of the stage are making their effect, how the audience are being placed with regard to the performed material.

6.5.4 Producing culture

To ask how something works is to assume that it does something, that it works *on* something. Plays work on their audience – or, to put it more precisely, they work on what is in the audience's heads, on their values, assumptions, beliefs, desires. They sustain these values and they challenge them, they make themselves seductive and they ask questions. In this sense plays are not only made within a specific culture (in the ways we have outlined in this chapter) but they also help to shape, to sustain and transform, that culture.

Let us recall where we started. The playtext *produces* the performance, in the sense that it scripts it. Most of this book has tried to show how that scripting is done. At the same time we have also tried to show how the performance sets up reactions in, uses and challenges the assumptions of, the audience. The performance produces a response in the audience, in the sense that it sets ideas and feelings in play. We are talking here about something bigger than a message from a writer to an audience. The script derives from, and interacts with, shapes, ideas and values in the culture around it. The performance is shaped by, and stretches, the various elements that bring it into being. Once script and performance come into existence they become part of the cultural resource on which new productions will draw, against which they will react: they help create the conditions in which the next plays will be able to imagine themselves. Once we understand how plays work, both on the page and then on the stage itself, we can think powerfully about drama as a part of cultural production – and then, of course, we can make powerful cultural productions of our own.

Glossary

This glossary defines words and phrases that we guess may be unfamiliar but are not explained in the main body of the text. We also elaborate on a few words and phrases already defined. But do get used to working with dictionaries, including specialist theatre dictionaries such as Hartnoll 1972.

apostrophe passage of text or speech addressing an absent person (or idea).

articulate give shape to an idea, *form* it as utterance, see 2.5.

binary system of two linked terms, usually in opposition: e.g. hot/cold, good/bad.

bourgeois middle class (from the French); in English, a 'burgher' is a town dweller. The middle class was first formed in towns.

box-set stage-set depicting the inside of a room, usually constructed with flats, where the audience looks through an invisible 'fourth wall'.

canonical a 'canon' of texts consists of those texts deemed by authoritative (and institutional) opinion to be important.

crescendo musical term taken from the Italian, meaning a build-up or steady increase of loudness. Note that, despite its common incorrect usage, it does not simply mean 'loud' – something ending with a *crescendo* ends with a build-up.

cultural formation particular and significant shape that a culture takes for a period of time, later to be succeeded by a fresh formation. Involves the relationships between classes and other groupings, their institutions and the dominant ideas. Sometimes also used to mean a formation *within* a culture.

dénouement moment of untangling of plot, unravelling of mystery.

dramaturgy practice of writing plays. A 'dramaturg' is someone who advises directors and others on the stage interpretation of the dramatic text.

economy system of significant differences. That it matters whether we call people by their forenames, surnames or titles according to who they are and when we do it means that there is an economy of naming to be borne in mind.

eponymous having the same name. Hamlet is the eponymous hero of *Hamlet*.

existential concerning the sheer fact of existence.

focal economy way that different points of focus work in relation to one another, and that focus differs from non-focus. See *economy*.

folio sheet of paper. Renaissance 'folio' editions, such as the posthumous First Folio of Shakespeare which collected all his plays, were large-format, printed on unfolded sheets. *Quarto* editions of single plays – often published just after first performances – are printed on sheets folded twice, making the pages one-quarter size.

gestic performance employing 'gestus'; see 4.2.3.2.

humanist originally a mode of thinking that was alternative to 'religious', then a notion of history as human self-development, and now implying a mistaken belief in humans as being separate from the forces (economic, social) of history.

humours according to medieval medicine, the four principal bodily fluids – blood, phlegm, choler and melancholy – whose relative proportions determined a person's physical and mental temperament. Hence e.g. 'phlegmatic', 'choleric'. A 'comedy of humours' organises its characters according to these biologically based predispositions.

kinaesthetic sympathetically feeling movement. Usually also implies a bodily reaction: the clown slips on the banana skin; our stomachs turn.

limelight introduced around 1816, lime gave a bright white light, much favoured for spotlighting individual actors.

mediating relating together two apparently unconnected kinds of activity or thinking in such a way that the interaction alters them. A chorus mediates between the dissimilar activities of performing and spectating. Good writing about a work of art and social relationships will understand each in relation to the other.

monological having a single meaning.

morality play late fifteenth-, early sixteenth-century drama of moral instruction, employing personified abstractions.

Neoclassical pertaining to a European-wide intellectual and artistic movement most apparent in the mid- to late eighteenth century. Its adherents studied and imitated Classical antiquity as a means to discovering and expressing the eternal truths of life. Their aesthetic values had ethical overtones, aspiring to purity, nobility, rationality.

parabolic in the form of a parable, like Aesop's fables or Christ's parables recounted in the Bible. Parables are not meant to be taken literally. They abstract general principles from life and their stories and situations are meant to be understood as if in 'inverted commas'.

pastoral tradition of writing and art depicting country life which is often idealised, idyllic; it becomes the ornamental play-acting of courtly society, but it also develops towards more realistic comment on agrarian problems.

proscenium (**arch, stage, theatre**) the space in front of the Greek *skena*, or scene, is the pro-skena. It meant an acting area. Nowadays it has come to refer to the architectural partition which designates the outer limit of this territory: the proscenium wall separates the auditorium from the acting area. This wall is penetrated by a great hole (to allow the audience to watch the action); the action goes on underneath, and behind, the proscenium arch. A proscenium theatre has this architectural arrangement built into it.

protagonist see 4.1.21: Greek *proto* (first) *agonistes* (actor/combatant); nowadays used of the leading character.

reception understanding of a text in reading or performance; the reader/spectator *constructs* the significant shapes and meanings of the text in the act of reading or spectating.

reciprocal two-way.

referent actual thing a sign (such as a word and its concept) refers to. 'Fire' makes us think of fires in general. 'Light the fire' sends you to an actual fire.

rhetorical of rhetoric, or the art of persuasion, especially at first by the organisation and ornamentation of language. A rhetorical effect is not merely eloquence, but a carefully constructed device intended to influence the receiver. Thus, simplicity also can be persuasive. We might, for instance, be persuaded that what we are being told is true – by a 'rhetorical guarantee'.

semiotics study of signs. *Semiology* assumes that this study can be a science.

signifier, signified a 'sign' consists of two elements: a word or visual image (a red traffic light) and a concept (stop: danger). Without the concept the traffic light is a metal pole with a red light on it: the signifier and signified have an arbitrary relationship, but they also depend on each other to make the sign. Performance depends substantially on the use of signs: an audience will understand two armchairs and a small table to signify a living room, or an antique shop.

syntax organisation of a sentence, or any unit of language.

stage left/right to the left or right of a person facing the audience from the stage. *Upstage* is towards the back of the stage, since it slopes.

tabs stage curtains.

Town the eighteenth-century concept of the Town implied a social group rather than a place; this group were, largely, the literate and wealthy. The Town had its unspoken rules about taste and standards. 'Town' first referred to the area, now the 'West End', between the palaces and the City of London which was developed after the Restoration.

unities of time, place and action. First formulated and insisted upon by Lodovico Castelvetro in his commentary on Aristotle's *Poetics* (1571) as rules for proper drama. The rules were that the action should take place over 24 hours in the fiction, in a single place, and that there should be a clear and single plot.

Vice stage figure from the moralities (*q.v.*) who combined together several personified abstractions (see 2.7) representing vices. The Vice tempts the hero, may sometimes represent the devil, and typically interacts with the audience. The Vice is attractively – though seriously – wicked.

Bibliography

1 Primary texts

When we refer to a play in the main text of this book, we give the actual or guessed date of first performance. In the rare cases where this was much later than the play was written, we give the date of its completion. In this bibliography, the second date given is of the printed edition of the play we have used. Where possible we have used collected editions. Note that various editions – especially of older plays – often present differing versions of the same play.

Anon. c.1440: *The Castle of Perseverance*. In Happé, P. (ed.), *Four Morality Plays*. Harmondsworth: Penguin Books, 1979.

Anon. 15th century: *Corpus Christi Play (York)*. In Beadle, R. and King, P. (eds), *York Mystery Plays*. Oxford: Clarendon Press, 1984.

Anon. c.1498: *Everyman*. In Cawley, A.C. (ed.), *Everyman and Medieval Miracle Plays*. London: Dent, 1977.

Anon. c.1470: *Mankind*. In Wickham, G. (ed.), *English Moral Interludes*. London: Dent, 1976.

Anon. 1606: *The Revenger's Tragedy*. In Salgado, G. (ed.), *Three Jacobean Tragedies*. Harmondsworth: Penguin Books, 1965.

Anon. c.1590: *The True Chronicle History of King Leir and his Three Daughters*. In Bullough, G. (ed.), *Narrative and Dramatic Sources of Shakespeare*, VII: *Major Tragedies: 'Hamlet', 'Othello', 'King Lear', 'Macbeth'*. London: Routledge & Kegan Paul, 1973.

Arden, John 1959: *Serjeant Musgrave's Dance. An Un-historical Parable*. London: Methuen, 1960.

Arden, John 1963: *The Workhouse Donkey. A Vulgar Melo-Drama*. London: Methuen, 1964.

Beaumont, Francis 1607: *The Knight of the Burning Pestle*. Ed. M. Hattaway. London: Ernest Benn, 1969.

Beckett, Samuel 1958: *Act Without Words*; 1960: *Act Without Words 2*; 1955: *Waiting for Godot. A Tragi-comedy in Two Acts.* In Beckett, S., *The Complete Dramatic Works.* London: Faber & Faber, 1986.

Behan, Brendan 1958: *The Hostage.* In Behan, B., *The Complete Plays*, intr. A. Simpson. London: Methuen, 1978.

Behn, Aphra 1677: *The Rover.* In Behn, A. *The Rover and Other Plays*, ed. J. Spencer. Oxford: Oxford University Press, 1995.

Bolt, Robert 1960: *A Man for All Seasons.* In Maschler, T. (ed.), *New English Dramatists* VI. Harmondsworth: Penguin Books, 1967.

Boucicault, Dion 1860: *The Colleen Bawn.* In Rowell, G. (ed.), *Nineteenth Century Plays.* Oxford: Oxford University Press, 1990.

Brecht, Bertolt 1943: *The Good Person of Setzuan.* In Brecht, B., *The Collected Plays* VI.1, trs. J. Willett. London: Eyre Methuen, 1985.

Brecht, Bertolt 1943: *Life of Galileo.* In Brecht, B., *The Collected Plays* V.1, trs. J. Willett. London: Eyre Methuen, 1980.

Brecht, Bertolt 1926: *Man Equals Man.* In Brecht, B., *The Collected Plays* II.1, trs. G. Nellhaus. London: Eyre Methuen, 1979.

Brecht, Bertolt 1932: *The Mother.* Trs. Baxandall, L. New York: Grove Press, 1965.

Brenton, Howard 1974: *The Churchill Play: As it will be performed in the winter of 1984 by the internees of Churchill Camp somewhere in England.* London: Eyre Methuen, 1974.

Carrie. 1976: dir. Brian de Palma. United Artists/Red Bank.

Chekhov, Anton 1903: *The Cherry Orchard. A Comedy in Four Acts*; 1901: *Three Sisters. A Drama in Four Acts.* In Chekhov, A., *Plays*, trs. E. Fen. Harmondsworth: Penguin Books, 1959.

Churchill, Caryl 1983: *Fen*; 1982: *Top Girls.* In Churchill, C., *Plays: 2.* London: Methuen Drama, 1990.

Cowley, Hannah 1788: *The Fate of Sparta; or, The Rival Kings. A Tragedy.* London: G. G. J. and J. Robinson.

Dryden, John 1668: *An Evening's Love.* In Dryden, J., *Works* X. Berkeley: University of California Press, 1970.

Dumas, Alexandre *fils* 1852: *La dame aux camélias* [*Camille*]. In Stanton, S. S. (ed.), *Camille and Other Plays.* New York: Hill & Wang, 1957.

Etherege, George 1676: *The Man of Mode or, Sir Fopling Flutter. A Comedy.* In Gosse, E. (ed.), *Restoration Plays.* London: Dent, 1974.

Frisch, Max 1958: *The Fire Raisers. A Morality without a moral, with an afterpiece.* Trs. M. Bullock. London: Eyre Methuen, 1962.

Fugard, A. 1982: *'Master Harold'* . . . *and the Boys.* Oxford: Oxford University Press, 1983.

Galsworthy, John 1910: *Justice: A Tragedy.* In Galsworthy, J., *The Plays.* London: Duckworth, 1929.

García Lorca, Federico 1933: *Blood Wedding. Tragedy in Three Acts and Seven Scenes.* In García Lorca, F., *Plays: One*, intr. G. Edwards. London: Methuen, 1987.

Greig, Noël 1983: *Poppies*. London: Gay Men's Press.

Griffiths, Trevor 1975: *Comedians*. London: Faber & Faber.

Haines, J.T. 1835: *My Poll and My Partner Joe*. In Booth, M. (ed.), *Hiss the Villain: Six English and American Melodramas*. London: Eyre & Spottiswoode, 1964.

Hazlewood, Colin 1863: *Lady Audley's Secret*. In Rowell, G. (ed.), *Nineteenth Century Plays*. Oxford: Oxford University Press, 1990.

Hodge, Herbert 1937: *Cannibal Carnival*. (sc. iv and v plus synopsis). In Osborne, E. A. (ed.), *In Letters of Red*. London: Michael Joseph.

Holcroft, Thomas 1802: *A Tale of Mystery*. London: R. Phillips.

Ibsen, Henrik 1879: *A Doll's House*. In Ibsen, H., *Plays: Two*, trs. M. Meyer. London: Eyre Methuen, 1980.

Ibsen, Henrik 1882: *Ghosts*; 1885: *The Wild Duck*. In Ibsen, H., *Plays: One*, trs. M. Meyer. London: Eyre Methuen, 1980.

Ibsen, Henrik 1876: *Peer Gynt* [written 1867]. In Ibsen, H., *Plays: Six*, trs. M. Meyer. London: Eyre Methuen, 1987.

Ibsen, Henrik 1877: *The Pillars of Society*. In Ibsen, H., *Plays: Four*, trs. M. Meyer. London: Eyre Methuen, 1991.

Jerrold, Douglas 1829: *Black-Ey'd Susan or, 'All in the Downs'. A Nautical Drama*. In Rowell, G. (ed.), *Nineteenth Century Plays*. Oxford: Oxford University Press, 1990.

Jonson, Ben 1606: *Volpone, or the Fox*. In Jonson, B., *Three Comedies*, ed. M. Jamieson. Harmondsworth: Penguin Books, 1966.

Kipphardt, Heinar 1966: *In the Matter of J. Robert Oppenheimer*. Trs. R. Speirs. London: Methuen, 1967.

Kyd, Thomas *c*.1587: *The Spanish Tragedy*. In McIlwraith, A. K. (ed.), *Five Elizabethan Tragedies*. Oxford: Oxford University Press, 1976.

Lawrence, D. H. 1974: *The Daughter-in-Law. A Play in Four Acts* [written 1912]; *The Widowing of Mrs Holroyd. A Play in Three Acts* [written 1914]. In Lawrence, D. H., *Three Plays*, intr. R. Williams. Harmondsworth: Penguin Books.

Lewis, Leopold 1871: *The Bells*. In Mayer, D., *Henry Irving and the Bells. Irving's Personal Script of the Play*. Manchester: Manchester University Press, 1980. (Also in Rowell 1990, with different text.)

MacColl, Ewan 1945: *Johnny Noble. An Episodic Play with Singing*. In Goorney, H. and MacColl, E. (eds), *Agit-Prop to Theatre Workshop. Political Playscripts 1930–50*. Manchester: Manchester University Press, 1986.

McGrath, John 1973: *The Cheviot, the Stag and the Black, Black Oil*. Isle of Skye: West Highland Publishing Company, 1977.

Marlowe, Christopher *c*.1587: *Tamburlaine the Great: Parts 1 and 2*. In Marlowe, C., *Plays*, ed. J. B. Steane. Harmondsworth: Penguin Books, 1969.

Mason, Libby 1982: *Double Vision*. In Davis, J., *Lesbian Plays*. London: Methuen, 1987.

Middleton, Thomas ?1621: *Women Beware Women*. In Middleton, T., *Three Plays*, ed. K. Muir. London: Dent, 1975.

Miller, Arthur 1949: *Death of a Salesman*. Harmondsworth: Penguin Books, 1973.

Molière 1666: *Le Misanthrope*. Trs. and adapted Bartlett, N., 1988. Bath: Absolute Classics, 1990.

Moraga, Cherríe 1984: *Giving up the Ghost*. Los Angeles: West End Press, 1986.

O'Casey, Sean 1926: *The Plough and the Stars*. In O'Casey, S., *Three Plays*. London: Macmillan, 1977.

Osborne, John 1956: *Look Back in Anger*. London: Faber & Faber, 1976.

Palmer, T. A. 1874: *East Lynne* (adapted from the novel by Mrs Henry Wood). In Scullion, A. (ed.), *Female Playwrights of the Nineteenth Century*. London: Dent, 1996.

Pinero, Arthur W. 1898: *Trelawny of the 'Wells'. A Comedietta in Four Acts*. In Pinero, A. W., *Trelawny of the 'Wells' and Other Plays*, ed. J. S. Bratton. Oxford: Oxford University Press, 1995.

Pinnock, Winsome 1991: *Talking in Tongues*. In Brewster, Y. (intro.), *Black Plays: Three*. London: Methuen, 1995.

Pinter, Harold 1958: *The Birthday Party*; 1960: *The Dumb Waiter*. In Pinter, H., *Plays: One*. London: Eyre Methuen, 1976.

Posener, Jill 1975: *Any Woman Can*. In Davis, J., *Lesbian Plays*. London: Methuen, 1987.

Robertson, Tom 1867: *Caste. An Original Comedy in Three Acts*. In Robertson, T., *Plays*, ed. W. Tydeman. Cambridge: Cambridge University Press, 1982.

Rowe, Nicholas 1703: *The Fair Penitent*. Ed. M. Goldstein. London: Edward Arnold, 1969.

Sartre, Jean-Paul 1942: *The Flies*. Trs. S. Gilbert. Harmondsworth: Penguin Books, 1968.

Sartre, Jean-Paul 1944: *Huis clos [In Camera]*. In Sartre, J.-P., *In Camera and Other Plays*, trs. S. Gilbert. Harmondsworth: Penguin Books, 1989.

Schiller, Friedrich 1800: *Mary Stuart*. In Lamport, F. J. (trs.), *Five German Tragedies*. Harmondsworth: Penguin Books, 1969.

Shakespeare, William 1606/7: *Antony and Cleopatra*; 1608/9: *Cymbeline*; 1601: *Hamlet*; 1597: *1 Henry 4*; 1613: *Henry 8*; c.1599: *Julius Caesar*; 1605/6: *King Lear*; 1606: *Macbeth*; 1596–8: *The Merchant of Venice*; 1594: *A Midsummer Night's Dream*; 1602–4: *Othello*; 1592/3: *Richard 3*; c.1595 *Romeo and Juliet*; 1592: *The Taming of the Shrew*; 1610/11: *The Tempest*; c.1600: *Troilus and Cressida*; 1602: *Twelfth Night*. In Shakespeare, W. *The Complete Works*, ed. P. Alexander. London and Glasgow: Collins, 1974.

Shakespeare, William 1601: *Hamlet*. Ed. G. R. Hibbard. Oxford: Oxford University Press, 1987.

Shakespeare, William 1597: *1 Henry 4*. Ed. D. Bevington. Oxford: Oxford University Press, 1987.

Shakespeare, William 1610/11: *The Tempest*. Ed. F. Kermode. London: Methuen, 1964.

Shaw, George Bernard 1902 *Mrs Warren's Profession. A Play* [written 1894]. In Shaw, G. B., *Plays Unpleasant*. Harmondsworth: Penguin Books, 1975.

Sheridan, Richard B. 1799: *Pizzaro. A Tragedy in Five Acts* [after Kotzebue]. In Sheridan, R. B., *The Dramatic Works*, ed. J. Knight. London: Oxford University Press, 1931.

Simpson, N. F. 1959: *One Way Pendulum. A Farce in a New Dimension*. London: Faber & Faber, 1960.

Sims, George 1881: *The Lights o'London. A New and Original Drama in Five Acts*. In Booth, M. R. (ed.), *The Lights o'London and Other Victorian Plays*. Oxford: Oxford University Press, 1995.

Sophocles *c*.450 BCE: *Antigone*. Trs. D. Fitts and R. Fitzgerald. In Corrigan, R. W. (ed.), *Classical Tragedy Greek and Roman: 8 Plays*. New York: Applause, 1980.

Sophocles 427 BCE: *Oedipus Rex*. Trs. K. Cavander. In Corrigan, R. W. (ed.), *Classical Tragedy Greek and Roman: 8 Plays*. New York: Applause, 1980.

Strindberg, August 1902: *A Dream Play*. In Strindberg, A., *Plays: Two*, trs. M. Meyer. London: Eyre Methuen, 1982.

Toller, Ernst 1921: *Masses and Man. A Fragment of the Social Revolution of the Twentieth Century*. Trs. V. Mendel. London: Nonesuch Press, 1926.

Vega, Lope da 1612–14: *Fuente Ovejuna*. In Vega, L. da, *Fuente Ovejuna and Lost in a Mirror*, version by A. Mitchell. London: Absolute Classics, 1989.

Webster, John 1614: *The Duchess of Malfi*. In Webster, J., *Three Plays*, ed. D. C. Gunby. Harmondsworth: Penguin Books, 1972.

Wertenbaker, Timberlake 1988: *Our Country's Good*. London: Methuen Drama, 1992.

Wilde, Oscar 1895: *The Importance of Being Earnest. A Trivial Comedy for Serious People*. In Wilde, O., *Plays, Prose Writings, and Poems*, ed. I. Murray. London: Dent, 1978.

Williams, Tennessee 1945: *The Glass Menagerie*. In Williams, T., *A Streetcar Named Desire and Other Plays*, ed. E. Martin Browne. Harmondsworth: Penguin Books, 1962.

Zephaniah, Benjamin 1987: *Job Rocking*. In Brewster, Y. (intro.), *Black Plays: Two*. London: Methuen, 1989.

2 Secondary texts

Here we list critical and reference works that we have mentioned in the main text of this book. Texts marked with * may well be useful for further reading.

Aristotle. *c.*350 BCE: *Poetics [On the Art of Poetry].* In Dorsch, T. S. (trs.), *Classical Literary Criticism.* Harmondsworth: Penguin Books, 1983.

Aston, E. 1994: *An Introduction to Feminism and Theatre.* London: Routledge.

Aston, E. and Savona, G. 1991: *Theatre as Sign System: A Semiotics of Text and Performance.* London: Routledge.

Austin, J. L. 1962: *How to Do Things with Words.* London: Oxford University Press.

Barker, H. 1989: *Arguments for a Theatre.* London: John Calder.

Bharucha, R.* 1993: *Theatre and the World. Performance and the Politics of Culture.* London: Routledge.

Boal, A. 1992: *Games for Actors and Non-Actors,* trs. A. Jackson. London: Routledge.

Boal, A.* 1979: *Theater of the Oppressed,* trs. C. A. and M.-O. Leal McBride. London: Pluto Press.

Carlson, M.* 1996: *Performance. A Critical Introduction.* London: Routledge.

Cima, G. G. 1993: Ibsen and the critical actor. In *Performing Women. Female Characters, Male Playwrights, and the Modern Stage.* Ithaca and London: Cornell University Press.

Clemen, W. 1986: *A Commentary on Shakespeare's Richard III.* London: Methuen.

Counsell, C. 1996: *Signs of Performance. An Introduction to Twentieth Century Theatre.* London: Routledge.

Edwards, G. 1987: *Lorca. The Theatre beneath the Sand.* London: Marion Boyars.

Elam, K.* 1980: *The Semiotics of Theatre and Drama.* London: Methuen.

Esslin, M. 1968: *The Theatre of the Absurd.* Harmondsworth: Penguin Books.

Ford, A. 1995: Katharsis: the ancient problem. In Parker, A. and Sedgwick, E. K., (eds), *Performativity and Performance.* London: Routledge.

Freeman, S. 1996: *Putting Your Daughters on the Stage. British Lesbian Theatre from the 1960s to the Present.* London: Cassell.

Gorfain, P. 1983: *Hamlet* and the tragedy of ludic revenge. In Manning, F. E., (ed.), *The World of Play.* West Point, NY: Leisure Press.

Harris, J. W. 1992: *Medieval Theatre in Context.* London: Routledge.

Hartnoll, P. *(ed.) 1972: *The Concise Oxford Companion to the Theatre.* Oxford: Oxford University Press.

Herman, V. 1995: *Dramatic Discourse. Dialogue as Interaction in Plays.* London: Routledge.

Leacroft, R.* 1988: *The Development of the English Playhouse. An Illustrated Survey of Theatre Building in England from Medieval to Modern Times.* London: Methuen.

Lucas, I. 1994: *Impertinent Decorum. Gay Theatrical Manoeuvres.* London: Cassell.

Marker, F. J. and Marker, L.-L. 1989: *Ibsen's Lively Art. A Performance Study of the Major Plays*. Cambridge: Cambridge University Press.

Nagler, A. M. 1959: *A Sourcebook in Theatrical History*. New York: Dover.

Pfister, M.* 1988: *The Theory and Analysis of Drama*, trs. J. Halliday. Cambridge: Cambridge University Press.

Rudlin, J. 1994: *Commedia dell'Arte. An Actor's Handbook*. London: Routledge.

Schechner, R. 1988: *Performance Theory*. London: Routledge.

Shaw, G. B. 1957: *The Quintessence of Ibsenism*. New York: Hill & Wang.

Shepherd, S. and Womack, P.* 1996: *English Drama. A Cultural History*. Oxford: Blackwell.

Shepherd, S. 1989: *Because We're Queers: The Life and Crimes of Kenneth Halliwell and Joe Orton*. London: Gay Men's Press.

Short, M. 1989: Discourse analysis and the analysis of drama. In Carter, R. and Simpson, P. (eds), *Language, Discourse and Literature. An Introductory Reader in Discourse Stylistics*. London: Unwin Hyman.

Sinfield, A. 1992: *Faultlines. Cultural Materialism and the Politics of Dissident Reading*. Berkeley and Los Angeles: University of California Press.

Southern, R.* 1962: *The Seven Ages of the Theatre*. London: Faber & Faber.

Taylor, J. R. 1967: *The Rise and Fall of the Well-made Play*. London: Methuen.

Weimann, R. 1987: *Shakespeare and the Popular Tradition in the Theater. Studies in the Social Dimension of Dramatic Form and Function*, ed. R. Schwartz. Baltimore: Johns Hopkins University Press.

Wallis, M. 1995: Watching like detectives: *Othello* and the audience. In *Othello and The Winter's Tale. Essays*. Loughborough: Loughborough Theatre Texts.

West, S. 1991: *The Image of the Actor. Verbal and Visual Representation in the Age of Garrick and Kemble*. London: Pinter Publishers.

Wickham, G.* 1985: *A History of the Theatre*. Oxford: Phaidon.

Willett, J.* 1977: *The Theatre of Bertolt Brecht*. London: Eyre Methuen.

Williams, R. 1981: *Keywords*. London: Fontana.

Williams, R. 1977: *Marxism and Literature*. Oxford: Oxford University Press.

Williams, R. 1966: *Modern Tragedy*. London: Chatto & Windus.

Williams, R. 1980: Social environment and theatrical environment. The case of English Naturalism. In Williams, R., *Problems in Materialism and Culture*. London: Verso.

Index